Postmetaphysical Thinking

Postmetaphysical Thinking:
Philosophical Essays

Jürgen Habermas

translated by William Mark Hohengarten

The MIT Press
Cambridge, Massachusetts
London, England

This edition © 1992 Massachusetts Institute of Technology
This work originally appeared in German under the title *Nachmetaphysisches Denken: Philosophische Aufsätze*, © 1988 Suhrkamp Verlag, Frankfurt am Main, Germany. The author has dropped several of the essays from the German edition and added the essay "Peirce and Communication" for this edition.

This book was set in Baskerville by DEKR Corporation and was printed and bound in the United States of America.

Library of Congress Cataloging-in-Publication Data

Habermas, Jürgen.
   [Nachmetaphysisches Denken. English]
   Postmetaphysical thinking / Jürgen Habermas ; translated by
William Mark Hohengarten.
      p.   cm. — (Studies in contemporary German social thought)
   Translation of: Nachmetaphysisches Denken.
   Includes bibliographical references and index.
   ISBN 0-262-08209-8
   1. Philosophy, Modern—20th century. 2. Civilization, Modern—
Philosophy. I. Title. II. Series.
   B3258.H323N3313   1992
   190—dc20   91-40800
                                         CIP

Contents

Translator's Introduction   vii

I A Return to Metaphysics?

1 The Horizon of Modernity Is Shifting   3

2 Metaphysics after Kant   10

3 Themes in Postmetaphysical Thinking   28

II The Turn to Pragmatics

4 Toward a Critique of the Theory of Meaning   57

5 Peirce and Communication   88

III Between Metaphysics and the Critique of Reason

6 The Unity of Reason in the Diversity of Its Voices   115

7 Individuation through Socialization: On George Herbert Mead's Theory of Subjectivity   149

8 Philosophy and Science as Literature?   205

Index   229

Translator's Introduction

William Mark Hohengarten

The essays collected in this volume take up and expand upon a line of argument begun by the author in *The Philosophical Discourse of Modernity*. Like most contemporary thinkers, Habermas is critical of the Western metaphysical tradition and its exaggerated conception of reason. At the same time, however, he cautions against relinquishing that conception altogether. Against the radical critics of Western philosophy he argues that the wholesale rejection of the metaphysical tradition inevitably undercuts the possibility of rational critique itself. He thus defends the view that genuinely postmetaphysical thinking can remain critical only if it preserves the idea of reason derived from the tradition while stripping it of its metaphysical trappings. In order to steer between the twin dangers of a nostalgic return to or a radical critique of metaphysics, we must transform our inherited conceptions of reason and the rational subject. In these essays Habermas contributes to this task by further developing his intersubjectivistic approaches to meaning and validity and, especially, to subjectivity and individuality. In this introduction I shall make a few brief remarks clarifying each of these undertakings.

The linguistic turn in philosophy paved the way for postmetaphysical thinking; yet, in many of its manifestations, the philosophy of language is still wedded to the very metaphysical figures of thought it sought to overcome. For instance, intentionalistic theories of meaning uncritically adopt a conception

of action drawn from the subject-object model of consciousness, while truth-semantic accounts of meaning uncritically accept the logocentric perspective dominant in the tradition.
Even the semiotics of Charles Sanders Peirce remains ensnared
by the legacy of metaphysics; for although Peirce insisted that
interpretability (or the "interpretant relation") must be a part of
the structure of any sign, he also believed that this requirement
could be met without taking into account the communicative
relationship between a speaker and an interpreting hearer.
Ultimately this led Peirce back to metaphysical realism concerning universals. Against this, Habermas argues that the "interpretant relation" cannot be understood independently of
the conditions of *intersubjective communication* oriented toward
mutual understanding. In the fourth essay of this volume,
"Toward a Critique of the Theory of Meaning," he examines
three competing accounts of meaning—intentionalism, the use-
theory, and truth-semantics—with the aim of showing that each
of them captures only one of the three functions performed
by language when a *speaker* comes to an understanding with
another person about *something* in the world. Habermas's own
universal pragmatics, with its theory of three distinct validity
claims and three corresponding world-relations, is meant to
avoid the one-sidedness of these competing theories. The essays in this volume provide many compelling arguments in
support of Habermas's meaning-theoretic position. At the same
time, they also tend to presuppose some prior familiarity with
it. It may therefore be helpful to summarize its most significant
features.

Habermas argues that linguistic meaning is constituted communicatively. The smallest unit of communication is the utterance put forth by a speaker *together with* the "yes" or "no"
position taken toward that utterance by a hearer. Every utterance contains a (stated or implied) propositional component *p*
that predicates something of an object. However, even in the
case of an assertion, the meaning of the utterance is not determined by *p* alone. The full meaning of an utterance depends
equally upon *how* this propositional content is being put forth—
whether it is being asserted, commanded, confessed, promised,
etc. This *force* of the utterance is given by its *illocutionary com-*

ponent, which may be made explicit by a performative clause: "I assert . . .," "I command . . .," "I confess . . .," "I promise . . .," and so on. But every utterance in fact makes three distinct *validity claims,* only one of which is thematized by the illocutionary component. That is, with her utterance a speaker makes a *truth* claim relating to the objective world of states of affairs, a *rightness* claim relating to the social world of normatively regulated interpersonal relations, and a *truthfulness* or *sincerity* claim relating to the subjective world of experiences to which the speaker has privileged access. Each of these validity claims is universal, in two senses. First, each of them is raised, either implicitly or explicitly, in every speech act; they are *universal formal features* of linguistic communication. But, secondly, each also lays claim to *universal validity* for what it claims to be true, right, or truthful. That is, the validity that is claimed cannot be restricted to "validity for the speaker," or "validity for this specific group." Validity means validity for every subject capable of speech and action. With any utterance, then, a speaker lays claim to three dimensions of validity that *transcend* the particular context or the linguistic community in which the utterance is made.

The correlates of this transcendence are the three "worlds" to which the speaker relates with her utterance: the objective, social, and subjective worlds. Habermas traces his pragmatic concept of world back to the One of metaphysics: participation in the metaphysical One is what allowed a diverse plurality of entities to be constituted as a totality, or as one world. In the Kantian critique of reason, the place of the metaphysical One was taken by the transcendental subject, while the totality of entities lost its objective character and took on a regulative function as an Idea of Reason. Habermas stresses the crucial distinction in Kant between the *ideal* synthesis of reason, whereby this world-totality is first *constituted,* and the empirical syntheses of the understanding, which concern objects *in the world* and are therefore made possible only by the antecedent world-constituting synthesis. Ultimately, this figure of thought undergoes a pragmatic transformation in Habermas's own theory. The concept or idea of a world is no longer projected by a monological consciousness but by interacting subjects who raise validity claims in communicative acts. And the concept of the one objective world consisting of all existing objects or all true states of affairs is augmented by two analogous world-concepts corresponding to the two other validity claims: the concept of a social world consisting of all normatively sanctioned actions or of all legitimate norms themselves and the concept of a subjective world consisting of all experiences to which the subject has privileged access and to which she can give expression in truthful utterances. The metaphysical One and the Kantian Idea of Reason reappear more modestly in everyday communicative practice as these three worlds, that is, as "more or less trivial suppositions of commonality that make possible the cognitive, the regulative and the expressive uses of language."

But what does it mean to claim that one's utterance is valid? For the sake of simplicity, let us consider the truth-claim a speaker makes for a statement. Habermas argues that, in general, we evaluate truth claims not by directly comparing a statement with a state of affairs in the objective world but by examining the *reasons* that a speaker can give in support of what she says. Claiming that one's statement is true, or valid, is tantamount to claiming that good reasons can be given in support of it. In Habermas's words: "The speaker refers with his validity claim to a potential of reasons that could be brought to bear for it." These reasons are in turn evaluated in terms of their *intersubjective* acceptability as good reasons for holding something to be the case. That is why an understanding of the speaker's utterance cannot be abstracted from the "yes" or "no" position that the hearer takes toward it. Even when reasons are neither actually demanded nor given—even in settings where giving reasons is not institutionalized or is relatively undeveloped—the meaning of every speech act is tied to the potential of reasons that *could* be given in support of it. In this sense, every speech act points implicitly to the argumentative procedure of giving and evaluating reasons in support of validity claims.

The process of argumentation itself requires one final idealization, which concerns the relevant speech situation. According to Habermas, argumentation provides a suitable medium for determining which reasons are good reasons for accepting an utterance only if this determination is based solely upon the force of the better argument and not, for instance, upon power relations among speakers. Therefore, when speakers engage in argumentation, they must suppose that certain conditions hold that guarantee that the agreements they reach are based on reasons alone. These conditions define what Habermas calls the ideal speech situation, centering on the supposition that symmetry conditions hold between competent speakers whenever they engage in argumentation.[1]

It is crucial to Habermas's position that the status of the various *idealizations* named by him not be misunderstood. He uses "ideal" in a specifically Kantian sense to designate something that has a regulative function but is unattainable in actual fact. Thus, "the idealizing presuppositions of communicative action must not be hypostatized into the ideal of a future condition." The ideal of universal agreement that is projected by every validity claim, and the correlative ideals of world-totalities corresponding to all true statements, to all correct norms, and to all truthful expressions, function in communication as *critical* reference points. "Critical," because the concept of validity is not defined in terms of what a particular group accepts as valid in a given situation. Validity claims can of course only be raised within particular language games and forms of life; yet, while *immanent* in particular contexts of communication, they always claim a validity that *transcends* any and all of them.

The foregoing summary emphasizes the *universalistic* dimension of Habermas's pragmatics. In the eyes of some critics, this universalism indicates an insensitivity to the claims of the *individual* over and against the universal—and thus an insensitivity to the related themes of otherness and difference. It is true, of course, that Habermas's defense of a postmetaphysical universalism has often been explicitly and emphatically directed against relativistic and ethnocentric brands of *particularism*. Yet, despite his criticism of these types of particularism—or, perhaps more precisely, because of it—Habermas does not champion the universal *against* the individual, otherness, and difference. On the contrary, he attempts to rescue the individual from complete absorption into the particular contexts in which it is always embedded. It may be true that the universalistic dimensions of Habermas's pragmatic theory lie closer to the surface of his writings; but this should not obscure the fact that this theory accords a role to the individual that is at least as significant as the role it attributes to universal validity claims. Fortunately, the essays in this volume include discussions of the individual, otherness, and difference that will make it more difficult to overlook this dimension of Habermas's thought. Of central importance on this score is the article "Individuation through Socialization: On George Herbert Mead's Theory of Subjectivity." This essay brings together various lines of thought developed elsewhere in the collection and in many ways serves as its focal point, as is suggested by the frequent references to it throughout the volume. For this reason, and because of its complexity, I shall sketch its argument here.

Habermas readily concedes that the universal is opposed to the individual and tends to suppress it—*if the basic concepts of metaphysics are presupposed.* Operating with the concepts of genus and species, the metaphysical tradition could explicate individuation only in two equally unsatisfactory ways. *Numerically,* things are individuated through the material instantiation of universal formal substances. But since being is attributed only to these universal substances, while matter is conceived as that which is not, numerical individuation can only be conceived as privation. Things stand no better with *qualitative* individuation. The genera and species that characterize any thing are themselves universals and cannot distinguish that thing as a unique individual entity. On the other hand, if the chain of genera and species is extended to include an ultimate individuating specification (such as Duns Scotus' *haecceitas*), then the triumph of the universal is all the more complete; for this specification is itself a universal that extends to *every* individual as such and thus distinguishes none of them as something unique and irreplaceable. This metaphysical dilemma still continues to make itself felt in Hegel, where the individual totality is made dependent on an absolute totality that ultimately robs the former of its individuality. Habermas concludes:

Hegel's philosophy of history and his philosophy of right merely illustrate in a drastic way something that is generally valid: as long as the problematic of metaphysical unitary thinking remains in force, and as long as idealist modes of thought remain in use, the universal will triumph over the individual, which is banished to ineffability. Along the course of metaphysical thinking, the endangered individual reveals itself at best *ironically* as the nonidentical—as the marginal that is pressed to the side and drops out of the running at every attempt to identify an individual as itself and distinguish it from *all* other individuals.[2]

Unfortunately, just these metaphysical concepts are unreflectively presupposed by the classics of sociology when they interpret a central phenomenon of modernity, namely, social individualization. The paradigm is provided by Durkheim. On the one hand, he treats individuality as a privative concept, defined in terms of *deviation* from the universal features of one's social environment. On the other hand, he interprets societal differentiation (or the "division of labor") and the concomitant multiplication of socially sanctioned roles as a source of increased individualization; the greater the number of possible roles, the more nearly unique or "individualized" will be the combination of roles fulfilled by any one person. In either case, however, universal characterizations retain the upper hand. In particular, a multiplication of roles does not result in any increase in *autonomy* for the individual in relation to these socially binding roles. In fact, societal differentiation appears to make this sort of "individualization" into just one more socially binding norm—the paradoxically "institutionalized individual." What is needed instead is a concept of individuation that captures the missing dimensions of autonomy and the capacity to be oneself. Such a concept should, moreover, allow us to distinguish between two phenomena: societal differentiation and progressive individuation.

The route to such a concept proceeds via the modern philosophy of the subject. Since Descartes, the emphatic sense of individuality has been associated with the spontaneous ego, or the I. The affiliated subject-object model of consciousness, however, proved inadequate for developing this insight. In German Idealism, this paradigm took shape as the mirror-model of self-consciousness: consciousness gets hold of itself by being reflected back on itself out of the world of objects of which it is conscious. However, what is "gotten hold of" proves not to be the spontaneous ego as the subject of consciousness (i.e., Kant's transcendental ego), since that would require that the subject be an object of consciousness. The spontaneous subject recedes from consciousness of itself. At best, then, consciousness can come to know the empirical ego; but this appears as merely one more object. So there remains no place for the individual between consciousness in the first-person, as the receding subject, and consciousness in the third-person, as a causally determined object.

Habermas believes that the limits of this approach become particularly clear in the work of Fichte, who wanted to go beyond the transcendental starting point by uniting it with both an intersubjectivistic account of individuality and an existentialist notion of self-choice—a union which, however, foundered precisely on the primacy accorded to consciousness and the subject-object relation. With the model of an ego that posits itself in an act that is practically executed *and* reflexively recapitulable, Fichte brought together the practical and the theoretical dimensions of subjectivity that were separated in Kant. At the same time, he saw that the ego is only able to posit itself *as* something individual; but individuality requires that the ego encounter *other egos* which delimit it. Precisely because the original ego is conceived as transcendental subjectivity, however, it can encounter these other egos only as *objects*. Its individuality thereby reflects objective restrictions placed upon it, rather than an increase in self-determination and self-realization. Moreover, the ego's reflexive certainty of itself distinguishes between its essential determination as ego and its further, inessential attributes; it is essentially an instance of "egohood in general," and only accidentally *this* ego. In this way, the singularity and the universality of the transcendental starting point ultimately reasserted themselves at the expense of both intersubjective plurality and individuality.

In order to escape the aporias of an ego that posits itself, Wilhelm von Humboldt and Soren Kierkegaard rejected the transcendental starting point in favor of a self that is *situated* within a concrete form of life or within an individual life-history. Kierkegaard reinterpreted self-positing as self-choice, in which I critically appropriate my life-history through the paradoxical act of choosing myself as the one who I am and who I want to be. Because the authentically chosen life-history serves thereby as the source of individuation, the distinction between my essential character as ego and my accidental character as this historical individual is cancelled. Self-choice involves a *performative* rather than a descriptive concept of individuality. In choosing myself as the one who I am and want to be, I make a claim to radical authenticity, rather than to descriptive accuracy. But this claim requires recognition from an Other. For Kierkegaard, this Other is God. Already in the eighteenth century, however, Rousseau had appealed for recognition not to God but to an unrestricted universal public. The really decisive innovation was, however, made by Humboldt. He replaced the subject-object model of consciousness with a model of linguistic communication involving speakers and hearers. In linguistic communication, speakers encounter one another in a nonobjectifying way. The one perspective of the transcendental subject gives way to a plurality of participants' perspectives. Unity within this plurality is conceived not as subsumption but as unforced agreement in dialogue. Communication unites diverse forms of life without cancelling their diversity. "Thus," Habermas argues, "although the nonidentical . . . always slipped through the net of basic metaphysical concepts, it remains accessible in a trivial way in everyday communicative practice."[3]

It is this model of intersubjective communication that Mead used to explicate the structure of the individual. In a certain sense, Mead retains the mirror-model of self-consciousness familiar from German Idealism in which the subject only comes upon itself via the mediation of its object. Now, however, this "object" is understood not from the third-person perspective of an observer but from the *second-person* perspective of a participant in linguistic communication—the other is an alter ego.

The self is then conceived as the alter ego of this alter ego. We might call this the subject in the second person. Mead employs the term "me" to give expression to this structure of the self as a second person to another second person. With the "me" he is able to bypass the dilemma posed by the philosophy of the subject, which conceives of the self either in the first person, as the singular and universal receding subject of knowledge and action, or in the third person, as one mere empirical object among others. Of course, Mead still has to explain how this subject in the second person could first arise out of structures of intersubjectivity. After all, intersubjectivity itself would seem to presuppose antecedently constituted subjects. Mead's solution to this problem is to show that an organism first takes up a relationship to itself, and is thus first constituted as a subject, in the moment when communicative relations are established between organisms. Subjectivity (in the second person) and intersubjectivity (between second persons) are therefore coeval.

The "me" has two distinct components: the theoretical "me," or a person's consciousness of herself, and the practical "me," or the agency through which she monitors her behavior. Habermas devotes considerable effort to showing that Mead's genetic account of the theoretical "me" avoids the paradoxes that plagued Kant's and Fichte's theories of self-consciousness. From the point of view of a theory of the individual, however, it is the practical "me" that is of particular interest. This practical "me" comes into existence when the subject establishes a practical relation to herself by adopting the normative attitude of an alter ego toward her own behavior. Later, this second-person perspective is enlarged to encompass the *generalized* expectations of all members of her society, or the attitude of the "generalized other." Understood in this way, the practical "me" is a conservative moment of selfhood since it represents the pregiven normative expectations of society as a whole. A practical self or identity constituted solely by this "me" would have to be wholly conventional in character. In Habermas's view, such a conventionally constituted self is nonetheless a precondition for the emergence of a nonconventional aspect of the practical self: the practical "I," which *opposes* the "me" with both presocial drives and innovative fantasy. The inter-

subjectivity of the practical self is reflected in this tension between the "me" and the "I." At the conventional stage, however,
the relationship is one in which the "I" is suppressed or repressed. This is why Habermas detects a critical moment
lodged in Mead's use of these pronouns: the suppression of
the "I" indicates that this conventional identity can at best be
a substitute for a true one.

Yet, the self is intersubjectively constituted through and
through; the relationship to a community is what makes the
practical relation-to-self possible. If the individual is to realize
her true identity, she cannot do so by withdrawing from this
community. Habermas follows Mead in arguing that this apparent dilemma is solved by appealing to a wider, *universal*
community consisting of all possible alter egos. The "I" *projects*
a new intersubjective context; it thus makes possible a new
"me" reflecting the norms of this projected community. In this
postconventional identity, the relationship between the "I" and
the "me" still remains, but the order of priority has been
reversed.

Habermas distinguishes between two dimensions in which
the postconventional self appeals to a universal community:
the moral and the ethical. In *moral* discourse an individual
seeks a consensus with the larger community about the rightness of binding norms. This in turn makes possible an autonomous self capable of self-determination. *Ethical* discourse, on
the other hand, concerns identities, be it of groups or of individuals. Again, whenever I lay claim to a unique identity as
an irreplaceable individual rather than as the instantiation of
a social type, I must appeal to a larger community. In this case,
however, what I seek is not so much the agreement of this
larger community as its recognition of me as the one who I am
and who I want to be. In this sense, the self is not the property
of an isolated subjectivity: the claim of radical authenticity
depends upon recognition by others.

Because true individuation depends on the development of
a postconventional identity, it ultimately requires the individuated person to leave behind the conventional stage of socialization in order to take up a critical attitude toward the
merely given norms of her particular society. For this reason,

individuation cannot be equated with societal differentiation, whether this be described as the pluralization of socially sanctioned roles or as the break-up of society into functional subsystems that relegate individuals to their "environments" (and vice versa). On Habermas's view, societal differentiation *does* result in overburdening the conventional individual with conflicting demands, and the impossibility of reconciling these demands *can* lead to the disintegration of a conventional identity. Yet, this "release" from traditional determinants of personal identity is in itself an ambiguous phenomenon: both an emancipation and a loss of self. Its emancipatory potential can be realized only if the released individuals are capable of making the transition to postconventional identity structures. This transition requires not isolation but projected reintegration into a larger community.

It is not difficult to make the connection between this account of individuation and Habermas's universal pragmatics: both require the ideal supposition, or projection, of a universal community of discourse. But, one might ask, does not this construction allow the universal to triumph over the individual one final time? In Habermas's view, it does not. The relationship between the supposition of a universal community and the individual is not one of subsumption but of complementarity. This complementarity is evident in each of the two dimensions in which individuation occurs: in moral self-determination and in ethical self-realization. According to Habermas, moral autonomy is the correlate of normative validity claims, claims that transcend the status quo of a particular society precisely because they refer to the ideal of a universal normative consensus. Yet, the relative approximation to this ideal in universally acknowledged norms does not imply that differences in concrete forms of life must be leveled, or that every person must conform to a single ideal lifestyle. On the contrary, the universalization of norms leads to their becoming ever more *abstract,* and thus more compatible with increasing concrete diversity. Ultimately, this process leads to a growing *toleration* of other forms of life—as long as these do not themselves embody the intolerant oppression of some individuals in the interest of others. Habermas thus argues that the transitory unity that is generated in the porous and refracted intersubjectivity of a linguistically mediated consensus not only supports but furthers and accelerates the pluralization of forms of life and the individualization of lifestyles. More discourse means more contradiction and difference. The more abstract the agreements become, the more diverse the disagreements with which we can *nonviolently* live.[4]

The same can be said of the ethical dimension of self-realization. Ethically, the individual appeals to the projected universal community not for agreement about norms but for *recognition* of her claim to authenticity and of herself as a unique and irreplaceable individual. Habermas correlates this performative concept of individuality with the performative employment of "I" in the making of universal validity claims: when making *any* validity claim, I also lay claim to recognition for my individual identity. Even when, after weighing the evidence, the other person rejects my specific validity claim, this very rejection still implies her acknowledgement of me as an accountable actor and therefore constitutes an acceptance of my *identity claim.* My understanding of myself as an irreplaceable individual is in this way anchored in the recognition I receive from others in linguistic interaction. No one else can take my place, or represent me, in this interaction. Hence, the unity engendered by communication does not eliminate the difference between individuals, but instead confirms it: "linguistically attained consensus does not eradicate from the accord the differences in speaker perspectives, but rather presupposes them as ineliminable."[5]

Except for three omissions and one addition, the essays included in this volume are the same as those in the German *Nachmetaphysisches Denken* (Frankfurt: Suhrkamp, 1988). The omissions are "Handlungen, Sprechakte, sprachlich vermittelte Interaktionen und Lebenswelt" and "Bemerkungen zu J. Searles 'Meaning, Communication, and Representation'," which are to appear in English elsewhere; an appendix consisting of a review article by Habermas has also been omitted.[6] The addition is "Peirce and Communication," a paper first delivered at the Peirce Sesquicentennial Congress held at Harvard University in 1989.

In translating these essays I have taken the ideal of a faithful rendering as my primary guide. To the greatest extent possible, I have retained Habermas's own figures of speech, particularly the metaphors he draws from the natural world. I have also tended to retain the basic style of his sentences. This style, often consisting of several subordinate and relative clauses joined together in a well-crafted whole, is one that he deems appropriate to the scholarly treatment of complex subjects—as can be seen by comparison with, say, his political writings or *Feuilliton* contributions, which reflect stylistic ideals more appropriate to other topics and other forums.

I would like to thank the author for reading through a draft of this translation and suggesting changes he thought appropriate. While these changes have been introduced in order to capture his meaning more precisely or to make the translation more readable, they do sometimes result in minor departures from the original text. At such points, the correspondence between the German and the English versions is not exactly that of translation.

Notes

1. See "Vorlesungen zu einer sprachtheoretischen Grundlegung der Soziologie," in *Vorstudien und Ergänzungen zur Theorie des kommunikativen Handelns* (Frankfurt: Suhrkamp, 1984), 118ff.; "Wahrheitstheorien," also in *Vorstudien und Ergänzungen*, 174ff.; *Moral Consciousness and Communicative Action*, trans. Christian Lenhardt and Shierry Weber Nicholsen (Cambridge, Mass.: MIT Press, 1990), 88; and *Theory of Communicative Action*, 2 vols., trans. Thomas McCarthy (Boston: Beacon Press, 1984–1987) 1: 25.

2. This volume, pp. 157–158.

3. This volume, p. 48.

4. This volume, p. 140.

5. This volume, p. 48.

6. The English version of "Handlungen, Sprechakte, sprachlich vermittelte Interaktionen und Lebenswelt" will appear in a volume edited by G. Floistad, *Philosophical Problems Today*. The English version of "Bemerkungen zu J. Searles 'Meaning, Communication, and Representation'" will appear in a Festschrift for John Searle edited by E. LePore.

I

A Return to Metaphysics?

1

The Horizon of Modernity Is Shifting

How modern is the philosophy of the twentieth century?

This question may seem naive. And yet, was the development of philosophical thinking at the beginning of this century marked by turning points similar to those found in painting on its way toward abstraction, in music with the transition from the octave to the twelve-tone system, and in literature with the shattering of traditional narrative structures? And if an enterprise like philosophy, so very indebted to antiquity and its renaissances, really has opened itself to the inconstant spirit of modernity, which is oriented toward innovation, experimentation, and acceleration, could one not pose a more far-reaching question: Has philosophy, too, succumbed to the aging of modernity, as for instance present-day architecture has? Are there similarities with a postmodern architecture that, with vaguely provocative gestures, is again turning to historical decoration and to the ornamentation that had once been condemned?

There are at least terminological parallels. Contemporary philosophers, too, are celebrating their farewells. Members of one group call themselves postanalytic philosophers, others call themselves poststructuralists or post-Marxists. The fact that the phenomenologists have not yet arrived at their own "post-ism" almost makes them suspect.

Four Philosophical Movements

Platonism and Aristotelianism, even rationalism and empiricism, have lasted for centuries. Today things move faster. Philosophical movements are phenomena of effective history. They mask the constant pace of academic philosophy, which with its long rhythms stands athwart the more rapid shifts in issues and schools. Nonetheless, both when it formulates its problems, and when it has an effect on the public at large, philosophy draws from the same sources—in our century, four great movements. Even with all the differences we perceive at close range, four complexes, each with its own physiognomy, emerge from the flow of thought: analytic philosophy, phenomenology, Western Marxism, and structuralism. Hegel spoke of "shapes of spirit." This expression forces itself on us. For as soon as a shape of spirit is recognized in its uniqueness and is named, it is placed at a distance and condemned to decline. To this extent, the "posties" are not only deft opportunists with their noses to the wind; as seismographers tracking the spirit of the age, they must also be taken seriously.

In their courses, compositions, and implications, these movements of thought differ from one another in nontrivial ways. Phenomenology and above all analytic philosophy have left the deepest tracks behind in the discipline. They found their historians and their standard portrayals long ago. Individual titles have achieved the rank of founding documents: G. E. Moore's *Principia Ethica* and Russell and Whitehead's *Principia Mathematica* on the one hand, Husserl's *Logical Investigations* on the other hand. The paths between Wittgenstein's *Tractatus* and his *Philosophical Investigations,* between Heidegger's *Being and Time* and his "Letter on Humanism," mark peripeties. Movements of thought branch off. Linguistic analysis splits into a theory of science and a theory of ordinary language. Phenomenology anthropologizes broadly and ontologizes deeply; along both paths it becomes permeated with existential topicality. And although phenomenology—after a final productive impetus in France (Sartre, Merleau-Ponty)—seems to be breaking up, it is only in the decades following World War II that analytic philosophy has gained the imperial position that it claims to this day with Quine and Davidson.

An unparalleled concentration of powers characterizes the course of the latter tradition, which would seem to be guided solely through disciplined self-criticism from within, and which continually re-forms itself through self-produced problematics. In the end, it empties into the historicism of a postempirical philosophy of science (with Kuhn) and into the contextualism of a postanalytic philosophy of language (with Rorty). Yet, even in the aftermath of this self-overcoming, the achievements of linguistic analysis still triumphantly determine the explanatory level of the discipline as a whole.

Structuralism and Western Marxism embody an entirely different type of thinking. While the former received its impetus completely from without (from Saussure's linguistics and Piaget's psychology), the latter (Lukács, Bloch, and Gramsci) re-Hegelianizes Marxist thinking by leading it from political economy back to philosophical reflection. Both movements, however, make their way through human- and social-scientific disciplines before the seed of speculative thought grows in the bed of social theory.

As early as the twenties, Western Marxism entered into a symbiosis with Freudian metapsychology, and this served as the inspiration for the interdisciplinary works of the Frankfurt Institute for Social Research once it had emigrated to New York. There are in this respect similarities with a structuralism that has spread radially outward via Bachelard's critique of science, Levi-Strauss' anthropology, and Lacan's psychoanalysis. Yet, while Marxist social theory regrouped as pure philosophy in Adorno's negative dialectics, structuralism was only brought completely into the domain of philosophical thought by those who wished to overcome it—Foucault and Derrida. Here too, leave is taken in opposite directions. Wherever the impulses of Western Marxism have not lost their force, its production takes on stronger social scientific and professional philosophical characteristics, whereas poststructuralism presently seems to be absorbed in a critique of reason radicalized through Nietzsche. Thus, while analytic philosophy is itself overcoming itself, and phenomenology is unraveling, in these latter cases the end comes with the turn either to science or to *Weltanschauungen.*

Themes in Modern Thought

These four movements of thought belong to our century. Does that imply more than a chronological classification? Are they, in a specific sense, modern? And if they are, does placing them at a distance also imply a departure from modernity?

What catches the eye are the new instruments of representation and analysis that twentieth-century philosophy borrows from the post-Aristotelian logic developed in the nineteenth century and from Fregean semantics. But the specifically modern element that seized all movements of thought lies not so much in the method as in the themes of thinking. *Four themes* characterize the break with the tradition. The headings are: postmetaphysical thinking, the linguistic turn, situating reason, and reversing the primacy of theory over practice—or the overcoming of logocentrism.

(1) The fact that the authority of the empirical sciences has achieved autonomy is not new—nor is the positivistic glorification of this authority. But even Nietzsche, in his rejection of Platonism, remained attached to the tradition's strong concept of theory, its grasp of the totality, and its claim to a privileged access to truth. This emphatic concept of theory, which was supposed to render not only the human world but nature too intelligible in their internal structures, finally sees its decline under the premises of a postmetaphysical thinking that is dispassionate. Henceforth, it would be the procedural rationality of the scientific process that would decide whether or not a sentence has a truth-value in the first place. This antimetaphysical affect was not restricted to the logical empiricists in the Vienna Circle and their vain attempt to lay hold of a criterion of meaning that would supposedly allow metaphysics to be demarcated from science once and for all. The early Husserl, the young Horkheimer, and later the structuralists as well, all in their ways made philosophical thinking bow to the sciences' claim to exemplary status. Now we think more tolerantly about what might count as science.

(2) An equally profound caesura is formed by the paradigm shift from the philosophy of consciousness to the philosophy of language. Whereas linguistic signs had previously been taken as instruments and accessories of mental representation, the intermediate domain of symbolic meanings now takes on a dignity of its own. The relation of language to the world or of a proposition to a state of affairs takes the place of the relation between subject and object. World-constitutive accomplishments are transferred from transcendental subjectivity to grammatical structures. The reconstructive work of the linguist replaces a kind of introspection that cannot be readily checked on. That is, the rules according to which signs are linked, sentences are formed, and utterances are brought forth can be read off from linguistic formations as if from something lying before one. Analytic philosophy and structuralism are not alone in thus creating a new methodological foundation; bridges are also built to formal semantics from Husserl's theory of meaning, and even critical theory is finally overtaken by the linguistic turn.

(3) In the name of finitude, temporality, and historicity, an ontologically oriented phenomenology further robs reason of its classical attributes. Transcendental consciousness concretizes itself in the practices of the lifeworld and takes on flesh and blood in historical embodiments. An anthropologically oriented phenomenology locates further media of embodiment in action, language, and the body. Wittgenstein's language-game grammars, Gadamer's contexts of tradition in effective history, Levi-Strauss' deep structures, and the Hegelian Marxists' historical totality all mark so many attempts to re-embed an abstractly exalted reason in its contexts and to situate it in its proper domains of operation.

(4) The reversal of the classical relationship of theory to practice is at bottom indebted to the honing of a Marxian idea. But additional evidence for the rootedness of our cognitive accomplishments in prescientific practice and in our intercourse with things and persons was provided by pragmatism from Peirce to Mead, by Piaget's developmental psychology and Vygotski's theory of language, by Scheler's sociology of knowledge, and by Husserl's analysis of the lifeworld. This fact

also explains the interrelationships that have been established in the name of a philosophy of praxis between phenomenology and Marxism (beginning with the early Marcuse and the later Sartre).

Insights—Prejudices

These themes—postmetaphysical thinking, the linguistic turn, situating reason, and overcoming logocentrism—are among the most important motive forces of philosophizing in the twentieth century, in spite of the boundaries between schools. To be sure, they have not only led to new insights but also to new prejudices.

For instance, the methodological example of the sciences did further the development of philosophy into a special discipline without cognitive privilege. Yet it also provided fuel for a type of scientism that did not simply submit the presentation of philosophical thought to sharper analytic standards, but which set up astonishing ideals of science as well—whether disciplines such as physics or neurophysiology, or a methodological procedure such as behaviorism.

Further, the linguistic turn has placed philosophizing on a more secure methodological basis and has led it out of the aporias of theories of consciousness. But an ontological understanding of language has also been built up in this way, one which makes the world-disclosing function of language independent of innerworldly learning processes and which mystifies the transformation of linguistic [world-] pictures as a poetic originary happening (*Ursprungsgeschehen*).

The skeptical concepts of reason have certainly had a salutary and sobering effect upon philosophy and have at the same time confirmed philosophy as the guardian of rationality. On the other hand, a radical critique of reason has also been on the rise, one which does not simply protest against the inflation of the understanding (*Verstand*) into instrumental reason, but which equates reason as a whole with repression—and then fatalistically or ecstatically seeks refuge in something wholly Other.

Finally, enlightenment about the relationship of theory to practice preserves philosophical thinking from illusions of independence and opens its eyes to a spectrum of validity claims extending beyond the assertoric. However, this has also led some to slide back into a type of productivism that reduces practice to labor and that covers up the links between the symbolically structured lifeworld, communicative action, and discourse.

Today, in a situation that has become more and more obscure, new convergences are becoming apparent. Yet, disputation continues by way of issues that do not age: the debate over the unity of reason in the diversity of its voices; the debate over the position of philosophical thinking in the concert of the sciences; the debate over the esoteric and the exoteric, special scientific discipline versus enlightenment; finally, the debate over the boundary between philosophy and literature. In addition, the wave of restoration that has rolled over the Western world for a good decade is also washing an issue up on shore that has accompanied modernity from the beginning: the imitation substantiality of a metaphysics renewed one more time.

2

Metaphysics after Kant

Dieter Henrich has generously treated a review by me as the occasion for a metacritical debate, with the aim of bringing essential intentions of his philosophizing to the fore.[1] His twelve theses addressing the question, "What is metaphysics—what is modernity?," provide a forceful sketch of a counter-project, to which I cannot respond in an equivalent manner in this space.[2] My remarks might better be characterized as aiming at establishing a pre-understanding about the common enterprise and motives of philosophizing. A festschrift should not simply promote detailed argumentative disputation;[3] it should also offer the opportunity to get clear about thematic motives in the thinking of an outstanding colleague—and, in the mirror of an extraordinary path of thought, observed with respect and admiration from a distance marked by friendship, it also offers the opportunity to arrive at a better understanding of one's own thematic motives.

Henrich has become, in recent years more markedly than earlier, the advocate of a metaphysics that might be capable of enduring after Kant. This metaphysics takes its starting point from Kant's and Fichte's theory of self-consciousness, in order then to take up the threefold chord of reconciliation provided by Hegel's *Phenomenology*, Hölderlin's hymns, and Beethoven's symphonies. Henrich wants to place the enterprise of a post-Kantian metaphysics in the proper light, in order to counter the naturalistic background philosophy of contemporary Anglo-Saxon thinking—indeed, to vindicate its validity in the face of analytic materialism. This alternative marks the way; it requires that we begin with the knowing and acting subject's relation to, and understanding of, itself. Rather than being understood from the perspective of the world of contingent things and events, this subject must return to its world-constituting subjectivity as the definitive horizon of self-interpretation.

Metaphysics, the rejection of naturalism, and the retreat into subjectivity thus form the headings for a philosophizing that has never denied what it is up to:

The self which, with a view toward its own criteria of correctness, is concerned about its existence, might in the end find an internal ground for its own possibility, one which does not confront it in as alien and indifferent a manner as the aspect of nature, against which it has to turn the energy of its self-assertion.[4]

This formulation still leaves open the conditions that would have to be satisfied by "an internal ground of its own possibility." Does Henrich formulate these conditions so restrictively that, in the end, the only thing considered an appropriate candidate would be some kind of spirit or mind that is opposed to matter, or, perhaps, one that permeates nature from within—in any event, one conceived in the Platonic tradition? However that may be, for Henrich the modern position of consciousness is defined in terms of how a life that is *conscious* and originarily at home with itself can be maintained; it is *not* defined in terms of contingencies of naked self-preservation. To the extent, then, that this conscious life can only reach enlightenment about itself through metaphysical means, metaphysics retains an internal connection with modernity. This connection is Henrich's concern in his "Theses."

The reclamation of this connection distinguishes Henrich's undertaking *a limine* from the sort of return to metaphysics that is repelled by a modernity that, it seems, breeds disaster and *only* that—just as it is also distinguished from an "overcoming of metaphysics" feeding off similar motives. Henrich justifiably defends himself against confusing these. In this respect I see an affinity in basic convictions. It is a question here of alternatives in thought that have far-reaching implications, including implications for politics. Under the headings of self-consciousness, self-determination, and self-realization, a normative content of modernity has developed that must not be identified with the blind subjectivity of self-preservation or the disposition over oneself.

Whoever equates these two, whether with prefixes directed forward or backward, either aims at getting rid of the normative content of modernity altogether or wants to trim it down to the cognitive-instrumental heritage of bourgeois ideologies (even if these are in need of supplementation). In the wake of Hegel, philosophers should no longer become indignant when they are also judged in light of the political implications of their thought. Henrich does not belong to the grand alliance that is opposed to what, in better times, one dared to call "the ideas of 1789." In this alliance, minds as diverse as Leo Strauss, Martin Heidegger, and Arnold Gehlen stand shoulder to shoulder. Even an apparently paradoxical path such as that from Carl Schmitt to Leo Strauss, which has become possible during my lifetime, is made coherent through this equation of modern reason and instrumental reason—an equation that says farewell [to modernity]. With convincing arguments, Henrich defends himself against this; of course, he would also have some reservations about the close look I give to the political implications of a philosophical thought that is supposedly pure. Thus, even in the face of the confederate spirit signalled by Henrich, the discussion has to focus on the project itself. I organize my questions according to three descriptive headings: metaphysics, antinaturalism, and the theory of subjectivity.

I

It has become customary to transfer to the history of philosophy the concept of a paradigm stemming from the history of science and to undertake a rough division of epochs in terms of "being," "consciousness," and "language." It is possible, following Schnädelbach and Tugendhat, to distinguish the corresponding modes of thought as ontology, the philosophy of consciousness, and linguistic analysis.[5] Even with all the oppositions between Plato and Aristotle, metaphysical thinking in the wake of Parmenides takes its point of departure as a whole from the question of the being of beings and is to this extent ontological. True knowledge relates to what is purely universal, immutable, and necessary. It does not matter whether this is conceived according to the mathematical model as intuition and anamnesis or according to the logical model as thoughtfulness and discourse—the structures of beings themselves are what is layed hold of in knowledge. Important motives for the transition from ontological thinking to mentalism then resulted from skepticism about the priority of being over thought and from the specific nature of reflection upon questions of method. The relation of the knowing subject to itself provided access to an internal sphere of representations, a sphere which is peculiarly certain and belongs entirely to us, and which is antecedent to the world of represented objects. Metaphysics had emerged as the science of the universal, immutable, and necessary; the only equivalent left for this later on was a theory of consciousness that states the necessary subjective conditions for the objectivity of universal synthetic judgments *a priori*.

If we stick with this way of using these words, then under modern conditions of the philosophy of reflection there can be no metaphysical thinking in the strict sense but at most the reworking of metaphysical problems that have been transformed by the philosophy of consciousness. In this way it is also possible to explain Kant's ambiguous relationship to metaphysics as well as the change in meaning that this term undergoes at the hands of Kant's critique of reason. In contrast one might insist, as Henrich does, upon retaining the expression "metaphysics" for every manner of working through metaphysical questions, or those directed to the totality of (hu)man and world. That, too, has something to be said for it. For the conceptions of Leibniz or Spinoza or Schelling, as well as Kant's doctrine of two realms, stand within the tradition of the great systems that began with Plato and Aristotle. For Heidegger, even Nietzsche still counts as a metaphysical thinker because he is modern and stands under the principle of subjectivity. This terminological dispute does not lead any further into the matter itself. What is the real issue?

The *reconstructive tasks* of philosophy, or what Henrich calls the "clarification of the elementary modes of accomplishment by intelligence," are not in dispute. What has to be considered therein is not limited to the models provided by a metaphysics of (the objectivating knowledge of) nature and by a metaphysics of morals; it is in general not limited to Kant's architectonic of reason, with the separate faculties of objectivating knowledge, moral insight, and aesthetic judgment. *All* species competences of subjects capable of speech and action are accessible to a rational reconstruction if, namely, we recur to the practical knowledge to which we intuitively lay claim in tried-and-true productive accomplishments. In this respect philosophical work is continuous with scientific work. Besides posing questions directed toward what is universal, philosophy has no advantage over the sciences, and it certainly does not possess the infallibility of a privileged access to truth. Although the spontaneous expansion of the number series cannot very well be "disputed," "every theory of the series of natural numbers is in fact fallible" (Henrich, Second Thesis). What applies to the foundations of algebra is all the more valid for ethics.

Thus, except for details, the theoretical role of philosophy provides no occasion for more profound differences in opinion. It is rather the *enlightening* role of philosophy in the strict sense, directed toward the whole of life practices, which is controversial.[6] In another context, I have distinguished philosophy's role as "interpreter" from its role as "stand-in."[7] At issue here are those questions that Kant canonized as "unavoidable," which arise to a certain extent spontaneously and aim at answers that provide orientation. Philosophy is supposed to make possible a life that is "conscious" and "controlled" (*beherrschtes*), in a nondisciplinary sense, through coming to a reflexive self-understanding. In this respect philosophy is still faced with the task of taking the answers of the tradition, i.e., the sacred knowledge of religions and the mundane knowledge of cosmologies developed in the high cultures, and appropriating them within the narrowed and sharpened spotlight of what can still convince the daughters and sons of modernity with good reasons. Behind the verbal dispute over whether "metaphysics" is still possible after Kant, there is concealed a substantial disagreement about the existence and extent of those old truths that are capable of being critically appropriated, as well as a disagreement about the character of the change of meaning to which old truths are subjected when they are critically appropriated.

If we want to circumscribe this set of problems in terms of its genealogy, it is better to speak, for the sake of clarity, of metaphysical *and* religious questions. Thus, I do not believe that we, as Europeans, can seriously understand concepts like morality and ethical life, person and individuality, or freedom and emancipation, without appropriating the substance of the Judeo-Christian understanding of history in terms of salvation. And these concepts are, perhaps, nearer to our hearts than the conceptual resources of Platonic thought, centering on order and revolving around the cathartic intuition of ideas. Others begin from other traditions to find the way to the plenitude of meaning involved in concepts such as these, which structure our self-understanding. But without the transmission through socialization and the transformation through philosophy of *any one* of the great world religions, this semantic potential could one day become inaccessible. If the remnant of the intersubjectively shared self-understanding that makes human(e) intercourse with one another possible is not to disintegrate, this potential must be mastered anew by every generation. Each must be able to recognize him- or herself in all that wears a human face. To keep this sense of humanity alive and to clarify it—not, to be sure, through direct intervention, but through unceasing, indirect theoretical efforts—is certainly a task from which philosophers should not feel themselves wholly excused, even at risk of having the dubious role of a "purveyor of meaning" attributed to them.

In Germany today, however, the latter label is applied less to those who stand in an unbroken relationship to metaphysics than to those who, with the early Horkheimer, persevere in the critique of metaphysics because they believe that the universal concepts of idealism all too slickly and willingly conceal the concrete suffering that stems from degrading conditions of life. Skepticism, too, has its grounds.[8] Because new formations of the ancient alliance between metaphysics and obscurantism are uncovered again and again by critiques of ideology and of reason, Horkheimer's response is completely plausible. In order to safeguard the conceptual motifs of great philosophical thought, he wanted to transplant them into the perspective-constituting basic concepts of an interdisciplinary social theory. Certainly the Marxist philosophy of history, in whose framework he intended to undertake this transformation, has not stood up to criticism. But that does not devalue the grounds for a materialistic skepticism toward the ideological misuse of effusive ideas; nor does it devalue the correct intuition that philosophy has lost its autonomy in relation to the sciences, with which it must cooperate. Science in the singular—or *the* exemplary science that is supposed to provide a standard for other empirical sciences, whether it be physics or neurophysiology—is a fiction popular among philosophers, but no more than that. Within a highly differentiated and broadly extended spectrum, philosophy and the particular scientific disciplines are linked by relationships of affinity that vary greatly in degree: some are more or less dependent upon philosophical thoughts, others more or less open to such speculative boosts. Philosophy no longer directs its own pieces. This holds true even for the one role in which philosophy does step out of the system of sciences, in order to answer *unavoidable* questions by enlightening the lifeworld about itself as a whole. For, in the midst of certainties, the lifeworld is opaque.

Let us leave aside the concept of the lifeworld, which I have analyzed in various places.[9] For my purpose it is sufficient that individual life histories and intersubjectively shared forms of life are joined together in the structures of the lifeworld and have a part in its totalization. The horizons of our life histories and forms of life, in which we always already find ourselves, form a porous whole of familiarities that are prereflexively present but retreat in the face of reflexive incursions. As matter-of-course and as something about which we must be reassured, this totality of the lifeworld is near and far at the same time; it is also something alien from which insistent questions emerge—for example, "What is a human being?" Thus, the lifeworld is the almost naturelike wellspring for problematizations of this familiar background to the world as a whole; and it is from this source that basic philosophical questions draw the relation they have to the whole, their integrating and conclusive character. As Kant shows, one can circle in on them only along self-referential, and thus antinomic, paths of thought.[10]

However, the possibilities for answering such questions are also affected by changes that take place within the lifeworld itself. Only up to the threshold of modernity are a culture's accomplishments of reaching self-understanding joined together in interpretive systems that preserve a structure homologous to the lifeworld's entire structure of horizons. Until that point, the unity, unavoidably supposed, of a lifeworld constructed concentrically around "me" and "us," here and now, had been reflected in the totalizing unity of mythological narratives, religious doctrines, and metaphysical explanations. With modernity, however, a devaluing shift befell those forms of explanation that had allowed these very theories to retain a remnant of the unifying force possessed by myths of origin. The basic concepts of religion and metaphysics had relied upon a syndrome of validity that dissolved with the emergence of expert cultures in science, morality, and law on the one hand, and with the autonomization of art on the other. Already, Kant's three *Critiques* were a reaction to the emerging independence of distinct complexes of rationality. Since the eighteenth century, the forms of argumentation specializing in objectivating knowledge, moral-practical insight, and aesthetic judgment have diverged from one another. This has moreover occurred within institutions that could take upon themselves, without contradiction, the authority of defining the relevant criteria of validity. Today, philosophy could establish its own distinct criteria of validity—in the name of genealogy, of recollection (*Andenken*), of elucidating *Existenz*, of philosophical faith, of deconstruction, etc.—only at the price of *falling short* of a level of differentiation and justification that has already been reached, i.e., at the price of surrendering its own plausibility. What remains for philosophy, and what is within its capabilities, is to mediate interpretively between expert knowledge and an everyday practice in need of orientation. What remains for philosophy is an illuminating furtherance of lifeworld processes of achieving self-understanding, processes that are related to totality. For the lifeworld must be defended against extreme alienation at the hands of the objectivating, the moralizing, *and* the aestheticizing interventions of expert cultures.

Today, the illumination of common sense by philosophy can only be carried out according to criteria of validity that are no longer at the disposition of philosophy itself. Philosophy must operate under conditions of rationality that it has not chosen. It is for this reason unable, even in the role of an interpreter, to reclaim some sort of access to essential insights that is *privileged* in relation to science, morality, or art; it now disposes only over knowledge that is fallible. It must also do without the traditional doctrinal form that intervenes in and affects socialization; it must remain theoretical. Finally, it can no longer place the totalities of the different lifeworlds, which appear only in the plural, into a hierarchy of those which are of greater or lesser value; it is limited to grasping universal structures of lifeworlds in general. These are three respects in which there can no longer be, after Kant, a metaphysics in the sense of "conclusive" and "integrating" thought.[11]

II

We encounter in Henrich the conviction, which is otherwise still found only in dialectical materialism, that philosophical thinking is ultimately determined by a dualism amounting to two "ultimate" theories: general theories either of mind or of matter. This division into idealistic and materialistic approaches is supposed to dominate modern thought as well. Now it is certainly not to be denied that, within the highly diversified discussion of mind and body, the old contest for the primacy of *res cogitans* or of *res extensa* does stir up passions. This is especially true in the Anglo-Saxon world, where the presuppositions of a Cartesian ontology retain their force unbroken, in spite of a pragmatism that extends back to Hegel.[12] Under these premises, a knowing or acting subject is precisely that which stands over and against the world *qua* the totality of all objects or facts; yet, at the same time, it must also comprehend itself as a single object among all others (or as one complex of

facts among others). The conceptual constraints that result
from setting the ontological switches in this way remain the
same, whether this double position of the subject as "one confronting everything and one among many" is interpreted in
empiricist terms and described either via a theory of mental
representations or via an analysis of language, as it has been
from Hume to Quine, or whether it is conceived from the
perspective of transcendental philosophy as the fundamental
condition (*Grundverhältnis*) of subjectivity, as it is by Henrich.
In the construction of the theory, either the innerworldly or
the world-transcending position of the subject is accorded primacy. The subject either attempts to understand itself naturalistically, in terms of the knowledge it has of processes in the
world. Or, from the beginning, it retreats from this self-objectification by idealistically characterizing the condition of being-
in-and-outside-of-the-world-at-the-same-time, which is presented in reflection, as the fundamental phenomenon of conscious life. In any case, the opponents in this dispute find
themselves in agreement about the issue. Henrich aims to
recover its significance. For, of course, the demise of the premises of such an ontology would also spell the demise of this
alternative, understood by Henrich as naturalism versus
metaphysics.

Henrich believes that those who slip by the Cartesian language-game that places mind and body in exclusive opposition
are evading the pressing problem of naturalism. That does not
seem entirely plausible to me. In the first place, one would
have to examine whether those who step out of the Cartesian
language-game do not have good reasons for according philosophical status to "third" categories, such as "language," "action," or the "body." Attempts to think of transcendental
consciousness as "embodied" in language, action, or the body,
and to "situate" reason in society and history, are supported
by a set of arguments that is not entirely insignificant. These
arguments have been developed, from Humboldt through
Frege to Wittgenstein and through Dilthey to Gadamer, from
Peirce through Mead to Gehlen, and, finally, from Feuerbach
through Plessner to Merleau-Ponty. These attempts need not
get stuck in the cul-de-sac of a phenomenological anthropol-

ogy. They can also lead to a revision of deep-seated ontological prejudices by employing the pragmatics of language, for example, to overcome the logocentric bottleneck of a tradition that is ontologically fixated on the being of beings, epistemologically fixated on the conditions of objectivating knowledge, and semantically fixated on the truth-claim of assertoric sentences. Along the path to a pragmatics of language, it is possible to arrive at world-concepts that are more complex, and so to set aside the premises that have to be presupposed if the mind-body problematic is to be posed.[13]

In the second place, it should be borne in mind that, even then, the pressure of the problem of naturalism does not simply vanish into thin air. It merely arises in another way for those theories that do indeed *begin* with questions posed transcendentally, yet do not get stuck cutting the intelligible off from the phenomenal once and for all. These theories must find an answer to the question of how Kant can be reconciled with Darwin. It seems to me that it has been clear since Marx that the normative content of modernity can be taken up and preserved even and especially under materialistic premises. "Nature in itself" does not coincide with objectivated nature. What Marx has in mind is the emergence in natural history of the sociocultural form of life of *Homo sapiens,* which goes beyond physically objectified *natura naturata* to conceptually include, as it were, a piece of *natura naturans.* A naturalism of this sort need not be accompanied by an objectivistic self-description of culture, society, and the individual. As subjects capable of speech and action, we have, prior to all science, an *internal* connection to the symbolically structured lifeworld, to the products and competencies of socialized individuals. I have never understood why in the sciences we should be limited to the *external* connection we have to nature, why we should separate ourselves from our pretheoretical knowledge and make the lifeworld artificially unfamiliar—even if we could do so. Rat psychology might well be good for rats. On the whole, however, naturalism by no means requires the subject to give a naturalistically alienated description of itself. The subject who wants to recognize itself in its world need not insist upon using the grammar of a language that is suitable for describing things and events, or equivalent theoretical languages.

Linguistic behaviorism also seems to me to belong to these reductionistic forms of theory construction. The naturalism of this unquestionably impressive theory of language, developed from Morris to Quine, is not derived from the procedure of linguistic analysis but from the presuppositions of an empiricist ontology. This route is by no means *prescribed* by the conversion of the philosophy of consciousness into linguistic analysis; this is shown not only by the rudiments of linguistic philosophy in Humboldt and by the semiotics of Peirce but also by those implications of the linguistic turn that are critical of psychologism in semantics (Frege) and in logical empiricism's theory of science. Frankly, analytic materialism never impressed me very much—precisely because it is a metaphysical position, whereby I mean one that sticks to what is universal when the real issue is *carrying through* an abstractly posed program with scientific means. Such abstract attempts to establish an objectivistic self-understanding of the human being with one blow, as it were, thrive upon the scientistic background assumption that the natural sciences (with modern physics as their core) do in general furnish the model and the ultimate authority for all knowledge that is still acceptable. Nevertheless, they do not attempt an actual reduction of familiar social-scientific and historical facts to physics, biochemistry, neurophysiology, or even just sociobiology; rather, their only concern is the possibility in principle, based on a reversal of the natural attitude to the world, of taking *everything* that is intuitively known, the life-world context *as a whole,* and using the perspective of the natural-scientific observer to make it unfamiliar and explain it objectivistically.

I do not detect the pressure of the problem of naturalism in naturalistic thought-games but elsewhere altogether: namely, wherever naturalistic explanatory strategies within the social sciences are established with a prospect of success. Here I am thinking not so much of a hopelessly under-complex learning theory, nor even of game theory (which is on the rise but will also run up against its limits), since not everything can be reduced to strategic action. Rather, I have in mind a systems theory of society, whose basic concepts allow an approach that is both more sensitive and *more comprehensive*. This theory starts from the basic phenomenon of the self-maintenance of self-referential systems in hypercomplex environments and uses a metabiological perspective—which outdoes every ontology—to make the lifeworld into something unfamiliar.

III

By borrowing from Maturana and others, Niklas Luhmann has extended his basic concepts so far and made them so flexible that they are capable of supporting a competitive *philosophical* paradigm. The idea of a world process that takes place by way of system-environment distinctions annuls the usual ontological premises of a world of rationally ordered beings, or of a world of representable objects relating to the subject of knowledge, or of a world of existing and linguistically representable states of affairs. A theory of systems that generate themselves self-referentially is easily able to take up and absorb the heritage of the philosophy of the subject, in particular.[14] For this reason, a theory of conscious life that stands up for a nonobjectivistic self-description of the human-being-in-its-world should hardly still be seen as the paradigmatic *counter*-position to this naturalism, which both operates at the level of philosophy and is actually being worked out in detail. The conscious life of the subject in its dual position already resembles all too closely, I fear, the boundary-maintaining self-assertion of a system with its dual reference to itself and its environment.

Here we are not discussing my reasons for believing that a linguistic paradigm developed in communications-theoretic terms would be capable of offering greater resistance to this type of naturalism. However, Henrich's reservations do give me cause to indicate more precisely, at least in one respect, wherein the paradigm of consciousness and the paradigm of mutual understanding do distinguish themselves from each other.

For almost a century, various arguments have come together that have motivated the transitions from classical inferential logic to modern propositional logic, from the theoretical inter-

pretation of knowledge in terms of objects to that in terms of
states of affairs, from the intentionalistic to the linguistic explanation of accomplishments of understanding and communication, and, in general, from the introspective analysis of
facts of consciousness to the reconstructive analysis of publicly
accessible grammatical facts. To this extent, an asymmetry exists between the explanatory power of the philosophy of consciousness, which begins with the relation-to-self of a subject
that mentally represents and deals with objects, on the one
hand, and the capacity for solving problems possessed by a
theory of language, which begins with the conditions for understanding grammatical expressions, on the other hand. Certainly, I share with Henrich the belief that the phenomenon of
self-consciousness cannot be satisfactorily clarified through a
semantic analysis of the employment of *single* linguistic expressions (e.g., of the first-person singular personal pronoun).
Conversely, Henrich also drops the premise that the form of
logical and grammatical expressions could be explained by the
theory of consciousness. Instead, he favors the thesis that relation-to-self and linguistic capability are equiprimordial. It is
even intuitively plausible that "the functioning of linguistic
communication includes a relation-to-self on the part of the
speaker, as one of its constitutive conditions, which is just as
primordial as the form of the sentence with subject and predicate" (Henrich, Tenth Thesis). This seems to suggest something like an equality of status for the two paradigms that
crystalize around the relation-to-self of the speaking subject
and around the form of linguistic expressions. With the very
first test of its soundness, however, such a compromise would
certainly shatter. In constructing the theory of language, for
example, we have to decide whether to concede priority to the
incorporeal intention qua free-floating element of consciousness or to the meaning embodied in the medium of linguistic
symbols. We will come to opposing solutions, depending upon
whether the meaning that is shared intersubjectively in a linguistic community is brought to bear as the basic concept, or
whether the intersubjective understanding of an expression of
identical meaning is derived from the intentions, reflected in
one another in unending iteration, of different speakers.

This makes a third solution all the more advantageous. As soon as the theory of language is no longer semantically oriented toward the understanding of sentences but is pragmatically oriented toward the utterances with which speakers come to an understanding with each other about something, it will be able to take relation-to-self and sentence form into account on the same level. In order to reach an understanding about something, participants must not only understand the meaning of the sentences employed in their utterances, they must also be able to relate to each other in the role of speakers and hearers—in the presence of bystanders from their (or from a) linguistic community. The reciprocal interpersonal relations that are established through the speaker-hearer perspectives make possible a relation-to-self that by no means presupposes the lonely reflection of the knowing and acting subject upon itself as an antecedent consciousness. Rather, the self-relation arises out of an *interactive* context.[15]

That is, a speaker can in a performative attitude address himself to a hearer only under the condition that he learns to see and understand himself—against the background of others who are potentially present—from the perspective of his opposite number, just as the addressee for his part adopts the speaker's perspective for himself. This relation-to-self, which *results* from the adoption of the other's perspective in communicative action, can be investigated through the system of the three personal pronouns, which are linked through transformation relations, and can be differentiated according to each mode of communication.

This account escapes from the difficulty that has been connected from the start with the conceptualization of subjectivity and relation-to-self in the philosophy of consciousness. The subject that relates itself to itself *cognitively* comes across the self, which it grasps as an object, under this category as something already derived, and not as it-itself in its originality, as the author of spontaneous self-relation. Kierkegaard adopted this problem from Fichte by way of Schelling and made it into the starting point for a meditation that propels whoever existentially reflects upon himself into the "Sickness unto Death." Let us remind ourselves of the steps with which section A of that work begins. First: The self is only accessible in self-consciousness. Since, then, it is impossible to go behind this self-relation in reflection, the self of subjectivity is only the relation that relates itself to itself. Second: Such a relation, which relates itself to itself as to the self in the sense just indicated, must either have posited itself or have been posited by something else. Kierkegaard regards the first alternative (the Fichtean *Wissenschaftslehre*) as untenable and therefore turns immediately to the second. The self of the existing human is this sort of derived, posited relation and therewith one that, by relating itself to itself, relates itself to something other. This other that precedes the self of self-consciousness is, for Kierkegaard, the Christian God of Redemption, while for Henrich it is the pre-reflexively familiar anonym of conscious life, which is open to Buddhistic as well as Platonistic interpretations.[16] Both interpretations refer to a religious dimension and thereby to a language that may be derived from the old metaphysics but also transcends the modern position of consciousness.

I do not feel the slightest impulse to hinder Henrich in pursuing these far-ranging thoughts. Henrich speaks of "discouragement." Even the rhetorical force of religious speech retains its right, as long as we have not found a convincing language for the experiences and innovations conserved in it. One will nonetheless be allowed to note that the original Fichtean problem is rendered pointless by a change of paradigm.[17] If, namely, the self is part of a relation-to-self that is performatively established when the speaker takes up the second-person perspective of a hearer toward the speaker,[18] then this self is not introduced as an *object,* as it is in a relation of reflection, but as a subject that forms itself through participation in linguistic interaction and expresses itself in the capacity for speech and action. Prelinguistic subjectivity does not need to precede the relations-to-self that are posited through the structure of linguistic intersubjectivity and that intersect with the reciprocal relations of Ego, Alter, and Neuter because everything that earns the name of subjectivity, even if it is a being-familiar-with-oneself, no matter how preliminary, is indebted to the unrelentingly individuating force possessed by the linguistic medium of formative processes—which do not let up as long as communicative action is engaged in at all. According to Mead, no individuation is possible without socialization, and no socialization is possible without individualization.[19] For this reason, moreover, a social theory that captures this insight in a linguistic pragmatics must also break with the sort of Rousseauism that Henrich attributes to me.

Notes

1. Jürgen Habermas, "Rückkehr zur Metaphysik—Eine Tendenz in der deutschen Philosophie?" *Merkur*, 439/440 (1985), pp. 898ff. Reprinted as an appendix in Habermas, *Nachmetaphysisches Denken* (Frankfurt: Suhrkamp, 1988), 267ff.

2. Dieter Henrich, "Was ist Metaphysik—was Moderne? Thesen gegen Jürgen Habermas," in his *Konzepte* (Frankfurt, 1987), 11–43.

3. [Translator's note: This essay originally appeared in a festschrift dedicated to Dieter Henrich (*Theorie der Subjektivität*, ed. K. Cramer et al. [Frankfurt, 1987], 425ff.)]

4. Dieter Henrich, "Die Grundstruktur der modernen Philosophie. Mit einer Nachschrift: Über Selbstbewußtsein und Selbsterhaltung," in *Subjektivität und Selbsterhaltung*, ed. Hans Ebeling (Frankfurt: Suhrkamp, 1976), 114.

5. Ernst Tugendhat and Ursala Wolf, *Logisch-semantische Propädeutik* (Stuttgart: Reclam, 1983), 7ff.

6. Herbert Schnädelbach, "Philosophie," in *Grundkurs Philosophie*, ed. Ekkehard Martens and H. Schnädelbach (Reinbeck bei Hamburg: Rowohlt, 1985), 46–76.

7. Jürgen Habermas, "Philosophy as Stand-In and Interpreter," in *Moral Consciousness and Communicative Action*, trans. Christian Lenhardt and Shierry Weber Nicholsen (Cambridge, Mass.: MIT Press, 1990), 1–20.

8. H. Brunkhorst, "Dialektischer Positivismus des Glücks," *Zeitschrift für philosophischer Forschung* 39 (1985), 353ff.

9. Jürgen Habermas, *Theory of Communicative Action*, 2 vols., trans. Thomas McCarthy (Boston: Beacon Press, 1984, 1987), 2: 119–160; and *The Philosophical Discourse of Modernity*, trans. Frederick Lawrence (Cambridge, Mass.: MIT Press, 1987), 324ff.; also, "Handlungen, Sprechakte, sprachlich vermittelte Interaktionen und Lebenswelt," in *Nachmetaphysisches Denken*, 88ff.

10. A. Kulenkampff, *Antinomie und Dialektik* (Stuttgart, 1970).

11. Cf., however, Dieter Henrich, *Fluchtlinien* (Frankfurt: Suhrkamp, 1982), 99ff.

12. P. Bieri, ed., *Analytische Philosophie des Geistes* (Mannheim, 1981).

13. J. Habermas, *Theory of Communicative Action* 1: 76–101.

14. Cf. my excursus on Luhmann in J. Habermas, *Philosophical Discourse of Modernity*, 368ff.

15. J. Habermas, *Theory of Communicative Action* 2: 72ff.; cf. below, "Individuation through Socialization," section VI.

16. Dieter Henrich, "Dunkelheit und Vergewisserung," in *All-Einheit. Wege eines Gedankens in Ost und West,* ed. D. Henrich (Stuttgart: Klett-Cotta, 1985), 33ff.

17. Dieter Henrich, *Fichtes ursprüngliche Einsicht* (Frankfurt, 1967).

18. By no means does this exclude prelinguistic roots of cognitive development for early childhood: even with primitive rule consciousness, a rudimentary relation-to-self must already develop itself. Such ontogenetic assumptions do not, however, prejudice the description of the functioning of metacognitive abilities at the developmental stage of the mastered mother tongue, where achievements of intelligence are already linguistically organized.

19. Cf. below, pp. 177ff.

3

Themes in Postmetaphysical Thinking

The situation of present-day philosophizing, too, has become obscure. What I have in mind is not disputation among the philosophical schools—that has always been the medium through which philosophy has advanced. Rather I have in mind the debate over a premise on which all parties after Hegel previously relied. Today, what has become unclear is the position taken toward metaphysics.

The attitude of *positivism* and its successors was for a long time unambiguous; it had unmasked the questions formulated by metaphysics as meaningless—they could be pushed aside as being without any objective basis. Of course, the unenlightened scientistic motive of elevating empirical scientific thinking itself to the position of an absolute betrayed itself in this antimetaphysical furor. Nietzsche's endeavors were ambiguous from the beginning. Heidegger's destruction of the history of metaphysics[1] and the critique of ideology Adorno directed against the veiled forms of the modern philosophy of origins (*Ursprungsphilosophie*)[2] had as their aim a *negative metaphysics,* encircling that which metaphysics had always intended and had always failed to achieve. Today the spark of a *renewal of metaphysics* is rising from the ashes of negativism—whether this be a version of metaphysics asserting itself in the wake of Kant or one that is blatantly scrambling back behind Kant's transcendental dialectic.[3]

These more serious movements of thought oscillate amidst a surreal corona of *closed worldviews* that are put together by shabby speculation from bits of scientific theory. Ironically, New Age movements fill the need for the lost One and Whole by abstractly invoking the authority of a scientific system that is becoming ever more opaque. But in the sea of decentered world-understandings, closed worldviews can only stabilize themselves upon sheltered subcultural islands.

Despite this New Obscurity, I suspect that our situation is not essentially different from that of the first generation of Hegel's disciples. At that time the basic condition of philosophizing changed; since then there has been no alternative to postmetaphysical thinking.[4] I want to begin here by recalling some aspects of metaphysical thinking in order then to discuss four reasons for uneasiness with which this thinking was confronted—reasons that problematized and finally devalued metaphysics as a form of thought. In a rough simplification that neglects the Aristotelian line, I am using *metaphysical* to designate the thinking of a philosophical idealism that goes back to Plato and extends by way of Plotinus and Neo-Platonism, Augustine and Thomas Aquinas, Cusanus and Pico de Mirandola, Descartes, Spinoza, and Leibniz, up to Kant, Fichte, Schelling, and Hegel. Ancient materialism and skepticism, late-medieval nominalism, and modern empiricism are antimetaphysical countermovements, but they remain within the horizons of possible thought set by metaphysics itself. I venture to draw together under a single heading these diverse approaches to metaphysical thinking because, from the requisite distance, I am concerned with only three aspects. I want to take up the theme of unity within the philosophy of origins, the equation of being with thought, and the redemptive significance of the contemplative life; in short, identity thinking, the doctrine of Ideas, and the strong concept of theory. Of course, in the transition to the subjectivism of the modern period, these three moments underwent a peculiar refraction.

I Aspects of Metaphysical Thinking

Identity thinking
Ancient philosophy inherits from myth its view of the whole, but it distinguishes itself from myth by the conceptual level at

which it relates everything to one. Origins are no longer recol-
lected in narrative vividness as the primordial scene and beginning of the generational chain, as what is first *in the world.*
Rather, these beginnings are removed from the dimensions of
space and time and abstracted into something first which, as
the infinite, stands over and against the world of the finite and
forms its basis. Whether it is conceived as a world-transcendent
creator-god, as the essential ground of nature or, lastly and
most abstractly, as being—in each case a perspective emerges
from which innerworldly things and events, which in their
diversity are placed at a distance, can be made univocal *as
particular entities* and at the same time be conceived as parts of
a single whole. In myth the unity of the world had been produced *differently:* as the continuous contact of the particular
with the particular, as the correspondence of the like and the
unlike, as the mirroring of image and reflection, as concrete
linking, overlapping, and intertwining. The unitary thinking
of idealism breaks with the concretism involved in this way of
viewing the world. The one and the many, abstractly conceived
as the relationship of identity and difference, is the fundamental relation that metaphysical thinking comprehends both as
logical and as ontological: the one is both axiom and essential
ground, principle and origin. From it the many is derived—in
the sense both of grounding and of originating. And, thanks
to this origin, the many is reproduced as an ordered
multiplicity.[5]

Idealism
The one and the whole result from a heroic effort of thought;
the concept of being emerges with the transition from the
grammatical form and conceptual level of narration to that of
deductive explanation modeled after geometry. Thus, since
Parmenides an *internal* relation has been established between
abstractive thinking and its product, being. Plato concluded
from this that the unifying order, which as essence underlies
the multiplicity of phenomena, is itself of a conceptual nature.
The genera and species in terms of which we order phenomena
follow the ideal order of things themselves. Of course, the
Platonic Idea is neither pure concept nor pure image but rather

the typical, the form-giving, which is extracted from perceptible multiplicity. The Ideas, which are built into what is material, bring with themselves the promise of universal unity because they taper toward the apex of the hierarchically ordered conceptual pyramid and internally refer to this apex: to the Idea of the good, which comprises in itself all others. From the conceptual nature of the ideal, being derives the further attributes of universality, necessity, and supratemporality.

The history of metaphysics derives its inner dynamic both from the tension ingrained in the doctrine of Ideas between two forms of knowledge—the discursive, which is empirically based, and the anamnestic, which aims at intellectual intuition—and from the paradoxical opposition of Idea and appearance, form and matter. That is to say, from its inception idealism deceived itself about the fact that the Ideas or *formae rerum* had themselves always contained and merely duplicated what they were supposed to exclude as matter and as nonbeing *per se*—namely the material content of those empirical individuals from which the Ideas had been read off through comparative abstraction.[6]

Prima philosophia as philosophy of consciousness
Nominalism and empiricism deserve credit for having exposed this contradiction within the starting point of metaphysics and for having drawn radical conclusions therefrom. Nominalist thinking demoted the *formae rerum* to *signa rerum*, which are merely associated with things by the knowing subject—to names that we tack on to things. Hume further dissolved the desubstantialized individuals left over from nominalism into the sense impressions out of which the perceiving subject initially constructs its representation of objects. In a counter maneuver, idealist philosophy renewed both identity thinking and the doctrine of Ideas on the new foundation that was exposed by the shift in paradigms from ontology to mentalism: subjectivity. Self-consciousness, the relationship of the knowing subject to itself, has since Descartes offered the key to the inner and absolutely certain sphere of the representations we have of objects. Thus, in German Idealism metaphysical thinking could take the form of theories of subjectivity. Either self-

consciousness is put into a foundational position as the spontaneous source of transcendental accomplishments, or as spirit it is itself elevated to the position of the absolute. The ideal essences are transformed into the categorial determinations of a productive reason, so that in a peculiarly reflexive turn everything is now related to the one of a generative subjectivity. Whether reason is now approached in *foundationalist* terms as a subjectivity that makes possible the world as a whole, or whether it is conceived *dialectically* as a spirit that recovers itself in a procession through nature and history, in either case reason is active as a simultaneously totalizing and self-referential reflection.

This takes up the legacy of metaphysics to the extent that it secures the precedence of identity over difference and that of ideas over matter. Even Hegel's Logic, which is supposed to mediate symmetrically between the one and the many, the infinite and the finite, the universal and the temporal, the necessary and the contingent—even this Logic cannot but confirm the idealistic predominance of the one, the universal, and the necessary, because the operations that are both totalizing and self-referential assert themselves in the concept of mediation itself.[7]

The strong concept of theory
Each of the great world religions stakes out a privileged and particularly demanding path to the attainment of individual salvation—e.g., the way to salvation of the wandering Buddhist monk or that of the Christian eremite. Philosophy recommends as its path to salvation the life dedicated to contemplation—the *bios theoretikos*. It stands at the pinnacle of ancient forms of life, above the *vita activa* of the statesman, the pedagogue, or the physician. Theory itself is affected by being embedded in an exemplary form of life. For the few, it offers a privileged access to truth, while for the many the path to theoretical knowledge remains closed. Theory demands a renunciation of the natural attitude toward the world and promises contact with the extra-ordinary. The sacred origins of theory linger on in the contemplative present-ation of the proportions of stellar

orbits and cosmic cycles in general—*theoros* denoted the representative sent by the Greek cities to the public festivals.[8]

In the modern period the concept of theory loses this link to sacred occurrences, just as it loses its elite character, which is moderated into social privilege. What remains is the idealistic interpretation placed on distancing the everyday network of experience and interests. The methodic attitude ought to shield the scientist or scholar from local prejudices; but in the German university tradition up to Husserl, this attitude was inflated into the internally justified precedence of theory over practice. In the contempt for materialism and pragmatism there survives something of the absolutistic understanding of theory, which is not only elevated above experience and the specialized scientific disciplines but is also "pure" in the sense of having been purged cathartically of all traces of its earthly origin. Therein is completed the circuit of an identity thinking that self-referentially incorporates itself within the totality it grasps, and that wants in this way to satisfy the demand for justifying all premises from within itself. The modern philosophy of consciousness sublimates the independence of the theoretical mode of life into a theory that is absolute and self-justifying.[9]

I have characterized the metaphysical thinking that retained its force up until Hegel by the translation of identity thinking, the doctrine of ideas, and the strong concept of theory into the terms of the philosophy of consciousness. Since then, metaphysical thought has been problematized by historical developments that have come to it from outside and have in the final analysis been socially conditioned:

• Totalizing thinking that aims at the one and the whole was rendered dubious by a *new type of procedural rationality*, which has asserted itself since the seventeenth century through the empirical methods of the natural sciences, and since the eighteenth century through formalism in moral and legal theory as well as in the institutions of the constitutional state. The philosophy of nature and theories of natural law were confronted with a new species of requirements for justification. These requirements shattered *the cognitive privilege of philosophy*.

• In the nineteenth century the humanities were infused with a historical consciousness that reflected the new experiences of time and contingency within an ever more complex modern society. The intrusion of historical consciousness rendered the *dimension of finiteness* more convincing in comparison to an unsituated reason that had been idealistically apotheosized. A *detranscendentalization* of inherited basic concepts was thereby set in motion.

• Criticism of the *reification and functionalization of forms of life and interaction,* as well as of the objectivistic self-understanding of science and technology, spread during the nineteenth century. These themes have also promoted criticism of the foundations of a philosophy that forces everything into subject-object relations. *The shift in paradigms from the philosophy of consciousness to the philosophy of language* stands within this context.

• Finally, the *classical precedence of theory over practice* could no longer hold up against the mutual dependencies that were emerging ever more clearly. The embedding of theoretical accomplishments in the practical contexts of their genesis and employment gave rise to an awareness of the relevance of everyday contexts of action and communication. These contexts attain a philosophical status in, for example, the concept of a *lifeworld background.*

In what follows I want to go into these different aspects of the shattering of metaphysical thinking and, in doing so, to show that the transition to postmetaphysical thinking confronts us with new problems. In each case I want to indicate how, in the view of a theory of communicative action, we can react to the field of problems that arises *in the wake of* metaphysics.

II Procedural Rationality

Philosophy remains faithful to its metaphysical beginnings as long as it can assume that theoretical reason will rediscover itself in the rationally structured world, or that nature and history are given a rational structure by reason itself—whether through some type of transcendental foundation or in the course of a dialectical permeation of the world. A totality that is rational in itself, whether it be of the world or of a world-constituting subjectivity, guarantees participation in reason for its various parts or moments. Rationality is thought of as being material, as a rationality that organizes the contents of the world, from which it can itself be read off. Reason is of the whole and of its parts.

In contrast, both modern empirical science and autonomous morality place their confidence solely in the rationality of their own approaches and their *procedures*—namely, in the method of scientific knowledge or in the abstract point of view under which moral insights are possible. Rationality (*Rationalität*) is reduced to something formal insofar as the rationality (*Vernünftigkeit*) of content evaporates into the validity of results. The latter depends upon the rationality of the procedures one uses in trying to solve problems—empirical and theoretical problems for the community of inquirers and for the organized scientific enterprise, and moral-practical problems for the community of citizens of a democratic state and for the system of law. The order of things that is found in the world itself, or that has been projected by the subject, or has grown out of the self-formative process of spirit, no longer counts as rational; instead, what counts as rational is solving problems successfully through procedurally suitable dealings with reality. Procedural rationality can no longer guarantee an *antecedent* unity in the manifold of appearances.

The perspective from which metaphysics distinguished essence from appearance vanishes together with the anticipation of the totality of beings. In science phenomena are traced back to more and more fundamental structures whose depth matches the range of explanatory theories; but these structures no longer stand within the referential network of a totality. They no longer throw light upon the individual's position in the cosmos, upon one's place within the architectonic of reason or within the system. Essences elude the knowledge of nature just as they elude the theory of natural law. With the methodological separation of the natural sciences and the humanities, the perspectival difference between *outside* and *inside* develops and replaces the difference between *essence* and *appearance*.

Only an objectifying approach to nature based on observation is now seen as promising for the nomological empirical sciences, whereas the hermeneutical sciences only gain access to the historical-cultural world through the performative attitude of a participant in communication. A splitting-up of object realms corresponds to this privileging of the observer's perspective in the natural sciences and of the participant's perspective in the humanities. While nature resists an interpretive-reconstructive approach from within and only yields to nomological knowledge that is counterintuitive and guided by observation, the ensemble of social and cultural products is disclosed, as it were, from within through an interpretive procedure that links up with the intuitive knowledge of the participants. The knowledge of essences that explicates networks of meaning finds no hold on an objectified nature; and the hermeneutical replacement for it is now available only for that sphere of nonbeing in which, according to the conception of metaphysics, the ideal essences should never even have been able to get a foothold.

Finally, the methodically generated knowledge of the modern sciences loses even its characteristic autarky. In conceptually grasping the totality of nature and history, totalizing thought also operated self-referentially and was supposed to prove and justify itself as philosophical knowledge—whether through arguments providing ultimate justification or through the spiraling self-explication of the all-encompassing concept. In contrast, the premises with which scientific theories begin are treated as hypotheses and have to be justified through their consequences—whether through empirical confirmation or through their coherence with other statements that are already accepted. The fallibilism of scientific theories is incompatible with the type of knowledge *prima philosophia* believed itself capable of attaining. Every comprehensive, closed, and final system of statements must be formulated in a language that requires no commentary and allows of no interpretations, improvements, or innovations that might place it at a distance; it must bring its own effective history to a standstill. Such finality is incompatible with the unprejudiced openness characterizing the cognitive progress of science.

For these reasons, the reorientation of knowledge from material to procedural rationality was an embarrassment for metaphysical thinking. From the middle of the nineteenth century, the authority of the empirical sciences forced philosophy to assimilate.[10] Since that time, the idea of a return to metaphysics, which has been called for ever and again, has been stigmatized as something purely reactionary. Yet, attempts at assimilating philosophy to the natural or the human sciences, or to logic and mathematics, have only created new problems.

Both the vulgar materialism of Moleschott and Büchner and post-Machian positivism aimed at constructing a worldview along natural-scientific lines. Dilthey and historicism dissolved philosophy into the history of philosophy and the typology of *Weltanschauungen*. And the Vienna Circle set philosophy upon the narrow path of methodology and the theory of science. Yet, with each of these reactions, philosophical thinking seemed to surrender what is specific to it—namely the emphatic knowledge of the whole—without really being able to compete seriously with the sciences that were proclaimed as models in each case.

A division of labor that might guarantee to philosophy its *own* object realm with its *own* method presented itself as an alternative. As is well known, phenomenology and analytic philosophy have taken this route, each in its own way. But anthropology, psychology, and sociology have not particularly respected such special preserves; the human sciences have overstepped the demarcation lines of eidetic abstraction and of analysis; they have forced their way into the philosophical inner sanctum.

The turn to the irrational remained as a final way out. In this guise philosophy was supposed to secure its possessions and its relation to totality at the price of renouncing contestable knowledge. Philosophy has appeared in this form as existential illumination and philosophical faith (Jaspers), as a mythology that complements science (Kolakowski), as the mystical thinking of Being (Heidegger), as the therapeutic treatment of language (Wittgenstein), as deconstructive activity (Derrida), or as negative dialectics (Adorno). The antiscientism of these delimitations permits them only to say what philosophy is not and does not want to be; as a nonscience, however, philosophy must leave its own status undetermined. Positive determinations have become impossible because cognitive accomplishments can now prove themselves only through procedural rationality, ultimately through the procedure of argumentation.

Today, these embarrassments demand that the relationship of philosophy to science be determined anew. Once it renounces its claim to be a first science or an encyclopedia, philosophy can maintain its status within the scientific system neither by assimilating itself to particular exemplary sciences nor by exclusively distancing itself from science in general. Philosophy has to implicate itself in the fallibilistic self-understanding and procedural rationality of the empirical sciences; it may not lay claim to a privileged access to truth, or to a method, an object realm, or even just a style of intuition that is specifically its own. Only thus can philosophy contribute its best to a nonexclusive division of labor,[11] namely, its persistent tenacity in posing questions universalistically, and its procedure of rationally reconstructing the intuitive pretheoretical knowledge of competently speaking, acting, and judging subjects— yet in such a way that Platonic anamnesis sheds its nondiscursive character. This dowry recommends philosophy as an indispensable partner in the collaboration of those who are concerned with a theory of rationality.

Even if philosophy does find its niche in this way *within* the scientific system, it need not by any means completely surrender the relationship to the whole that had distinguished metaphysics. There is no point in defending this relationship without some definable claim to knowledge. But the lifeworld is always already intuitively present to all of us as a totality that is unproblematized, nonobjectified, and pretheoretical—as the sphere of that which is daily taken for granted, the sphere of common sense. In an awkward way, philosophy has always been closely affiliated with the latter. Like it, philosophy moves within the vicinity of the lifeworld; its relation to the totality of this receding horizon of everyday knowledge is similar to that of common sense. And yet, through the subversive power of reflection and of illuminating, critical, and dissecting analysis, philosophy is completely opposed to common sense. By virtue of this intimate yet fractured relation to the lifeworld, philosophy is also well suited for a role on *this side* of the scientific system—for the role of an interpreter mediating between the expert cultures of science, technology, law, and morality on the one hand, and everyday communicative practices on the other hand, and indeed in a manner similar to that in which literary and art criticism mediate between art and life.[12] Of course, the lifeworld with which philosophy maintains a type of nonobjectifying contact is not to be confused with the totality of the universal one, of which metaphysics wished to provide an image or, more precisely, a worldview. Postmetaphysical thinking operates with a different concept of the world.

III Situating Reason

Initially, postmetaphysical thinking was thoroughly characterized by its critique of Hegel's brand of idealism. The first generation of Hegel's disciples criticized in the work of their teacher the secret preponderance of what is universal, supratemporal, and necessary over what is particular, variable, and accidental, and thus the idealistic casting given to the concept of reason. Feuerbach emphasized the priority of what is objective: subjectivity is both embedded in an inner nature and confronted by an outer nature. Marx saw spirit rooted in material production and embodied in the ensemble of social relations. Finally, Kierkegaard counterposed the facticity of one's own existence and the inwardness of the radical will to be oneself against a chimerical reason within history. All of these arguments seek to recover the finite character of mind from the self-referential, totalizing thinking of the dialectic—Marx spoke of the "process of decay" of absolute spirit. Of course, all the Young Hegelians ran the risk in turn of hypostatizing the prius of nature, society, and history into something in-itself, and of thereby slipping back unacknowledged to the level of precritical thinking.[13] The Young Hegelians were strong enough to convince [their audience]—in the name of objectivity, finitude, and facticity—of the desideratum of a reason produced in natural history, incarnated bodily, situated socially, and contextualized historically. But they could not redeem this desideratum at the level marked out by Kant and Hegel. They thus opened the gates to Nietzsche's more radical critique of reason which, through inversion, ends up totalizing itself.

An appropriate concept of *situated reason* was established not along these lines but rather as the consequence of another critique, one directed against the foundationalist variety of thought within the philosophy of the subject. Through this discussion, which took Kant as its starting point, the basic concepts of transcendental philosophy were undermined, although perhaps not yet paradigmatically overcome.

The extramundane position of transcendental subjectivity, to which the metaphysical attributes of universality, supratemporality, and necessity were transferred, initially collided with the premises of the new cultural sciences. In their object realms, these sciences encounter formations that are already prestructured symbolically and that possess, as it were, the dignity of products resulting from transcendental accomplishments. Nevertheless, they are supposed to be subjected to a purely empirical analysis. Foucault describes how the human sciences plumb the empirical conditions under which diversified and individualized transcendental subjects bring forth their worlds, symbolic systems, forms of life, and institutions. In so doing, these sciences helplessly entangle themselves in a dual transcendental-empirical perspective lacking in clarity.[14] Dilthey sees this circumstance as an invitation to a critique of historical reason. He wants to reconstruct the basic concepts of transcendental philosophy in such a way that those synthetic accomplishments that have no origin and are removed from all contingency and natural necessity can henceforth find their place *within* the world, without having to surrender their internal connection to the process of world constitution.

Historicism and *Lebensphilosophie* have attributed an epistemological significance to the transmission of tradition, to aesthetic experience, and to the bodily, social, and historical existence of the individual; this significance had to explode the classical concept of the transcendental subject. Transcendental synthesis was replaced by the ostensibly concrete yet structureless productivity of "life." On the other hand, Husserl did not hesitate to equate the transcendental ego, to which he held fast, with the existing consciousness of each individual phenomenologist. Both these lines of argumentation come together in Heidegger's *Being and Time*. Under the rubric of *"Dasein,"* generative subjectivity is finally brought down from the realm of the intelligible; if not really placed on this side of history, still it is set within the dimensions of historicity and individuality. The definitive figure of thought is that of the "thrown projection" relating to care about an existence that is in each case mine.

This historicization and individuation of the transcendental subject makes it necessary to restructure the architectonic of basic concepts. The subject loses its familiar dual position as one over and against everything and as one among many. As transcendental consciousness, Kant's subject had indeed stood over and against the world qua the totality of objects of experience; but as empirical consciousness in the world, it also appeared as one entity among many. In contrast, Heidegger wants to conceive of world-projecting subjectivity itself as Being-in-the-world, as an individual *Dasein* that finds itself already within the facticity of historical surroundings, yet at the same time must not surrender its transcendental spontaneity. Regardless of its world-constituting originality, transcendental consciousness is supposed to be subjected to the conditions of historical facticity and innerworldly existence. Admittedly, these conditions themselves must not be conceived as something ontic, as something coming forth in the world. Rather, they restrict from within, as it were, the generative accomplishments of the subject that is in the world; they limit the world-projecting spontaneity at its source. The transcendental distinction between *constituens* and *constitutum* is replaced by another distinction: the ontological difference between the world-project, which opens the horizon of possible encounters in the world, and what is in fact encountered therein.

Now, however, the question arises whether the disclosure of the world, the letting-be of beings, can still be conceived as an *activity* at all and attributed to a subject that accomplishes it. In *Being and Time* Heidegger still favored this version. Despite its existential rootedness in the world, the individual *Dasein* retains the authorship of the sovereign world-project, the world-forming potency without the affiliated extramundane position. But with this decision Heidegger assumes a consequent problem, one on which Husserl labored in vain in the fifth Cartesian Meditation and for which Sartre, too, could find no solution in the third part of *Being and Nothingness*. Namely, as soon as consciousness in general breaks up into the pluralism of individual world-constituting monads, there arises the problem of how from each of their perspectives an intersubjective world can be constituted in which one subjectivity would be able to encounter another not just as an objectifying counterpower but in the other's originary world-projecting spontaneity. This problem of intersubjectivity is rendered unsolvable once one accepts the premise of a *Dasein* that can authentically project itself in response to its possibilities only in solitude.[15]

In his later philosophy Heidegger developed an alternative. Here he no longer encumbers the individual *Dasein* with the process of world-disclosure; he no longer conceives of world-constitution as an accomplishment at all but instead as the overpowering, anonymous happening of a temporalized originary power. The transformation of the ontological takes place in the medium of language as a happening beyond ontic history. With that, the problem of intersubjectivity is rendered irrelevant. Now, however, Being itself has become sovereign; it rules in an unforeseeable way over the grammatical transformation of linguistic worldviews. Language's power to create meaning is promoted by the later Heidegger to the rank of the absolute. But from this there results another problem: the prejudicing force of linguistic world-disclosure devalues all innerworldly learning processes. The ontological preunderstanding that dominates in any given period forms a *fixed* framework for the practices of the socialized individuals who are in the world. The encounter with what is innerworldly moves *fatalistically* along the paths of antecedently regulated contexts of meaning, such that these contexts themselves cannot be affected by successful problem solutions, by accumulated knowledge, by the transformed state of productive forces, or by moral insights. It thus becomes impossible to account for the dialectical interplay between the shifting horizons of meaning, on the one hand, and the dimension in which these horizons must in fact prove their viability, on the other.

All these attempts to detranscendentalize reason continue to get entangled in the prior conceptual decisions of transcendental philosophy, decisions in which they remain trapped. The false alternatives only fall by the wayside with the transition to a new paradigm, that of mutual understanding (*Verständigung*). Subjects capable of speaking and acting who, against the background of a common lifeworld, come to an understanding with each other about something in the world, relate to the medium of their language both autonomously and dependently: they can make use of grammatical rule-systems, which make their practices possible in the first place, for their own purposes as well. Both moments are equiprimordial.[16] On the one hand, these subjects always find themselves already in a linguistically structured and disclosed world; they live off of grammatically projected interconnections of meaning. To this extent, language sets itself off from the speaking subjects as something antecedent and objective, as the structure that forges conditions of possibility. On the other hand, the linguistically disclosed and structured lifeworld finds its footing only in the practices of reaching understanding within a linguistic community. In this way, the linguistic formation of consensus, by means of which interactions link up in space and time, remains dependent upon the autonomous "yes" and "no" positions that communication participants take toward criticizable validity claims.

Natural languages do more than open the horizons of the specific worlds in which socialized subjects find themselves. They also force these subjects to their *own* independent accomplishments—namely, to an innerworldly practice oriented toward validity claims, a practice in which projected world-disclosing meanings are subjected to an *ongoing test* in which they can prove their worth. A circular process comes into play between the lifeworld as the resource from which communicative action draws, and the lifeworld as the product of this action; in this process, no gap is left by the disappearance of the transcendental subject. Of course, it was the linguistic turn in philosophy that first prepared the conceptual means needed for an analysis of the type of reason embodied in communicative action.

IV The Linguistic Turn

In the last two sections I have shown how post-Hegelian thought broke away from the metaphysical concept of reason as it appeared in the philosophy of consciousness. Having treated identity thinking and idealism, I still want to discuss the relationship of theory to practice; but first I would like to go into the critique of the philosophy of consciousness that paved the way for postmetaphysical thinking. Specifically, the transition from the philosophy of consciousness to the philosophy of language results in advantages not only from the standpoint of method but from the standpoint of content as well. This transition breaks out of the circle of a hopeless to-and-fro between metaphysical and antimetaphysical thinking, i.e., between idealism and materialism. Moreover, it makes it possible to attack a problem that cannot be solved using the basic concepts of metaphysics: the problem of individuality. But several very different themes come together in the critique of the philosophy of consciousness. I want at least to name the four most important of these.

(1)   Whoever chooses the self-relation of the knowing subject as the starting point of his analysis has, since Fichte, had to deal with the following objection: self-consciousness could by no means be an original phenomenon, because whenever the knowing subject turns back upon itself in order to lay hold of itself as an object, the spontaneity of conscious life withdraws from the very objective form under which it would have to be subsumed.[17] Since Nietzsche, the fundamental conceptual necessity of objectification and self-objectification has also served as the target of a critique, extending to modern conditions of life in general, of thought that controls or instrumental reason.

(2)   Since Frege, logic and semantics have inflicted a beating on the object-theoretical conception that results from the conceptual strategy of the philosophy of consciousness. The acts of the judging, acting, and experiencing subject were always supposed to be directed toward objects (in Husserl's words,

intentional objects). Yet, this concept of the *represented* (*vorgestellten*) object does not do justice to the propositional structure of the states of affairs that are *meant* (*gemeint*) and stated.[18]

(3) Further, naturalism has cast doubt on whether it is at all possible to approach consciousness as a foundation, as something unconditioned and original: Kant had to be brought into accord with Darwin. Later, the theories of Freud, Piaget, and Saussure offered third categories that avoided the basic conceptual dualism of the philosophy of consciousness. The categories of the expressive body, of behavior, of action, and of language introduce relations that the socialized organism of a subject capable of speaking and acting *already* has to the world, before this subject takes up an objectivating relation to something in the world.[19]

(4) Of course, it was the linguistic turn that first provided reservations such as these with a firm methodological foundation. Traditionally, language was conceived in terms of the model of assigning names to objects and was viewed as an instrument of communication that remained external to the content of thought. The new foundation, already marked out by Humboldt, depended upon turning away from this traditional conceptualization. The new, transcendentally characterized conception of language attained paradigmatic relevance primarily through the methodological advantage it had over the philosophy of the subject, which has to invoke introspective access to facts of consciousness. The description of entities that appear within the space of mental representations or in the stream of lived experiences remains tainted with the stigma of what is merely subjective. This is equally true whether one looks for support from inner experience, intellectual intuition, or immediate evidence. The intersubjective validity of observations can be ascertained through experimental practice and thus through a regulated transformation of perceptions into data. A similar objectivation seems to work when the analysis of mental representations and thoughts is undertaken using the grammatical formations with whose help they are expressed. Grammatical expressions are something publicly accessible; one can read structures off from them without having to refer to what is merely subjective. The exemplary models of

mathematics and logic also helped to direct philosophy to the public object realm of grammatical expressions. The turning point is marked by Frege and Peirce.[20]

Admittedly, at first the linguistic turn was made within the limits of semanticism, that is, at the price of abstractions that kept the problem-solving potential of the new paradigm from being fully exploited. Semantic analysis remains in essence an analysis of sentence forms, above all the forms of assertoric sentences. It disregards the speech situation, the employment of language and its context, and the claims, dialogue roles, and positions of the speaker. In a word, it disregards the pragmatics of language, which formal semantics wanted to entrust to a different, namely an empirical, investigation. In the same way, the theory of science isolated the logic of inquiry from questions about the dynamics of inquiry; the latter were supposed to be left to psychologists, historians, and sociologists.

This semanticistic abstraction cuts language down to a format that makes its distinctive self-referential character unrecognizable.[21] Just one example of this: in the case of nonlinguistic actions, the intention of the actor cannot be extracted from his manifest behavior; at most it can be indirectly inferred. In the case of a speech act, however, the very act itself gives the hearer an understanding of the intention of the speaker. Linguistic utterances identify themselves because they are structured self-referentially and comment upon the sense in which the content expressed by them is employed.

The discovery, following Wittgenstein and Austin, of this performative-propositional double structure was the first step on the way to bringing pragmatic elements into a formal analysis.[22] Only with this transition to a formal pragmatics does linguistic analysis win back those dimensions and problematics of the philosophy of the subject that had been given up for lost. The next step is the analysis of the universal presuppositions that must be fulfilled if participants in communication are to be able to come to an understanding with each other about something in the world. A peculiarity exhibited by these pragmatic presuppositions of consensus formation is that they contain strong idealizations. For example, the supposition that all participants in dialogue use the same linguistic expressions with identical meanings is unavoidable but often counterfactual. The validity claims that a speaker raises for the content of his assertoric, normative, or expressive sentences are also bound to similar idealizations: what the speaker, here and now in a given context, asserts as valid transcends, *according to the sense of his claim,* all context-dependent, merely local standards of validity. These and similar idealizing yet unavoidable presuppositions for actual communicative practices possess a normative content that carries the tension between the intelligible and the empirical into the sphere of appearances itself. Counterfactual presuppositions become social facts. This critical thorn sticks in the flesh of any social reality that has to reproduce itself via action oriented toward reaching understanding.

The linguistic turn was made not only by propositional semantics but by semiotics as well, for example in Saussure. But structuralism also gets caught in the snare of abstractive fallacies. By elevating anonymous forms of language to a transcendental status, it downgrades the subjects and their speech to something merely accidental. How the subjects speak and what they do is supposed to be explained by the underlying system of rules. The individuality and creativity of subjects capable of speaking and acting, indeed absolutely everything that had been attributed to subjectivity as a possession, now become residual phenomena that are either neglected or devalued as narcissistic symptoms (Lacan). Whoever would nonetheless like to continue to pay them their due under structuralist premises must transfer everything that is individual and innovative into a prelinguistic sphere that is accessible only through intuition.[23]

The pragmatic turn leads the way out of this structuralist abstraction as well. Transcendental accomplishments have not by any means withdrawn into the system of grammatical rules as such. Rather, linguistic synthesis results from constructive accomplishments of mutual understanding, accomplishments that are achieved in the form of a refracted intersubjectivity. Certainly, grammatical rules guarantee an identity of meaning for linguistic expressions. But at the same time, they must leave room for individual nuances and innovative unpredictability in the use of these expressions, whose identity of meaning is only presumed. The shadow of difference that is cast on every linguistically attained agreement is explained by the fact that the intentions of speakers also diverge again and again from the standard meanings of the expressions they use: "All understanding is for this reason always simultaneously non-understanding, and all accord in thoughts and feelings is simultaneously a parting of the ways." (Wilhelm von Humboldt) The intersubjectivity of linguistically achieved understanding is by nature porous, and linguistically attained consensus does not eradicate from the accord the differences in speaker perspectives but rather presupposes them as ineliminable. For these reasons, action that is oriented toward reaching understanding is also suitable as a medium for those formative processes that at once make possible both socialization and individuation. The grammatical role of the personal pronouns forces the speaker and the hearer to adopt a performative attitude in which the one confronts the other as *alter ego:* only with a consciousness of their absolute difference and irreplaceability can the one recognize himself in the other. Thus, although the nonidentical is vulnerable, has been repeatedly distorted through objectification, and has therefore always slipped through the net of basic metaphysical concepts, it remains accessible in a trivial way in everyday communicative practice.[24] But the scope of this profane rescue of the nonidentical will only be recognizable when we give up the classical precedence of theory over practice and, in so doing, also overcome the logocentric constriction of reason.

V Deflating the Extra-Ordinary

To the extent that philosophy has withdrawn into the system of the sciences and has established itself as one academic discipline among others, it has had to renounce its privileged access to truth and the redemptive significance of theory. Today, philosophy is still a matter for the few only in the harmless sense of being special knowledge left to experts. Unlike the other scientific disciplines, to be sure, philosophy also still maintains a certain relation to pretheoretical knowledge and to the nonobjective totality of the lifeworld. *From there,* philosophical thinking can then *turn back* towards science as a whole and undertake a self-reflection of the sciences that goes beyond the limits of methodology and the theory of science and that—in a reversal of the ultimate grounding of all knowledge in metaphysics—exposes the meaning-foundation of scientific theory-formation in prescientific practice. Such internal connections between genesis and validity have been uncovered by pragmatism from Peirce to Quine, by philosophical hermeneutics from Dilthey to Gadamer, and also by Scheler's sociology of knowledge, Husserl's analysis of the lifeworld, the anthropology of knowledge from Merleau-Ponty to Apel, and postempiricist theory of science since Kuhn. Even esoteric cognitive accomplishments have roots in the practices of prescientific dealings with things and persons. With this, the classical precedence of theory over practice is undermined.

For philosophy itself, however, this type of insight has become a source of uneasiness; indeed, the modern form of skepticism is nourished primarily by this source. Once expert cultures are no longer in need of justification and have taken upon themselves the authority to define the relevant criteria of validity, philosophy no longer disposes over its own, distinct criteria of validity, criteria that might have remained unaffected by insights into the fundamental primacy of practice over theory. Thus, conclusions keep forcing themselves on us that contradict the universalistic claims made for situated reason. Today, many areas are dominated by a contextualism that confines all truth claims to the scope of local language games and conventionally accepted rules of discourse and assimilates all standards of rationality to habits or to conventions that are only valid *in situ*.[25]

I cannot go into this discussion here and will have to rest content with one counterthesis. The insight into the fundamental primacy of practice over theory, which has relevance for validity as well, leads to a radical skepticism about reason only if the gaze of philosophy is *restricted* to questions of truth that can be dealt with by science. Ironically, philosophy has itself fostered this kind of cognitivistic reduction and has pinned reason down to only one of its dimensions, at first ontologically, later epistemologically, and then even in linguistic analysis—to the logos that inheres in the totality of beings, to the capacity to represent and act upon objects, or to the fact-stating discourse that specializes in only one dimension of speech, the truth of assertoric sentences. The occidental deference towards logos reduces reason to something that language performs in only one of its functions, in representing states of affairs. Ultimately, methodically pursuing questions of truth is the only thing that still counts as rational. Questions of justice and questions of taste, as well as questions regarding the truthful presentation of self, are all excluded from the sphere of the rational. Whatever surrounds and borders on the scientific culture that specializes in questions of truth, every context in which this culture is embedded and rooted, then appears to be irrational as such. Contextualism is only the flipside of logocentrism.

But philosophy liberates itself from logocentrism when it is not completely absorbed by the self-reflection of the sciences, when its gaze is not fixated on the scientific system, when it reverses this perspective and looks back upon the thicket of the lifeworld. It then discovers a reason that is already operating in everyday communicative practice.[26] True, claims to propositional truth, normative rightness, and subjective truthfulness intersect here within a concrete, linguistically disclosed world horizon; yet, as criticizable claims they also transcend the various contexts in which they are formulated and gain acceptance. In the validity spectrum of the everyday practice of reaching understanding, there comes to light a communicative rationality opening onto several dimensions; at the same time, this communicative rationality provides a standard for evaluating systematically distorted forms of communication and of life that result when the potential for reason that became available with the transition to modernity is selectively utilized.

In its role as interpreter, in which it mediates between expert knowledge and everyday practices in need of orientation, philosophy can make use of that knowledge and contribute to making us conscious of the deformations of the lifeworld. But it can do so only as a critical agency, for it is no longer in possession of an affirmative theory of the good life. *After* metaphysics, the nonobjective whole of a concrete lifeworld, which is now present only as horizon and background, evades the grasp of theoretical objectification. Marx's saying about the realization of philosophy can also be understood in this way: what has, following the disintegration of metaphysical and religious worldviews, been divided up on the level of cultural systems under various aspects of validity, can now be put together—and also put right—only in the experiential context of lifeworld practices.[27]

In the wake of metaphysics, philosophy surrenders its extraordinary status. Explosive experiences of the extraordinary have migrated into an art that has become autonomous. Of course, even after this deflation, ordinary life, now fully profane, by no means becomes immune to the shattering and subversive intrusion of extraordinary events. Viewed from without, religion, which has largely been deprived of its worldview functions, is still indispensable in ordinary life for normalizing intercourse with the extraordinary. For this reason, even postmetaphysical thinking continues to coexist with religious practice—and not merely in the sense of the contemporaneity of the noncontemporaneous. This ongoing coexistence even throws light on a curious dependence of a philosophy that has forfeited its contact with the extraordinary. Philosophy, even in its postmetaphysical form, will be able neither to replace nor to repress religion as long as religious language is the bearer of a semantic content that is inspiring and even indispensable, for this content eludes (for the time being?) the explanatory force of philosophical language and continues to resist translation into reasoning discourses.

Notes

1. Martin Heidegger, *Nietzsche,* vols. 1 & 2, trans. David Krell (San Francisco: Harper & Row, 1979–1987).

2. Theodor Adorno, *Against Epistemology: A Metacritique,* trans. Willis Domingo (Oxford: Blackwell, 1982). [Translator's Note: *"Ursprungsphilosophie"* might also be translated as "First Philosophy" or even "metaphysics," but since the reference to origins is somewhat obscured in these more usual terms, I generally follow the English translation of Adorno cited here and use the phrase "philosophy of origins."]

3. Dieter Henrich, *Fluchtlinien* (Frankfurt: Suhrkamp, 1982); R. Spaemann, *Philosophische Essays* (Stuttgart: Reclam, 1956).

4. Reasons supporting this premise are given in J. Habermas, *Philosophical Discourse of Modernity*, trans. Frederick Lawrence (Cambridge, Mass.: MIT Press, 1987).

5. W. Beierwaltes, *Denken des Einen* (Frankfurt, 1985).

6. T. Adorno, *Against Epistemology*, 21: "The philosophy of origins—which through self-consistency, the flight before the conditioned, turns to the subject and pure identity—also fears that it will lose itself in the determinacy of the purely subjective, which, as isolated moment, has precisely never reached pure identity and bears its defect as well as its opposite. Great philosophy has not escaped this antinomy." On the significance of the nonidentical for the history of metaphysics, cf. also K. H. Haag, *Der Fortschritt in der Philosophie* (Frankfurt: Suhrkamp, 1983).

7. Cf. Dieter Henrich, *Hegel im Kontext* (Frankfurt: Suhrkamp, 1967), 35ff.

8. B. Schnell, *Die Entdeckung des Geistes* (Hamburg, 1955), 401ff.

9. On Fichte's idea of final grounding, cf. V. Hösle, *Hegels System* (Hamburg: Meiner, 1988), 1: 22ff.

10. Herbert Schnädelbach, *Philosophy in Germany 1831–1933, trans. Eric Matthews (Cambridge: Cambridge University Press, 1984).*

11. Jürgen Habermas, "Philosophy as Stand-In and Interpreter," in *Moral Consciousness and Communicative Action*, trans. Christian Lenhardt and Shierry Weber Nicholsen (Cambridge, Mass.: MIT Press, 1990), 1–20.

12. Cf. my excursus on Derrida: J. Habermas, *Philosophical Discourse of Modernity*, 185ff.

13. Even Marx did not adequately think through the relationship between nature in itself, nature for us, and society. Engels's dialectic of nature, which represented the extension of historical to dialectical materialism, then made the lapse into precritical thinking evident.

14. Cf. the final chapter of Michel Foucault, *The Order of Things* (New York: Pantheon, 1971).

15. Michael Theunissen, *The Other*, trans. Christopher Macann (Cambridge, Mass.: MIT Press, 1984), 187ff.

16. Cf. my reply to Taylor in: J. Habermas, "A Reply," in *Communicative Action*, ed. Axel Honneth and Hans Joas (Cambridge, Mass.: MIT Press, 1991), 215ff.; and in this volume below, "Individuation through Socialization," section IV.

17. Nonegological theories of consciousness that seek a way out of this aporia are discussed in Manfred Frank, *Die Unhintergehbarkeit von Individualität* (Frankfurt, 1986), 33–64.

18. Ernst Tugendhat, *Traditional and Analytical Philosophy*, trans. P. A. Gorner (Cambridge: Cambridge University Press, 1982), 50–75.

19. The themes of the philosophical anthropology developed by H. Plessner and A. Gehlen are again taken up in the anthropological phenomenology of Merleau-Ponty; cf. Bernhard Waldenfels, *Phänomenologie in Frankreich* (Frankfurt: Suhrkamp, 1983); and Axel Honneth and Hans Joas, *Social Action and Human Nature*, trans. Raymond Meyer (Cambridge: Cambridge University Press, 1988).

20. Cf. the writings of Charles S. Peirce from his middle period in Peirce, *Schriften zum Pragmatismus*, ed. Karl-Otto Apel (Frankfurt: Suhrkamp, 1976), 141ff. [Translator's note: This includes translations of the following articles by Peirce from his *Collected Papers*, 8 vols. (Cambridge, Mass.: Harvard University Press, 1931–1958): "The Fixation of Belief," 5: 223–247; "How To Make our Ideas Clear," 5: 248–271; selections from "The Doctrine of Chances," 2: 389–414; selections from "The Theory of Probable Inference," 2: 433–477; and "Deduction, Induction, and Hypothesis," 2: 372–388. It also includes C. S. Peirce, "Draft of a Preface to 'My Pragmatism'," appendix to Max Fisch, "Was There a Metaphysical Club?," in *Studies in the Philosophy of Charles Sanders Peirce. Second Series,* ed. E. C. Moore and R. S. Robin (Amherst: University of Massachusetts Press, 1964), 24–29.]

21. Karl-Otto Apel, *Transformation der Philosophie,* 2 vols. (Frankfurt: Suhrkamp, 1973) 2: 155ff. [The majority of these essays are available in English in K.-O. Apel, *Towards a Transformation of Philosophy,* trans. Glyn Adey and David Frisby (Boston: Routledge & Kegan Paul, 1980), 77–300.]

22. John Searle, *Speech Acts* (Cambridge: Cambridge University Press, 1969).

23. Manfred Frank, *What Is Neostructuralism?,* trans. Sabine Wilke and Richard Gray (Minneapolis: University of Minnesota Press, 1989), 359ff.

24. Cf. K. H. Haag, *Der Fortschritt in der Philosophie,* 50ff.; cf. below, "Individuation through Socialization."

25. Richard Rorty, "Solidarity or Objectivity?," in *Post-Analytic Philosophy,* ed. John Rajchman and Cornel West (New York: Columbia University Press, 1985), 3ff.; and in this volume below, pp. 134ff.

26. U. Matthiesen, *Das Dickicht der Lebenswelt und die Theorie des kommunikativen Handelns* (Munich, 1985).

27. Cf. below, pp. 140ff.

II
The Turn to Pragmatics

4

Toward a Critique of the Theory of Meaning

I Three Approaches to a Theory of Meaning

A theory of meaning should answer the question: what is it to understand the sense of a—well-formed—symbolic expression? In 1934, Karl Bühler proposed a functional scheme for language that classified linguistic expressions according to their relations to the speaker, to the world, and to the hearer.[1]

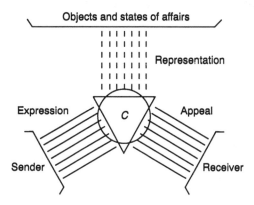

Figure 1
Buhler's functional scheme for language

This scheme for the employment of signs shows its usefulness when one removes it from the formative context of a specific psychology of language, expands upon the semiotic starting point, and gives a charitable interpretation to the three functions named. There then emerges from the diagram the general thesis that language represents a medium—Bühler spoke of the organon-model of language—that simultaneously serves three different, though internally related, functions. Expressions that are employed communicatively serve to express the intentions (or experiences) of a speaker, to represent states of affairs (or something the speaker encounters in the world), and to establish relations with an addressee. The three aspects of a *speaker* coming to an understanding with *another person* about *something* are reflected therein. Three rays of meaning intersect and are focused in linguistic expressions. What the speaker wants to say with the expression is connected with what is literally said in it, as well as with the action that what is said should be understood as. There arises a threefold relationship between the meaning of a linguistic expression and what is *intended* or *meant* (*Gemeinten*) by it, what is *said* in it, and the way it is *used* in the speech act. Normally, the linguistic meaning is not exhausted by any one of these three relations.[2]

However, intentionalistic semantics (from Grice to Bennett and Schiffer)[3] treats as fundamental only what the speaker means (*meint*) in a given situation by an expression he employs; formal semantics (from Frege via the early Wittgenstein to Dummett)[4] begins with the conditions under which a proposition is true; and the use-theory of meaning (inaugurated by the later Wittgenstein)[5] recurs to the habitualized contexts of interaction in which linguistic expressions serve practical functions. Once linguistic behaviorism (from Bloomfield via Morris to Skinner)[6] had failed to explain three fundamental phenomena[7]—namely, the identity of linguistic meanings, the situation-independence of the meaning of referential expressions that are employed relative to specific contexts,[8] and the acquisition of the competence to generate arbitrarily many linguistic expressions—the discussion has essentially been dominated by these three theories, for each of them has been able to appeal to a fundamental intuition. Bühler brings these intuitions together in his threefold functional scheme.

(1)   Intentionalism shares with Bühler a conception in which language has the character of a tool. The speaker uses the signs and concatenations of signs produced by him as a vehicle for

informing another player about his beliefs or intentions. In this conception, the premises of the modern philosophy of consciousness are still presupposed as unproblematic. The *representing subject* stands over and against a world of things and events; at the same time, he asserts his sovereignty in the world as a purposively *acting subject*. From the same perspective, he encounters other subjects who assert themselves in turn. As subjects capable of acting, they influence each other in the same manner in which they always intervene in innerworldly processes: causally. That their interactions are mediated by language appears to be something secondary in comparison to the representing and purposive activity of the individual subjects. Representations are connected with the substrate of linguistic signs in a conventional manner, such that one's own subjectivity is able to emerge from its inwardness and take on external form. In turn, as instruments for influencing an alien subjectivity, these signs have a place within the network of teleological action.

Once language has thus been assimilated to the physical means of purposive interventions, the explication of the meaning of linguistic expressions can be treated as a special task within a general theory of action. A speaker S intends to call forth an effect r in a hearer H by uttering 'x' in a particular context, whereby 'x' does not yet have a conventionally regulated meaning content, but has its meaning recognizably *conferred* by S for H in the given situation. According to the proposal of H. P. Grice, the effect intended by the speaker resides in the hearer's being induced by the utterance of 'x' to recognize the communicative intention (*Intention*) of the speaker, and in his accepting it (at least in part) as a reason either for thinking that S means something specific, or for regarding the fact that S means something specific as occasioning his (the hearer's) own intent (*Absicht*) to do something specific.[9] The effect r, which is produced by 'x' and triggered in H by S, is a particular belief or the intent to carry out a particular action. Two functions of signs that Bühler had separated, namely the presentation of self and the appeal to an addressee, thus fuse here into one and the same accomplishment: to bring a hearer to infer the communicative intention of the speaker and to motivate him in this way to form the corresponding belief or intent.

The gist of this strategy of explication is that what is meant is not primarily determined by what is said. The meaning content of an utterance of 'x' by S is supposed to be explicated solely by means of the intention with which S utters 'x' in a given context. This strategy is guided by the intuition that the employment of language is only a particular manifestation of the general sovereignty of purposively acting subjects—a sovereignty which, relative to the medium of language, reveals itself in the fact that we can for example assign objects any names we choose as well as arbitrarily bestow meanings on signs. Under the same premises drawn from the philosophy of consciousness, Husserl spoke in this context of meaning-conferring acts. If language obtains its meaning exclusively from the intentions of the purposive user of language, then it loses the autonomy of having its own internal structure.

(2) Formal semantics follows a different intuition. It attends to the grammatical form of linguistic expressions and ascribes to language a status that is basically independent of the intentions and ideas of speaking subjects. In relation to the rule-system of language itself, the practice of employing language and the psychology of understanding it occupy a status that is merely secondary. Initially, the object of the theory of meaning is constituted by the linguistic expressions themselves and not by the pragmatic relations between speakers and hearers that can be read off from the process of communication. Correct usage and correct understanding do not result from the intentions of the speaker or from the conventions agreed upon by users of language but from the formal properties of the expressions and their generative rules. The theory of meaning is thus detached from action-theoretical contexts and reserved for linguistic analysis in the narrower sense. A dimension is thereby revealed that Bühler left out of consideration in his semiotically foreshortened model: the logical-semantic construction of grammatical language. From Bühler's point of view, however, formal semantics pays for this advantage by limiting its analysis to the representational function of language.

That explains both the methodological abstraction of the propositional meaning from the meaning of the utterance and the choice of the assertoric sentence as the smallest unit of semantic analysis. That is, the emphasis on the function of representation also places the relationship between language and the world, or between an assertoric sentence and a state of affairs, at the center of the analysis. Only with sentences is the speaker able to say something specific or, in Frege's words, express a "thought." Only in relation to a sentence and its thought is a hearer able to take a position with "yes" or "no." When the croupier says "red" after the ball has come to a stop, the word takes on a specific sense if the roulette player relies on the context to expand it implicitly to the sentence: "Red has won."

The approach of propositional semantics revolutionizes the older and long dominant referential semantics, according to which language is related to reality as a name is related to its object. The relation of the signified (the meaning) to the signifier (the sign) was thought to be explicable in terms of the relation of the symbol (the meaningful sign) to the designatum (the object referred to). This basic semiotic notion was suitable for the object-centered theory of knowledge in the philosophy of consciousness.[10] In fact, names or designations, indeed all referential terms that we use to identify objects, do as it were establish contact between language and reality. If, however, this part is taken for the whole, a false picture arises. In order to represent an elementary state of affairs with a simple predicative sentence, a singular term must be completed with a universal predicate expression. The predicate should "apply" to the object for which the subject expression "stands." But then the relationship of the complete sentence to the state of affairs that is expressed in it must not be conceived according to the referential model of "standing for an object." And if assertoric sentences are representative of language as a whole, then the relationship of language to the world must be explicated in terms of a model different from that of the relation to an object: facts are what *make* assertoric sentences *true*.

This, then, is the key to answering the fundamental question of the theory of meaning. If the meaning of an assertoric sentence is the state of affairs that it describes, and if this sentence is true precisely when the expressed state of affairs exists or is the case, then we understand the sentence if we know the conditions under which it is true. The truth conditions of an assertoric sentence serve as the explanans for its meaning: "To understand a proposition means to know what is the case if it is true."[11]

This crucial insight by Frege into the internal connection between meaning and validity is based upon an intuition that can be provisionally elucidated from a pragmatic angle, which Frege himself did not adopt. Participants in communication reach understanding by employing sentences about something in the world; if, however, the validity of the sentences uttered by the speaker could not be judged by the hearer, they would be completely inadequate as the smallest units of communication. Mutual understanding about the contestable existence of states of affairs can be reached by participants only on the basis of an evaluation of the truth of sentences.

(3) Yet a different intuition underlies the use-theory of meaning, which Wittgenstein developed from his critique of the truth-semantic conception once shared by him. Wittgenstein uncovered the action character of linguistic expressions.[12] From this perspective, the representational function of language loses its privileged position among a multiplicity of uses. The medium of language does not facilitate first and foremost the description or affirmation of facts; it equally serves for giving commands, solving riddles, telling jokes, thanking, cursing, greeting, and praying.[13] Later on, Austin uses these performative verbs to analyze the dual accomplishment of speech acts, with which a speaker simultaneously does something in saying something.[14]

Wittgenstein's formula—that the meaning of a word is its use in the language—is admittedly in need of interpretation. The famous example of the builders in the second paragraph in the *Philosophical Investigations* suggests an intentionalistic reading. The assistant learns to bring "pillars," "slabs," and "beams" to the master on call; as soon as the participants intuitively master the cooperative context, they can assign words to objects through implicit definitions. The habitualized practice is thereby defined by the purpose of building a house as well as by the relationship of authority between the master and the apprentice. For the speaker who gives the directives, the words that are called out and the cooperative performances that are steered by them function as tools for the realization of his intentions. The words appear to derive their meaning from the purposes and the activities of the speaking subjects.

Formulations such as, "To understand a language means to be master of a technique," come close to the conception of intentionalistic semantics.[15] There is, however, a decisive difference. Wittgenstein conceives of the practice of the language game, which determines the use of the linguistic expressions, not as the result of individual teleological actions on the part of isolated, purposively acting subjects but as the "common behaviour of mankind."[16] With "language game" he names the whole, comprising the linguistic expressions and the nonlinguistic activities that are interwoven with each other. The network of activities and speech acts is constituted by an antecedent accord about an intersubjectively shared form of life, or by a preunderstanding of a common practice regulated by institutions and customs. Learning to master a language or learning how expressions in a language should be understood requires socialization into a form of life. The latter *antecedently* regulates the use of words and sentences within a network of possible purposes and possible actions.

Unlike the intentionalistic approach, the use-theoretical approach does not emphasize the tool character of language but the interconnection of language with an interactive practice in which a form of life is simultaneously reflected and reproduced. With this, the world-relation of linguistic expressions retreats once again, this time behind the relationships between speaker and hearer. These relationships are not interpreted intentionalistically from the perspective of a single speaker but as reflections of antecedently established and intersubjectively shared practices. The grammar of language games discloses the lifeworld dimension of intersubjectively shared background knowledge that supports the pluralized functions of language.

The example of the builders is better suited to concealing the real point of the use-theory of meaning: in a competently mastered language game, the speech acts *support* the interactive practice in a completely different way than they support activities that are first coordinated through them. Communicative acts derive their primacy from a property that has been brought to our attention by Austin through his investigation of the illocutionary character of speech acts. An observer can only understand a nonlinguistic action when he knows the intention that is supposed to be satisfied through it. Speech acts, on the other hand, identify themselves.[17] Because in carrying out an illocutionary act a speaker simultaneously *says* what he *is doing*, a hearer who understands the meaning of what is said can, without further ado, identify the performed act as some specific action. Thus, the use-theoretical approach is based on an intuition that has been recognized in its full import only after Wittgenstein. The acts carried out in a natural language are always self-referential. They say both how what is said is to be employed and how it is to be understood. This reflexive structure of everyday language is tangible in the grammatical form of the individual speech act. The illocutionary portion establishes the sense in which the propositional content is being employed and the sort of action which the utterance should be understood as.

II The Limits of Semantics and of Speech-Act Theory

Each of the three competing theories of meaning takes up exactly one aspect of the process of achieving mutual understanding of an utterance. They seek to explicate the meaning of a linguistic expression either from the perspective of what is meant (as intended meaning), or from the perspective of what is said (as literal meaning), or from the perspective of use (as utterance meaning). By introducing each of these theories as stylizations of one of the aspects attended to *simultaneously* in Bühler's functional scheme, I have implicitly suggested their one-sidedness. I now want to go through the theories once more in order (1) to discuss the limits of what they are capable of accomplishing, and then (2) to test the problem-solving potential of a fourth approach, namely that of the theory of speech acts.

Toward a Critique of the Theory of Meaning

(1) The intentionalistic program sets for itself the task of tracing the conventional meaning of a random grammatical expression 'x' (x-meaning timeless) back to the nonconventional meaning of the speaker's intention, which is connected with the utterance of 'x' in a particular context (S-meaning occasional). Grice selects his premises in such a way that communication can be explained with the concepts relevant to a purposive-rational influence of S upon H. The model is set up so that strategic action can serve as a functional equivalent for coming to an understanding in language. Given this preliminary decision, however, the phenomena that actually come into view are categorially different from those that are putatively being reconstructed. That is, even in the most complex cases, what is reconstructed is only the meaning of an utterance 'x' by S which, under the presupposition that a common language is not available, is capable of *inducing H* to believe something specific or to intend to do something specific, i.e., *to understand something indirectly* by way of inferences. But giving someone to understand something indirectly is a limit case that, for its part, refers back to the normal case of coming to an understanding directly in a common language by way of utterances that identify themselves.

This parasitic status reveals itself through a type of counter-example introduced by Strawson and dealt with by S. R. Schiffer, in which S can only achieve the desired effect as long as the intention that H is supposed to take for the intention of S is not identical with the strategic background intention that S is actually pursuing.[18] Through this asymmetry an infinite regress is, however, set in motion, one which could only be prevented if the participants were allowed to recur to shared knowledge, indeed in the final instance to the natural meaning of symptoms established through a causal chain (e.g., that smoke means fire). Yet, this recourse functions only under the condition that both sides, speaker and hearer, already conceive the shared natural meaning of such a symptom on analogy with language, i.e., in the manner of the intersubjectively known, nonnatural meaning of a conventionally regulated sign. Schiffer makes an illegitimate leap from the natural evidence of a symptom like smoke (accessible from the perspective of an observer) to the comprehension (possible only in the performative attitude) of a communicatively employed sign together with the corresponding propositional content (that smoke means fire) that is recognizably employed for informative purposes.[19] He thereby slips in just what is supposed to be explained, namely the reflexivity of a self-identifying utterance and the intersubjective knowledge that is made possible by the comprehension of that utterance. Interactions among purposively acting subjects (which are mediated solely through observations, the strategic deployment of signs, and inferences) can certainly lead to the reciprocally reflected attribution of propositional attitudes and contents, but they cannot lead to something like intersubjective knowledge in the strict sense.

In contrast, truth semantics pays heed to the linguistic medium's own rationality and internal structure, which the intentionalistic approach leaves out of consideration. The clear articulation of thoughts and intentions is made possible only through grammatical language, which forms a reality of its own kind and with its own dignity; states of affairs can only be mirrored by sentences. Yet this also bestows a privileged position upon the truth-validity of assertoric sentences. The diverse functions served by language are analyzed only in terms of the form of the sentences employed, and ultimately only in terms of the form of assertoric sentences that serve representational functions. That is, even the meanings of nonassertoric sentences are elucidated through recourse to the conditions that make assertoric sentences true. Frege himself had already analyzed assertoric sentences into two components: the assertoric force or the mode of assertion must supervene upon the propositional content 'that p,' in order to result in the statement 'p,' whereby 'that p' signifies a state of affairs and 'p' signifies a fact, i.e., an existing state of affairs. Only the mode-component distinguishes imperative and interrogative sentences from statements that have the same content.

In order to explicate such distinctions between modes in truth-semantic terms, Stenius and Kenny make use of an idea from Austin, who had assumed two opposing directions of fit between sentences and states of affairs.[20] They begin with statements and imperatives as the two basic modes, whereby true statements represent existing states of affairs and imperatives require that states of affairs be brought into existence. The conditions that make statements true correspond to the conditions under which imperatives are successfully carried out. In both cases, these are the conditions for states of affairs, either for the existence of known states of affairs or for the establishment of desired states of affairs. However, this strategy of analysis founders on the asymmetry between truth conditions and success conditions, which are supposed to "satisfy" statements and imperatives, respectively. Specifically, the force of imperatives cannot be adequately differentiated from the force of assertions through the opposed directions in which a speaker takes up, with imperatives or assertions respectively, a relation to (the same) state of affairs from different perspectives. A hearer is able to understand a sentence as an imperative only when he knows the conditions under which the speaker may expect that he could impose his will upon a hearer, even a reluctant one. The sense of the imperative demand for compliance cannot be explained in terms of the semantically analyzable knowledge of success conditions; it can only be explicated pragmatically, specifically with reference to the authority standing behind it.[21]

Of course, a purely semantic approach to the analysis runs up against limits even in the case of assertoric sentences themselves. In its classical form, truth semantics is supposed to be able to ignore altogether the circumstances under which a hearer *is in a position to recognize* when the truth conditions of a sentence are satisfied. But, at most, the knowledge of truth conditions is unproblematic in the case of simple predicative observation sentences, whose truth can be checked in surveyable contexts by means of readily accessible perceptual evidence. There are in any case no correspondingly simple tests for predictions, counterfactual conditionals, statements of laws, etc. Assertoric sentences of these kinds quantify over dimensions that are infinite or are inaccessible to observation. Michael Dummett points out, correctly, that simple verification rules for these and similar sentences are not at our disposal. It is therefore not enough to make the Fregean thesis more precise, to the effect that one understands an assertoric sentence when one knows what its verification rules are. Supported by the pragmatic distinction between the truth of a sentence and its 'assertability,' or the entitlement to put forward an assertion with that sentence, Dummett replaces the knowledge of truth conditions (or the knowledge of verification rules in a game of identification tailored to observation situations[22]) with indirect knowledge: the hearer must know the kind of reasons which, in a given case, the speaker could give to redeem his claim that particular truth conditions are satisfied. Briefly stated: one understands an assertoric sentence when one knows what kind of reasons a speaker would have to cite in order to convince a hearer that the speaker is entitled to raise a truth claim for the sentence.[23]

Just as Dummett implicitly makes reference to the game of argumentation, in which the speaker *qua* proponent is able to convince a hearer *qua* opponent of the entitlement for his truth claim, so Wittgenstein already comes upon the presupposition of a similar distribution of roles in his analysis of the concept of following a rule.[24] Following a rule means following the *same* rule in each case; the meaning of a rule is interwoven with the employment of the word 'same.' *A* cannot be certain whether he is following a rule at all unless a situation exists in which he exposes his conduct to the judgment of a critic *B* who can ascertain deviations from the rule. The identical meaning and the validity of a rule are conceptually connected. That is, the identity of a rule in the multiplicity of its realizations does not rest upon *observable* invariances, but upon the validity of a criterion according to which rule-conforming conduct can be judged. Rule-guided conduct is fallible and therefore requires two simultaneous, exchangeable roles: one for *A*, who follows a rule and thereby seeks to avoid mistakes, and one for *B*, who can critically judge the correctness of the rule-guided conduct of *A*. The point of this consideration is that a linguistic expression can only have an identical meaning for a subject who is capable, together with at least one additional subject, of following a rule that is *valid for both of them*. A monadically isolated subject can no more employ an expression with identical meaning than a rule can be followed privately.

In this way, Wittgenstein introduces the internal relation of meaning and validity independent of the world-relation of language; he therefore does not connect the rules for the meaning of words with the truth-validity of sentences. Instead, he compares the validity of meaning conventions with the social acceptability of practices and institutions and assimilates the grammatical rules of language games to social norms of action. To be sure, he thereby surrenders every relation to validity that transcends the context of a given language game. Utterances are valid or invalid only according to the standards of the language game to which they belong. It is thus hardly noticed that the relation to truth of fact-stating discourse is also lost. For Wittgenstein, the representational function is just one among many other functions of language that have developed, as it were, in the natural history of diverse and interlocking language games possessing equal status as a matter of principle.

(2) Linking up with the later Wittgenstein, Austin has examined various illocutionary acts to investigate more closely how language is joined with interactive practice in a form of life. But in addition, and unlike Wittgenstein, Austin does not want to ignore the relationship brought out by truth semantics between language and the objective world, between a sentence and a state of affairs. Austin takes the first steps enroute to a theory of speech acts that combines the insights of truth semantics with those of language-game pragmatics. At first this leads him to a dualistic conception that globally opposes illocutionary acts to the representation of facts. In so-called constative utterances, assertoric sentences are employed to represent states of affairs. Austin also speaks of locutionary acts here: the speaker uses locutionary acts in order to say something (say how things stand). On the other hand, illocutionary acts as such are not supposed to have any propositional content, not even a meaning. In such an act, the speaker does not say anything that could be true or false but instead performs a social action. "Hello!" does not *mean* anything; rather, it *is* a greeting, which the speaker can perform with this expression. Such an act can admittedly be unhappy, or infelicitous, if for example it is carried out with the wrong words, in

an inappropriate context, or without the correct emphasis, etc. Instead of having a meaning, an illocutionary act expresses a particular force (*Kraft*)—a force (*Gewalt*) of a kind with the binding character of a promise. While locutionary acts make possible a cognitive use of language that is, as it were, turned toward the world, speakers and hearers are able to establish relations among each other with illocutionary acts; the latter serve the interactive function of language. Initially Austin made the following provisional classification:

Locutionary Act—Assertoric Sentence—Meaning—True/False.

Illocutionary Act—Performative Sentence—Force—Felicitous/ Infelicitous.

This dualism could not be maintained.[25] Austin saw from the beginning, of course, that most illocutionary acts do not appear independently but incorporate clauses with propositional content. In general, the speaker carries out an illocutionary act *by saying something*. The illocutionary component only establishes the mode of a sentence that is employed as a promise, a recommendation, a confession, etc. The notation '*Mp*' indicates that we execute two acts in one, and these can only be separated analytically. But it is then no longer clear why the contrast of 'force' and 'meaning,' familiar from truth semantics, ought to be retained in a theory of speech acts. Performative sentences obviously have just as clear a meaning as assertoric sentences. And constative speech acts exhibit the same illocutionary-propositional double structure as all other speech acts. Fully independently of their truth value, assertions, descriptions, and narratives can be infelicitous in a way similar to other illocutionary acts: one can make such a mess of a story that it "is no longer a tale," or discuss a delicate matter so bluntly that those present "will not tolerate any further discussion of it."

If, however, *all* speech acts can be analyzed in the form '*Mp*,' then locutionary acts lose the special status that was initially claimed for them. They are, so to say, absorbed into the propositional content of any and every speech act, although their monopoly on the claim to truth is inherited by a particular class of speech acts, the constativa. But this gives rise to an interesting question: Are constative speech acts the only ones that can be valid or invalid (true or false), or do other speech acts also reveal dimensions equivalent to truth? If they did not, then we would have to work out a concept of language that attributes no essential meaning to the fact that what is said in language *always* transcends the boundaries of language itself and relates to something in the world. In light of this, both Austin and John Searle pursue the other alternative, although their respective positions differ in significant ways.

Austin moves in this direction when he reconceptualizes the two dimensions of judgment, which he had initially correlated with locutionary and illocutionary acts, respectively (truth vs. success), as aspects that are merely analytically separable. *Every* speech act can be judged according to whether it is "right" as well as whether it is "in order."[26] To be sure, Austin does not fill the dimension of "rightness," to which the truth-validity of constative speech acts is now generalized, with a definite number of well-defined validity claims; rather, the "loosening up of the idea of truth" is supposed to unlock a whole spectrum of validity types, ranging from propositional truth via the good and appropriateness to normative rightness. Out of a wealth of evaluative viewpoints, the analyzer of language is supposed to be able to locate the relevant criterion of judgment in each case and register it descriptively. In contrast, Searle wants to avoid the difficulties that result from this subsumption of truth-validity and ought-validity under a diversity of "values." In the dimension of the validity of speech acts, he admits only the one clear-cut universal validity claim that had already been privileged by truth semantics. In this respect, Searle takes a step backward from Austin and the later Wittgenstein to Frege.

We are nonetheless indebted to Searle for the version of speech-act theory that has been most precisely explicated up to now.[27] He takes Austin's conditions of felicity and renders them more precise as "preparatory conditions"; these refer to standardized contexts that must obtain if various kinds of speech acts are to be performed meaningfully and with a prospect of success. He then adds comprehensibility and sincerity conditions; these refer to the availability of a common linguistic medium and the suitability of the speech situation, on the one hand, and to the corresponding intention of the speaker, on the other. He names further conditions for the semantic form, which the clauses with propositional content must obey, and finally stands before the task of specifying the "essential conditions," according to which different illocutionary forces or modes of employing language can be demarcated. The five basic modes distinguished by Searle (constative, directive, commissive, expressive, and declarative speech acts) are open to more precise surface differentiations on the basis of pragmatic criteria (such as the direction of interest from speaker to hearer, the degree of intensity in making the illocutionary point, or the institutional bindingness of the speech act, etc.).

However, the differentiation of the basic modes themselves, particularly in a validity dimension tailored only to propositional truth (which admits of variation solely according to the direction of fit between language and the world), is the problem on which Searle labors in vain. In both directions (from "word to world" and from "world to word"), the relation of language to the objective world offers a basis that is too narrow for distinguishing the five proposed classes of speech acts. Indeed, for Wittgenstein, the fact that the rich variety of illocutionary forces could not be ordered from the viewpoint of truth semantics had already been a sufficient reason for giving up all attempts at classification in favor of describing an unordered collection of language-game grammars. Only constative speech acts can be characterized—partially—by the direction in which sentences and facts can be brought into agreement.[28] The assertoric force means that S presents to H a truth claim for 'p' and thereby gives the guarantee that the truth conditions of 'p' are satisfied—or simply: that the statement fits the facts.

Even the illocutionary force of authorized imperatives is incapable of being explicated solely through recourse to the fulfillment of success conditions, that is, by H effecting that 'p' becomes true. H understands an imperative sentence as a command, an instruction, a request, or the like, only when knowledge of the success conditions (given in the clause with propositional content) is augmented by knowledge of those conditions (contained in the illocutionary component) under which S could justify why he regards an imperative with the content p as legitimate or enforceable. A validity claim of a normative kind, which cannot be reduced to a truth claim, thus comes into play. The same goes for the illocutionary force of commissive speech acts, with which a speaker binds his own will with a normative obligation. The conditions for the binding character of obligating declarations of intention are of a different kind from success conditions, which the speaker fulfills as soon as he translates his intention into action, or makes it true.

The illocutionary force of expressive speech acts, with which S expresses an experience (*Erlebnis*) to which he has privileged access, can be defined neither through the cognitive nor through the interventionistic relationship of a subject to the world of existing states of affairs. Consequently, in these cases Searle uses a neither-nor sign to indicate the inapplicability of truth-semantic perspectives. In expressive speech acts a claim to truthfulness comes into play, a claim that Searle has however already employed nonspecifically for the sincerity condition that *all* comprehensible speech acts must satisfy. A similar objection can be made to his definition of the illocutionary force of declarative speech acts.[29]

These problems are avoided when one does not respond to the validity problematic inherited from Austin as Searle does, with a truth-semantic back-formation of speech-act theory, but instead interprets Bühler's linguistic functions in terms of the corresponding validity claims.

III Speech Acts, Communicative Action, and Strategic Interaction

The validity-theoretical interpretation of Bühler's functional scheme offers itself as a way out of the difficulties of speech-act theory because it does justice to all three aspects of *a speaker* coming to an understanding with *another person* about *something*. It incorporates within itself the truth contained in the use-theory of meaning and at the same time overcomes the types of one-sidedness specific to intentionalistic and formal semantics (1). The resulting formal-pragmatic analysis of speech acts provides a basis for the concept of communicative action. Communicative action forms an alternative to strategic action, yet it remains linked with the teleology of the various individual plans of action that come together in it (2).

(1)   Following the transition from the semantic to the pragmatic point of view, the question of the validity of a sentence no longer poses itself as a question about the objective relation of language to the world, detached from the process of communication. Nor can the validity claim, with which a speaker refers to the validity conditions of his utterance, be defined solely from the perspective of the speaker. Validity claims aim at being acknowledged intersubjectively by speaker and hearer; they can only be redeemed with reasons, that is, discursively, and the hearer reacts to them with rationally motivated "yes" or "no" positions. The smallest independent unit of processes of reaching understanding that are explicitly linguistic are composed of (a) the elementary speech act 'Mp' with which S raises at least one validity claim for his utterance, and of (b) the "yes" or "no" position that determines whether H understands and accepts the speech-act offer from S. Mutual understanding aims at consensus formation. The attempt by S to reach an understanding with H about something in the world terminates in the agreement brought about between them, and this agreement is sealed by the acceptance of a comprehensible speech act. For this reason, the comprehension of a speech act already points to the conditions for a possible agreement about what is said.

Of course, the pragmatic reinterpretation of the validity problematic also requires a complete reevaluation of what was originally meant by the 'illocutionary force' of a speech act. Austin had in fact conceived of the illocutionary force as the literally irrational component of the speech act, whereas the content of the assertoric sentence (or its nominalized form) monopolized the rational content. Meaning and understanding were concentrated only around this rational component. In contrast, the consistent execution of the pragmatic turn remakes validity claims into the stewards of a rationality that presents itself in the structural interconnection among conditions of validity, the validity claims related to these conditions, and the reasons given in redeeming these validity claims. The individual speech act is bound to this structure primarily through its mode-component. That is, the mode is defined according to the type of claim put forth (and according to the manner of reference to the validity claim, as well), and this claim is raised by the speaker through the misleadingly named 'illocutionary' act, in the standard case through the utterance of a performative clause. The home of rationality is thereby transferred from the propositional to the illocutionary component, and at the same time the attachment of the validity conditions to the propositional component is loosened. Room is thus made for the introduction of validity claims that are *not* directed toward truth conditions or tailored to the relationship of language to the objective world.

Bühler's functional scheme had already related linguistic expressions to the intention of the speaker, to the objective world, and to the addressee. And the three theories of meaning discussed here had each claimed that it could explain the comprehensibility of linguistic expressions through some one of these relations—namely, through the function of expressing intentions, or of representing existing states of affairs, or of establishing interactive relationships. What we are looking for is a theory of speech acts that takes into consideration the kernel of truth in all three of these theories of meaning. But from Searle's classification of speech acts it has also become apparent that the truth-semantic conceptualization of the internal relation between meaning and validity is *too specialized*.

To be sure, whether or not an utterance fulfills its representational function is measured against truth conditions; however, the fulfillment of the expressive and the interactive functions is also measured against conditions that are *analogous to truth*. I therefore want to introduce subjective truthfulness and normative rightness as truth-analogous concepts for the validity of speech acts. The relations of the speech act to the speaker's intention and to the addressee can also be conceived in terms of the model of relations to the objective world. That is, there also exists a relation to the subjective world (of the speaker), as the totality of lived experiences (*Erlebnisse*) to which he has privileged access, and a relation to the social world (of the speaker, the hearer, and other members), as the totality of interpersonal relationships that are currently accepted as legitimate. These world-concepts formed *through analogy* must not, of course, be misunderstood as partial regions (in Popper's sense) of the one objective world.[30] The lived experiences that *S* expresses in expressive speech acts (prototypically avowals and revelations) should no more be understood as a particular class of *entities* (or inner episodes) than should the norms that, through regulative speech acts (prototypically commands and promises), legitimate an interpersonal relationship established between *S* and *H*. From the perspective of the participants, the first-person experiential sentences employed in expressive speech acts can be uttered *truthfully* or *untruthfully*—according to whether the speaker says what he means. But they cannot be true or false, unless experiential sentences are to be assimilated to assertoric sentences. In the same way, the imperative sentences (commands) or intention sentences (promises) that are employed in the attitude of the second person in regulative speech acts can be *right* or *not right,* according to whether they satisfy or violate recognized normative expectations, or whether they have a binding character or only give the illusion of creating a commitment. But they, too, cannot be true or false. With their speech acts, participants in communication relate to something in the subjective world or to something in the social world in ways that are *different* from the way in which they relate to something in the objective world. That these world-concepts should be used only in an analogous sense is shown by this distinction in the *manner of referring:* objects are identified differently than lived experiences, which in an expressive attitude I reveal or disguise as "in each case mine," and also differently than the norms variously acknowledged "by us," which in a norm-conformative attitude we follow or contravene.

A validity-theoretic interpretation of Bühler's functional scheme further leads to the assumption that with a speech act '*Mp,*' *S* takes up relations *simultaneously* to something in the objective world, to something in the subjective world, and to something in a shared social world. Every speech act as a whole can always be criticized as invalid from three perspectives: as

untrue in view of a statement made (or of the existential presuppositions of the propositional content), as untruthful in
view of the expressed intention of the speaker, and as not right
in view of the existing normative context (or the legitimacy of
the presupposed norms themselves). Admittedly, only one of
the three validity claims can be thematically emphasized in any
explicit speech act. It is in terms of these thematized validity
claims (which can also be modified according to surface distinctions in a particular language and context) that the illocutionary forces are finally defined, and these illocutionary forces
must be capable of being traced back to three basic modes:
they belong either to constative, to expressive, or to regulative
speech acts.

If every speech act is thematically linked with some one
validity claim, then Dummett's proposal for explicating the
meaning of assertoric sentences employed in constative speech
acts can be *generalized:* we understand a speech act when we
know what makes it acceptable. Of course, this is a matter of
objective conditions of validity, and the hearer cannot infer
these directly from the semantic content of the expressions
employed, but only indirectly through the epistemic claim that
the speaker raises for the validity of his utterance in perform-
ing his illocutionary act. The speaker refers with his validity
claim to a potential of reasons that could be brought to bear
for it. The reasons interpret the conditions of validity, and to
this extent they themselves belong to the conditions that make
an utterance acceptable. The acceptability conditions point
thereby to the holistic structure of natural languages. In a
language, each individual speech act is connected by way of
logical-semantic strands to many other potential speech acts
that can take on the pragmatic role of reasons. Of course,
depending on the structure and content of a speech act, the
available but latent reasons that are suitable for the discursive
redemption of the validity claim raised in that speech act will
be more or less complex in kind and extent. When the speaker
puts forward an assertion with a simple predicative observation
sentence in the present indicative, the reasons that interpret
the truth conditions of the sentence are typically easy to survey.
When, in contrast, a court renders a judgment in a complicated

matter, or when a physicist explains a natural event with the aid of an empirical theory, the evaluation of the validity—and thus also the *comprehension*—of the court verdict or of the natural-scientific explanation will require knowledge of more demanding kinds of reasons. Otherwise we do not understand what is said—not even if we understand the individual words as a result of their frequent past appearance in *other* sentences.

We understand a speech act when we are acquainted with the kind of reasons that a speaker could cite in order to convince a hearer that he (the speaker) is entitled under the given circumstances to claim validity for his utterance. For this reason, familiarity with a language is interwoven with knowledge of how things do actually stand in the (linguistically disclosed) world. Perhaps knowledge of the world merely depends upon a longer chain of reasons than knowledge of language. That they cannot be sharply separated from each other becomes plausible when the basic idea of the formal-pragmatic explanation of meaning (already begun by Bühler) is made clear. Understanding an expression means knowing how one can make use of it in order to reach an understanding with somebody about something. Therefore, it can already be discerned from the conditions for comprehending linguistic expressions that the speech acts that can be performed by means of them are directed toward mutual understanding and thus toward a rationally motivated agreement about what is said. One would hardly know what it is to understand the meaning of an utterance if one did not know that the utterance can and should serve to bring about an agreement; and it lies within the concept of agreement that it "is valid" for the participants. The dimension of validity thus inheres in language. The orientation toward validity claims belongs to the pragmatic conditions of possible mutual understanding—and of understanding language itself.

(2) With the concept of mutual understanding oriented toward validity claims, formal pragmatics finds a connection with action theory, albeit in a way completely different from the attempt of intentionalistic semantics to explain processes of reaching understanding using action-theoretic concepts. A teleological action can be described as the realization of a plan

of action that is based on the actor's interpretation of the situation. By executing a plan of action, an actor comes to grips with a situation, whereby the action situation is a segment drawn from the environment as interpreted by the actor. This segment is constituted in light of possibilities for action that the actor regards as relevant to the success of his plan. The problem of coordinating action arises for interaction among several actors: how can alter's plans and actions be "linked up" with ego's plans and actions? Types of interaction can be distinguished according to the various mechanisms for this linkage. I speak either of "communicative action" or of "strategic action," depending upon whether the actions of different actors are coordinated by way of "reaching an understanding" or "exerting influence," respectively.[31] From the perspective of the participants, these two mechanisms and their corresponding types of action mutually exclude one another. Processes of reaching an understanding cannot be undertaken with the dual intention of both reaching an agreement about something with a participant in interaction and causally having an effect on him. From the perspective of the participants, an agreement cannot be imposed from without, cannot be foisted by one side upon the other—whether instrumentally, through direct intervention into the action situation, or strategically, through indirect influence, again oriented only toward success, on the propositional attitudes of the other. Whatever manifestly comes to be through external influence (gratification or threat, suggestion or deception) cannot count intersubjectively as an agreement; an intervention of this sort forfeits its effectiveness for coordinating action.

Communicative or strategic action is required when an actor can only carry out his plans of action interactively, i.e., with the help of the actions of another actor (or their omission). Beyond that, communicative action must satisfy certain conditions of cooperation and mutual understanding:

• The participating actors must conduct themselves cooperatively and attempt to reach an agreement about their plans (in the horizon of a shared lifeworld) on the basis of common (or sufficiently overlapping) situation interpretations.

• The participating actors must be prepared to achieve the intermediate goals of a common situation definition and of action coordination in the roles of speakers and hearers by way of processes of reaching understanding, i.e., by means of the unreserved and sincere pursuit of illocutionary aims.

This means specifically that:

• They pursue their illocutionary aims with the help of speech acts in a performative attitude, which demands an orientation toward reciprocally raised, criticizable validity claims.
• In doing this, they make use of the binding (or bonding) effects of speech-act offers, which come about when the speaker, with his validity claim, gives a credible guarantee for the validity of what is said.
• Whereby the binding (or bonding) effect of a comprehensible and accepted speech act carries over to the commitments relevant to the sequel of interaction that emerge from the semantic content of the speech act—whether asymmetrically for the hearer or for the speaker, or symmetrically for both sides.

Thus, communicative action distinguishes itself from strategic action through the fact that successful action coordination is not traced back to the purposive rationality of action orientations but to the rationally motivating force of achieving understanding, i.e., to a rationality that manifests itself in conditions for communicatively reached agreements. The manner in which mutual understanding in language functions as a mechanism for coordinating action is that the participants in an interaction agree about the validity claimed for their speech acts, that is, they recognize criticizable validity claims intersubjectively. What gives rationally motivating force to speech-act offers is, in turn, the structural connection linking the meaning of an utterance, on the one hand, with its validity conditions, the validity claim that is raised for what is said, and the reasons that can be mobilized for the discursive redemption of this claim, on the other hand.

Like all action, communicative action is purposive. But here the teleology of the individual action plans and of the operations for carrying them out is *interrupted* by the action-coordinating mechanism of mutual understanding. Orientations and action processes are at first egocentrically tailored to the various actors, but communicative "switching" via candidly executed illocutionary acts places them under the structural limitations of an intersubjectively shared language. The telos of reaching understanding, inherent in linguistic structures, compels the communicative actors to alter their perspective; this finds expression in the necessity of going from the objectivating attitude of success-oriented action, which seeks to *effect* something in the world, over to the performative attitude of a speaker who seeks to *reach an understanding* with a second person about something.[32]

In their standard form, illocutionary acts are carried out through the employment of performative sentences. For the formation of the predicate expression these sentences require performative verbs, for the subject expression they require the first-person singular, and for the position of the indirect object they require the second person. This grammatical form of the performative sentence mirrors the attitude of a speaker who takes up an interpersonal relationship with a hearer in order to reach an understanding with him about something, whereby the speaker is reflexively oriented to the possibility that the hearer may dispute the validity of what is said. This *performative attitude* of actors who are oriented toward reaching understanding can be conceptually differentiated from the objectivating attitude of success-oriented actors through the world-relations which each admits: with our speech acts we *simultaneously* relate, with changing thematizations, to something in the objective, the subjective, and the social worlds, whereas we purposively intervene in the objective world alone.

If, however, the attitude oriented toward reaching understanding and that oriented toward success are not merely to be distinguished from each other analytically, but correspond to two different interaction types, then from the perspective of the actors they must exclude each other. In opposition to this conclusion it has been objected that (1) any speech act can also be strategically deployed, and that (2) simple imperatives, which are not embedded in normative contexts, only express power claims rather than validity claims, and they therefore constitute illocutionary acts that are carried out with an orientation toward success, which would contradict the premises just set out.

(1) Whether conventionally regulated or not, perlocutionary effects that are *openly* aimed for within the framework of a common situation definition are of a kind which, *mutatis mutandis*, could also be effected through purposive intervention alone. But such nonlinguistically produced effects cannot be described as perlocutionary successes because the latter are always illocutionarily mediated. Admittedly, there is the case of the latently strategic speech act, which aims at perlocutionary effects that are not conventionally regulated. The latter come about only when the speaker does not declare his aims to the hearer within the framework of the common situation definition. For example, a speaker who wants to persuade his audience of something proceeds in this way, perhaps because in the given situation he lacks convincing arguments. Such *unmanifested* perlocutionary effects can only be achieved parasitically, namely, under the condition that the speaker feigns the intention of pursuing his illocutionary goals *without reserve* and leaves the hearer in the dark about his actual violation of the presuppositions of action oriented toward reaching understanding.[33] The latently strategic use of language is parasitic because it only functions when at least one side assumes that language is being used with an orientation toward reaching understanding. Whoever acts strategically in this way must violate the sincerity condition of communicative action *inconspicuously*.

The use of language that is manifestly strategic has a derivative status as well; in this case all participants are aware that reaching understanding in language is subordinated to conditions of strategic action—and therefore remains deficient. They know and reckon with the fact that they must supplement the illocutionarily mediated perlocutionary effects of their speech acts with purposively triggered empirical effects. That is, in the end they still rely upon indirect communication: only the proverbial shot before the bow is able to demonstrate the seriousness of a threat to the opponent.

This case of the manifestly strategic use of language is to be distinguished in turn from cases of an indirect communication that remains *subordinated* to the aim of communicative action. In unstructured initial situations, the common definition of the situation is first constructed (for example, in an accidental meeting in a bar) when a young man indirectly implies something to a young woman. In the same way, the pedagogically careful teacher instills self-confidence in his pupil through compliments, so that the pupil learns to take his own ideas seriously.[34] In cases such as these, in which communicative action has first of all to establish its own presuppositions step by step, the *terminus ad quem* is an agreement that is ultimately also available for communication and not a perlocutionary effect that would be destroyed by being admitted or declared.

(2) I analyze simple or nonauthorized imperatives according to the model of the derivative use of language that is manifestly strategic. The addressee of a command or a request must as a rule be familiar with the normative context that authorizes a speaker to make his demand, and which thereby legitimates the expectation that the addressee has reasons to carry out the action demanded. Knowledge of success conditions, which can be derived from the propositional component 'p' of the imperative 'Ip,' is not sufficient for understanding the illocutionary meaning of this speech act, namely, its specific character as an imperative. Knowledge of (1) the success conditions must be augmented by knowledge of (2) those conditions under which the speaker has reason to regard an imperative with contents (1) as valid, i.e., normatively justified—e.g., that children in the streets of Lima may beg from arriving foreigners.[35] Of course, the speaker may connect a validity claim with 'Ip' only if he knows his imperative to be covered by *some* normative context, be it ever so weak.

From the perspective of a sociological observer, there is a continuum between *de facto* power relations that are merely habitual and power relations that have been transformed into normative authority. But from the perspective of participants in communication, if only their lifeworlds are sufficiently interwoven, it is possible to understand *all* imperatives against the background of this intersubjectively shared lifeworld in terms of the paradigm of normatively authorized imperatives. Even passing strangers in foreign lands will expect from one another a readiness to help each other in emergencies. Such weak normative contexts are still sufficient to authorize a speaker's expectations for conduct, which the hearer can criticize if need be. Only in the limit case of manifestly strategic action does the normative validity claim shrivel into a pure power claim based upon a potential for sanction that is contingent and no longer conventionally regulated or grammatically readable. The "Hands up!" of a bankrobber, who at pistol point demands of the threatened bank clerk that he hand over the money, demonstrates in a drastic way that the conditions of normative validity have been replaced by sanction conditions. The dissolution of the normative background appears in a symptomatic way in the if-then structure of the threat, which in strategic action takes the place of the sincerity or earnestness of the speaker that is presupposed for communicative action. Strangely, imperatives or threats that are deployed purely strategically and robbed of their normative validity claims are not illocutionary acts, or acts aimed toward reaching understanding, at all. They remain parasitic insofar as their comprehensibility must be derived from the employment conditions for illocutionary acts that are covered by norms.

In latent strategic action the perlocutionary effects are dependent upon the illocutionary successes of a use of language that is oriented toward reaching understanding, however much it may be feigned on one side. In manifestly strategic action, illocutionarily weakened speech acts, if they are to be comprehensible, remain related to the meaning that they derive from an employment of language that is antecedently habitualized and originally oriented toward reaching understanding.

Notes

1. Karl Bühler, *Sprachtheorie* (Jena: Gustav Fischer, 1934), 28.

2. Karl-Otto Apel, *Die Idee der Sprache in der Tradition des Humanismus von Dante bis Vico* (Bonn, 1963).

3. Georg Meggle, ed., *Handlung, Kommunikation und Bedeutung* (Frankfurt, 1979).

4. Michael Dummett, *Frege* (London: Duckworth, 1973).

5. William P. Alston, *Philosophy of Language* (Englewood Cliffs: Prentice-Hall, 1964).

6. Charles W. Morris, *Signs, Language, Behavior* (Englewood Cliffs: Prentice-Hall, 1946).

7. Noam Chomsky, "A Review of B. F. Skinner's 'Verbal Behavior'," in *The Structure of Language*, ed. Jerry Fodor and Jerrold Katz (Englewood Cliffs: Prentice-Hall, 1964), 547ff.

8. Ernst Tugendhat, *Traditional and Analytical Philosophy*, trans. P. A. Gorner (Cambridge: Cambridge University Press, 1982), 163ff.

9. H. Paul Grice, "Utterer's Meaning and Intentions," in *Studies in the Ways of Words*, (Cambridge, Mass.: Harvard University Press, 1989), 86ff.; "Utterer's Meaning, Sentence-Meaning, and Word-Meaning," in ibid., 117ff.; and "Meaning Revisited," in ibid., 283ff.

10. Tugendhat, *Traditional and Analytical Philosophy*, 207ff.

11. Ludwig Wittgenstein, *Tractatus Logico-Philosophicus*, trans. D. F. Pears and B. F. McGuiness (New York: Humanities Press, 1961), 4.024.

12. Karl-Otto Apel, "Wittgenstein and the Problem of Hermeneutic Understanding," *Towards a Transformation of Philosophy*, trans. Glyn Adey and David Frisby (Boston: Routledge & Kegan Paul, 1980), 1ff.

13. Ludwig Wittgenstein, *Philosophical Investigations*, trans. G. E. M. Anscombe (New York: Macmillan, 1958), §§289ff.

14. J. L. Austin, *How to Do Things with Words* (Cambridge, Mass.: Harvard University Press, 1962).

15. Ludwig Wittgenstein, *Philosophical Investigations*, §199.

16. Ibid., §206.

17. D. S. Shwayder, *Stratification of Behavior* (New York: Humanities Press, 1965), 47ff.

18. S. R. Schiffer, *Meaning* (Oxford: Clarendon Press, 1972); cf. J. Habermas, "Intentionalistische Semantik," in *Vorstudien und Ergänzungen zur Theorie des kommunikativen Handelns* (Frankfurt: Suhrkamp, 1984), 332ff.

19. This argument is developed by C. B. Christensen, "On the Mechanism of Communication" (Manuscript) (Frankfurt, 1987).

20. E. Stenius, "Mood and Language Game," *Synthese* 17 (1964): 254ff.; Anthony Kenny, *Will, Freedom and Power* (Oxford: Blackwell, 1975); cf. also E. Tugendhat, *Traditional and Analytical Philosophy*, 398ff.

21. Jürgen Habermas, *Theory of Communicative Action*, 2 vols., trans. Thomas McCarthy (Boston: Beacon Press, 1984–87), 1: 298ff.

22. E. Tugendhat, *Traditional and Analytical Philosophy*, 207ff.

23. Michael Dummett, "What Is a Theory of Meaning?," in *Truth and Meaning*, ed. Gareth Evans and John McDowell (Oxford: Clarendon Press, 1976), 67ff.

24. L. Wittgenstein, *Philosophical Investigations*, §§380ff.; cf. Peter Winch, *The Idea of a Social Science* (London: Routledge & Kegan Paul, 1958); J. Habermas, *Theory of Communicative Action* 2: 15ff.

25. On the development of Austin's position, see Jürgen Habermas, "What Is Universal Pragmatics?," in *Communication and the Evolution of Society*, trans. Thomas McCarthy (Boston: Beacon Press, 1979), 1ff.

26. J. L. Austin, *How to Do Things with Words*, 145ff.; idem, "Performative-Constative," in *Philosophy and Ordinary Language*, ed. C. E. Caton (Urbana: University of Illinois Press, 1963), 22–33.

27. John Searle, *Speech Acts* (Cambridge: Cambridge University Press, 1969); idem, *Expression and Meaning* (Cambridge: Cambridge University Press, 1979); idem, *Intentionality* (Cambridge: Cambridge University Press, 1983); idem, *Minds, Brains and Science* (Cambridge, Mass.: Harvard University Press, 1984).

28. For the following, see J. Habermas, *Theory of Communicative Action* 1: 321ff.; see also idem, "Bemerkungen zu J. Searles 'Meaning, Communication and Representation'," in *Nachmetaphysisches Denken* (Frankfurt: Suhrkamp, 1988), 143ff.

29. Searle's own explanation already makes it apparent that the use of a double arrow to characterize the declarative mode expresses an embarrassment: Searle, *Expression and Meaning*, 19.

30. Cf. the discussion of Popper's doctrine of three worlds in: J. Habermas, *Theory of Communicative Action* 1: 76ff.

31. Jürgen Habermas, "Remarks on the Concept of Communicative Action," in *Social Action*, ed. G. Seebass and R. Tuomela (Dordrecht: Reidel, 1985), 151–178.

32. J. Culler, in "Communicative Competence and Normative Force," (*New German Critique*, 35 [1985]: 133ff.), claims that through a tendentious choice of examples I smuggle a normatively loaded concept of 'reaching understanding' ('*Verständigung*') into the analysis: "When I am reading the instructions for my word processing program I assume that statements are correct descriptions of the system's capabilities and that the manual has been checked for errors, but there seems no interesting sense in which I presuppose the sincerity of any individual communicator." (Ibid., 140) The impersonal form of the written instructions for the use of a computer is, however, no obstacle to adducing the model of face-to-face communication in order to analyze the illocutionary meaning, and the commitment arising out of it, of such technical instructions. Through the conditions of the sales contract a normative context is established, which appears to justify the normative expectations, mentioned by Culler that the user has toward the computer firm.

33. Jürgen Habermas, "A Reply," in *Communicative Action*, ed. Axel Honneth and Hans Joas (Cambridge, Mass.: MIT Press, 1991), 239ff. In an incisive article ("Habermas' Defense of Rationalism," in *New German Critique* 25 [1985]: 145ff.), Allen Wood has criticized my attempt to utilize the opposition of illocutionary and perlocutionary acts to justify the primacy of the use of language oriented toward reaching understanding. I admit that (in J. Habermas, *Theory of Communicative Action* 1: 288ff.) I rashly threw this meaning-theoretic distinction together with the action-theoretic distinction between action oriented toward reaching understanding and that oriented toward

success. It is sufficient to justify the primacy of the understanding-oriented use of language through the theory of meaning, as proposed here, and to distinguish communicative from strategic action through the fact that the former is mediated by illocutionary acts that are carried out without reserve, so that it is subject to the performative limitations of the action-coordinating mechanism of reaching understanding. This mechanism interrupts, as it were, the individual chains of action that are being linked up through consensus formation, whereas the speech acts that are instrumentalized for strategic action are robbed of their illocutionarily binding (or bonding) power. Perlocutionary effects, which are at first set off from illocutionary effects in purely meaning-theoretic terms, can then be described variously in action-theoretic terms, depending on whether they come on the scene openly and are capable of consensus within the framework of common situation definitions, or whether they are strategically pursued and may not be declared.

34. The example is taken from A. Wood, "Habermas' Defense of Rationalism," 161.

35. Cf. the example in Ernst Tugendhat, "J. Habermas on Communicative Action," in *Social Action,* ed. G. Seebass and R. Tuomela (Dordrecht: Reidel, 1985), 179ff.

5

Peirce and Communication

From Edward C. Moore, one of the editors of *A Chronological Edition*, we learn that the collected works of Charles Sanders Peirce could run to something like 104 volumes. I am no expert even about what is published and easily accessible. But, happily, Peirce was of the opinion that *all* signs are fragments of a larger, still undeciphered text—and, just the same, await their interpretation here and now. In this I find some slight encouragement.

I also have a reservation about the topic that has been suggested to me; as the subject index reveals, Peirce does not often speak of communication. That is surprising in the case of an author who is convinced of the semiotic structure of thought (CP 5.421),[1] and who asserts "that every logical evolution of thought should be dialogic." (CP 4.551) But, even in this last passage, Peirce is not talking about the relation between a speaker who uses an expression and an addressee who understands the expression. Rather, what he is saying here is that every sign requires two quasi-minds—"a Quasi-utterer and a Quasi-interpreter; and although these two are one (i.e., are one mind) in the sign itself, they must nevertheless be distinct. In the sign they are, so to say, *welded*." Peirce speaks of quasi-minds here because he wants to conceptualize the interpretation of signs abstractly, detached from a model of linguistic communication between a speaker and a hearer, detached even from the basis of the human brain. Today this makes us think of the operations of artificial intelligence, or of the mode of functioning of the genetic code; Peirce had crystals and the work of bees in mind.

Peirce wants to conceptualize the process of communication so abstractly that the intersubjective relationship between speaker and hearer vanishes and the relationship between sign and interpreter is absorbed without a trace into the so-called interpretant-relation. The "interpretant" is at first understood as the picture or impression that the sign calls forth in the mind of an interpreter. This intent explains the heavy sigh with which Peirce accompanies his definition of the sign in a letter to Lady Welby (from December 23, 1908), since this definition might well suggest a concretistic fallacy:

> I define a sign as anything which is so determined by something else, called its Object, and so determines an effect upon a person, which effect I call its Interpretant, that the latter thereby is mediately determined by the former. My insertion of "upon a person" is a sop to Cerberus, because I despair of making my own broader conception understood. (Letters, 29)

In another letter (from March 14, 1909), Peirce cautions against limiting the analysis to the repertoire of signs and the grammar of human language or, worse, to some *one* language. The title "Speculative Grammar" announces the ambitious project of a *universal* semiotics ranging over the universe of all signs. The concept of the sign ought to be so conceived that it is equally appropriate for natural and conventional signs, for prelinguistic and linguistic symbols, for sentences and texts, as well as for speech acts and dialogues.

A semiotics of this sort begins with the elementary sign. Yet, through the properties, the functions, the interpretive possibilities, and the transformative rules of the single sign, this semiotics should already bring those features to the fore that are constitutive for a full-fledged sign in language. A linguistic approach (for example, Saussure's structuralism) does not suffice for this. In contrast, the perspective of the logician adopted by Peirce has the advantage of examining expressions from the point of view of their possible truth *and*, at the same time, from that of their communicability. Thus, from the perspective of its capacity for being true, an assertoric sentence stands in an epistemic relation to something in the world—it represents a state of affairs. At the same time, from the perspective of its employment in a communicative act, it stands in a relation to a possible interpretation by a language user—it is suitable for the transmission of information. That which is thus differentiated on the level of grammatical speech into the epistemic relation to the world and the communicative relation to the interpreter is already taken into account by Peirce on the level of the elementary sign when he distinguishes between two relations: "standing for . . ." and "standing to. . . ." The interpretability (standing to . . .) of the sign is integrated with its representational function (standing for . . .) in the following way: the sign determines its interpretant in accordance with the relation in which the sign itself stands to the object represented by it. Everything that brings something else (its interpretant) to refer to an object in the same way that it itself refers to it, counts as a sign. (CP 2.303) A sign is only able to represent an object thanks to this three-placed relation.

What is thereby represented at first remains unspecified; in any event, we cannot assume from the start that the "object" ("*Objekt*") will be an identifiable thing (*Gegenstand*), or even a state of affairs. We must however bear in mind that Peirce does not explain the representative function of the sign in terms of the two-placed relation of standing for something. In order to fulfill its representative function, the sign must at the same time be interpretable: "A thing cannot stand for something without standing to something for something." (CE 1:466) This statement is already to be found in the seventh Lowell Lecture of 1866. The sign cannot establish its epistemic relation to something in the world if it is not at the same time directed toward an interpreting mind—that is, if it were not *capable* of being employed communicatively. Without communicability there is no representation—and vice versa. Even though Peirce's interest in semiotic problems is primarily epistemological in nature, he sets the basic conceptual switches in such a way that the epistemic relation of the sign to something in the world cannot be isolated from its communicative relation to a *possible* interpreter. At the same time, however, Peirce insists upon the anonymization of the interpretive process, from which he eliminates the interpreter. What remains after this abstraction are streams of depersonalized sign sequences in which every sign refers as interpreter to the foregoing sign and refers as interpretandum to the following sign. To be sure, these linkages are established only through the mediation of a mind in which signs are able to call forth interpretations ("intelligent consciousness must enter into the series" [CP 2.303]). Still, this *mind* remains anonymous because it consists of nothing other than the three-placed relation of representation in general; *it* is absorbed by the structure of the sign.

In terms of theoretical strategy, this abstract conceptualization has the advantage of not restricting semiosis from the very beginning to linguistic communication but instead leaves its elements open to further specifications. Nonetheless, the question arises whether Peirce's concept of the sign really does leave open the specifications that are requisite for the communicative level of propositionally organized language—or whether it does not prejudice them in a certain way instead. A methodological consideration can help us along here. Peirce pursues something like the logical genesis of sign processes. In doing so, he begins with the complex structures of language that are accessible to us, in order to feel his way towards the more elementary forms by means of privative determinations—Peirce speaks of "degeneration." In this procedure, one may totally abstract only from those aspects of a higher semiotic level for which it is not possible to locate a more primitive precursor or lower semiotic level. Now, Peirce seems to regard the intersubjective relationship between a speaker and a hearer, and the corresponding participant perspectives of the first and second person (in contrast to the perspective of an uninvolved third person), as such aspects that may be disregarded. He seems to believe that the fundamental semiotic structure can be completely defined without any recourse to forms of intersubjectivity, no matter how elementary. In any event, he generally leaves off from his logical-semiotic analyses at the point where speaker-hearer perspectives come into play.[2]

Like George Herbert Mead later on, the young Peirce, too, was clearly of a different opinion. He attached almost fundamental importance to the attitudes of the first, second, and third persons. On the one hand, the corresponding perspectives are equally fundamental, that is, none can be reduced to the others; on the other hand, they can be transformed into one another. The primitive expressions "I," "thou," and "it" thus form a system of relations, as the twenty-four-year-old Peirce notes:

Though they cannot be expressed in terms of each other, yet they have a relation to each other, for "Thou" is an "It" in which there is another "I." "I" looks in, "It" looks out, "Thou" looks through, out and in again . . . (CE 1:45)

Two years later Peirce connects his speculations about a future communitary age, which is supposed to supercede the tendencies to reification of the present materialistic age, with the name *Tuism,* which indicates the importance of the performative attitude one takes up toward a second person for the purposes of social interaction.[3] In 1861 Peirce planned to write a book about "I, It, and Thou" as "Elements of Thought." In the first Harvard Lectures of 1865 he attempts to introduce the concept of the sign in connection with the system of personal pronouns; not unreasonably, the interpretant relation, and thus the power of the sign to influence an interpreting mind, is explicated by means of the attitude of the second person. (CE 1:174) But after that, if I am not mistaken, the system of personal pronouns completely loses its significance for the foundations of semiotics.

Now, the question that interests me is, What considerations could have induced Peirce to turn away from the intersubjective aspects of the sign process? I want to defend the thesis that the interpretant relation of the sign cannot be explained without recourse to the conditions for reaching an intersubjective agreement, however rudimentary these conditions may be. This remains impossible as long as one conceives of sign-mediated representation, as Peirce does, in terms of truth and reality—for the latter concepts refer in turn to the regulative idea of a community of investigators that operates under ideal conditions. As long as Peirce maintains that his pragmatic turn cannot be consistently carried out without recourse to these or similar counterfactual presuppositions, he cannot do without an intersubjectively based semiotics. I would like to explicate this thesis in four steps.

First I want (1) to sketch the critique of the philosophy of consciousness that Peirce carried out in the 1860s and 1870s as well as (2) to recall the two resulting problems that emerge from the semiotic transformation of Kantian epistemology. The solutions proposed by Peirce depend upon (3) the premise of cumulative learning processes, which admits a weak, inter-subjectivistic reading. But instead of this interpretation, Peirce prefers a strong, or cosmological, one. He develops this version in terms of (4) a theory of natural evolution, which leads both to consequences that are problematic for semiotics and to a Platonistic concept of the person, a concept that cannot be brought into harmony with our best intuitions.

I

A third world of symbolic forms that mediates between the inner and the outer worlds (CE 1:168) discloses itself to the young Peirce along the dual path of religious experience and logical investigation:

Religion . . . is neither something within us nor yet altogether without us—but bears rather a third relation to us, namely, that of existing in our communion with another being. (CE 1:108)

While for Peirce the transcendentalist the forcelessly unifying power of communication stands in the foreground, for Peirce the logician something else provides the decisive factor, namely, the idea that "every thought is an unuttered word." (CE 1:169)

Peirce, prior to Frege and Husserl, carries through a devastating critique of psychologism in his first Harvard Lecture. Logic is not a matter of mental processes or particular facts of consciousness. Rather, it analyzes general sign operations and properties that are actualized in symbolic expressions and that can be read from them; logical characters "belong to what is written on the board at least as much as to our thought." (CE 1:165) But unlike Frege and Husserl, Peirce the epistemologist does not arrive at Platonistic conclusions about meaning. Every symbol of itself refers to possible interpretations, i.e., to indefinitely many reproductions of its meaning *over time*. Like all signs, symbols are what they mean only in relation to other signs. And these relations can in turn only be actualized with the aid of operations which for their part extend over time. Time is required for the transformation of symbolic expressions. For this reason the world of symbolic forms stands in an *internal* relation to time. Peirce had learned from Hegel "that the thought descends into time." In his debate with Kant, however, Peirce does not engage this theme from the perspective of a temporalization of mind. Instead, he is concerned with how the flowing stream of consciousness is stabilized in the form of a symbolically embodied mind.

Under the heading "On Time and Thought," Peirce considers how the flow of our ideas can take on the continuity and the connectedness of feelings, wishes, and perceptions that are in contact with each other. A mere succession of distinct ideas, each of which is absolutely present at a different time, cannot provide an explanation for how ideas can be determined by previous ideas—i.e., how one idea can be transformed into another according to a rule. Ideas that are at one point past must still be capable of being held fast in the mind, as it were, and of existing together and being linked up with the ideas that come after them. The semiotic interpretation of consciousness offers the key to explaining this reproduction of ideas that makes their recognition possible.[4] If cognitions are signs, then replicas can be generated from past cognitions and linked up with present and future ones: "thus the intellectual character of beliefs at least is dependent upon the capability of the endless translation of sign into sign." (CE 3:77) For their power to grant continuity, signs are indebted to the temporal reference that, with an object relation to the past and an interpretant relation to the future, is inherent in them.

With his semantic transformation of Kantian epistemology, Peirce paves the way for a critique of the philosophy of consciousness that introduces a specifically pragmatic turn.[5] The architectonic of the philosophy of consciousness had been defined by the subject-object relation, interpreted as mental representation. Within the traditional paradigm of representative thinking, the objective world is conceived as the totality of mentally representable objects, while the subjective world is conceived as the sphere of our mental representations of possible objects. Access to this internal sphere is gained through the representing subject's relation to itself (or through self-consciousness), i.e., through the representation of the act of representing objects. Peirce undermines this architectonic by giving a semiotic reinterpretation to the fundamental concept of "representation": the two-placed relation of mental representation (*Vorstellung*) is made into the three-placed relation of symbolic representation (*Darstellung*).

In explicit form, symbolic representation appears as a proposition representing a state of affairs. At first this only seems to replace the *psychological* perspective with a *semantic* perspective, as if the place of the subject-object relation were merely taken by the relation between language and the world. But a complication emerges directly from the propositional structure of that for which the sentence-sign stands. A simple predicative sentence does not just stand for an object; it does indeed refer to a singular object in the world, but it attributes to this object a property that can only be expressed in a predicate or a general concept. And it does this in such a way that it is not immediately clear whether this universal more properly belongs in the world or to language.

Another complication is more interesting. It arises from the fact that the sentence-sign does not refer only to something in the world but refers at the same time to an interpretive community. A fact is represented in terms of an assertoric sentence that can be true or false; the act of representation is, however, an assertion with which a speaker raises a contestable truth claim before an addressee. As early as the Ninth Lowell Lecture of 1866, Peirce emphasizes this *pragmatic aspect* of representation: "a symbol may be intended to refer to an interpretant or to have *force*. . . . It is intended . . . to inculcate this statement into an interpretant." (CE 1:477) An assertion receives illocutionary force through the fact that a speaker offers—at least implicitly—a reason or an argument by means of which he wants to bring the addressee to give assent. Peirce will later say that every proposition is the rudimentary form of an argument. (CP 2.344) Within the paradigm of the philosophy of consciousness, the truth of a judgment is based on the certainty that the mental representation corresponds to the object. After the pragmatic turn, however, the truth of a sentence-sign must be measured both against its object relation and against the reasons for its validity that could be accepted by an interpretive community. Thus in the new paradigm the role of the subject is assumed not by language *per se* but by communication among those who demand explanations from each other in order to reach an agreement with one another about something in the world. The place of subjectivity is assumed by an intersubjective practice of reaching understanding; this practice emits from itself infinite sequences of signs and interpretations. Peirce develops this conception via an incisive critique of the paradigm of the philosophy of consciousness. He is guided in particular by the following six points:

• The methodological critique is directed against a kind of *introspection* that relies on the private evidence of so-called facts of consciousness, without being able to present verifiable criteria for discriminating appearance from reality. In contrast, signs and symbolic expressions are generally accessible facts whose interpretation is open to public criticism, so that it is not necessary to appeal to a particular individual in place of the community of investigators as the final arbiter of correct judgment.

• The epistemological critique is directed against a form of *intuitionism* that claims that our judgments are constructed from immediately given and absolutely certain ideas or sense-data. The fact of the matter is that no idea, no matter how elementary, establishes contact with its object without semiotic mediation. There is no absolute beginning in an empirical process that is fundamentally discursive. Whether consciously or not, all cognitions are determined logically by previous cognitions.

• This gives rise to the critique of a *foundationalist* theory that privileges *self-consciousness*. The fact of the matter is that we only draw inferences about the inner world of mental states and psychic events from our knowledge of external facts. The hypothesis of a "self" is forced on us only through the experience of error, that is, when an opinion that is at first held to be true turns out to be merely "subjective."

• The critique of Kant's construction of a "thing-in-itself" is directed against a kind of *phenomenalism* that is led astray by the mirror-model of representative thinking: like the mirror itself, reality is thought to have a rear side that evades reflection, a reality hidden *behind* appearances. In fact reality does impose restrictions upon our knowledge, but only in such a way that it rejects false opinions when our interpretations founder upon it. But it does not follow that reality could fundamentally elude better interpretations. Rather, what is real is everything that can become the content of true representations, and nothing other than that.

• Further, the doubt about Cartesian doubt is directed against the *conception* of a *worldless subject* standing over and against the world as a whole. The individual consciousness does not form a monad encapsulated in itself, which could put into brackets the totality of beings by distancing itself *from everything* through a supposedly radical doubt. Rather, every subject always finds itself already within the context of a world that is familiar to it. The subject cannot skeptically problematize this massive background of beliefs by fiat and as a whole. An empty, abstract paper doubt cannot undermine life-world certainties; on the other hand, nothing is in principle immune to real, nagging doubt.[6]

• Finally, Peirce is opposed to the *privileging* of the *knowing subject* above the acting subject. All our beliefs are interwoven with our practices: "A belief which will not be acted upon ceases to be a belief." (CE 3:77) Thus, mind is situated and finds its embodiment in the symbolic medium of language *and* in that of *practice*. Any thought articulated in an utterance is recoupled with action and experience via the belief held by an interpreting mind. Every link in this chain exhibits the three-placed structure which explains the representative function of signs—and to this extent each is itself something of the same sort as a sign.

II

Even the semiotically transformed philosophy of consciousness does not, however, escape the old epistemological questions. How is the objectivity of experience supposed to be possible if the semiotically embodied mind remains caught in the spell of discourses and practices and bound by the chains of signs? How can we do justice to our intuitive understanding of reality as something independent of us if the truth of judgments and statements is mired in the rhetorical pros and cons of argumentation without end? True, Peirce destroyed two dogmas: the myth of the given and the illusion of truth as the certainty of our mental representations. But now he is faced with the question of whether he has not simply traded the dogmas of received empiricism for a second-order empiricism—a holistically renewed empiricism on the level of sign systems, which we can no more get behind than we can get behind "first principles" or "ultimate facts." Peirce suggests three innovative answers: (1) the theory of presymbolic signs, (2) the doctrine of synthetic inferences, and (3) the regulative idea of a final consensus (ultimate agreement or final opinion).

(1) How is the objectivity of experience supposed to be possible? On the one hand, the contact between sign and reality must be established via experience, just as before; on the other hand, experience is absorbed by a continuum of sign-mediated processes. Peirce thus has to show how strings of signs, which can be set forth without end through logical operations of inference, are nonetheless able to open themselves up osmotically to reality. He has to demonstrate the possibility of *anchoring* strings of signs in reality. Along the path of a logical genesis of perceptual judgments, Peirce, like the late Husserl in *Experience and Judgment,* must descend into the realm of prepredicative experience.

The starting point for this descent is provided by the structure of the simple predicative sentence, which is the semiotic form of perceptual judgments. A proposition consists of two elements. One of these, the subject expression, establishes the relation to the object, while the other contains the predicative determination of that object. In light of this Peirce develops the distinction between existence and reality. The two-placed relation between the referential term and its object is an existential relation, which does indeed reflect the "outward clash" of a confrontation with reality but does not mirror reality itself. For the real state of affairs is only represented by the sentence as a whole, including the predicate.

Drawing the well-known distinction between symbol, index, and icon is then the first move in the game of a logical genesis of the assertoric sentence. Below the level of complete sentences—that is, those representations that are capable of being true or false—there are signs that stand in either a relation of denotation or in a relation of similarity to corresponding aspects of reality. From this Peirce infers that the subject and predicate expressions, which must be joined together in sentences in order to fulfill an explicit representative function, are based upon a genetically more primitive layer of index signs and icons, each of which is of itself already capable of assuming a relation to an object and of finding an interpretant.[7] These are nonsymbolic yet still conventional signs.

Following this first step in the archeology of linguistic symbols, these conventional signs are augmented by three classes of nonconventional or natural signs. Whereas arguments, propositions, and terms, as well as independently appearing indices and iconic representations such as diagrams, still stand in conventional relations to their objects, those symptoms and analogues that Peirce introduces as "sin-signs" or "quali-signs" depend on a causal nexus or on preexisting similarities in form.[8] Later, Peirce further differentiates these classes of signs, but he never arrived at a conclusive system. That is only consistent when it is a matter of demonstrating that the roots of the semiotic family tree of predicative sentences branch off endlessly and extend down to a depth where, for the time being, they slip from the sight of the step-by-step process of abstracting from what is above. Similarly, empirical processes can have their roots in preconscious layers of sense stimuli and feelings without forfeiting the discursive character of a sign-mediated inferential process.

(2) Of course, these considerations can only provide support for experience's claim to objectivity if the infinitesimal

initial phases of our prepredicative experiences elude conscious control or explicitly discursive processing: in a certain sense, the percepts force themselves on us. But these elementary information inputs that are vested with sensory evidence are no less fallible than the perceptual judgments that are obtained from them.[9] Even percepts cannot take on the role of first premises. Even they depend upon those limit cases of abductive inference that strike us in the form of lightning insights, and which for that reason merely conceal their fallibility from us:

> If the percept or perceptual judgment were of a nature entirely unrelated to abduction, one would expect, that the percept would be entirely free from any characters that are proper interpretations, while it can hardly fail to have such characters. (CP 5.184)

Of course, these percepts and perceptual judgments run through the channels of practice again and again and eventually become habitualized; they are thus capable of gelling together with theoretical background suppositions and moral principles to form an unquestioned context of lifeworld certainties (common-sense beliefs). But none of these practically entrenched beliefs is immune to being problematized. That is, only in the case of misfires, or negative experiences, does the contact to reality furnish a good criterion for the evaluation of the opinions that are invested in plans of action.[10]

If however the objectivity of experience cannot be made secure by an indubitable basis of information, the manner in which information is processed might still provide a guarantee of truth. Peirce regards the rules of inferential reasoning as the core of such a procedural rationality. As is well known, he reconstructs this *logica utens* in the form of a doctrine of synthetic inferences. I cannot pursue that further here.[11] One reservation is nonetheless important: the circular process of hypothesis formation, inductive generalization, deduction, and renewed hypothesis formation might well lead us to expect that the processing of experiences will be self-correcting and that the growth of knowledge will be cumulative, but only if abduction is handled correctly. The abductive form of inference is the real knowledge-amplifying element, but at the same time it is far from yielding *necessary* conclusions. Peirce believes that considerations from probability theory can be used to show that induction is reliable "in the long run." Yet, only the rational formation of hypotheses could close the circle of inductive generalization and deduction. So the question arises once again, How is the objectivity of experience possible? There are now two possibilities. Either the doctrine of synthetic inferences needs an objective foundation in reality, so that it could be shown how nature itself directs our formation of hypotheses (the later Peirce would come back to this alternative). Or the burden of proof, which cannot be borne solely by experience (including the experience of practical failure) and inferential reasoning, has to be redistributed and *relocated* upon another link in the chain of the semiotic process: upon argumentation. Indeed, Peirce had always conceived of discussion as the "proofstone of truth" (Kant): "Upon most subjects at least sufficient experience, *discussion* and reasoning will bring men to an agreement." (CE 3:8) He does not conceive of such discussion as a contest (CP 5.406), in which one side seeks to overpower the other rhetorically; it appears rather as a cooperative search for truth by means of the public exchange of arguments. Only then is discussion able to serve as a "test of dialectical examination." (CP 5.392)

(3)   At first, in "The Fixation of Belief," Peirce gives a *historical* grounding for the thesis that procedural rationality, which is effective in everyday practices and elaborated in science, can only develop under conditions of rational discourse: in modernity, the rational authority of empirically guided discursive learning has asserted itself against the force of habits, thought control, and wish-fulfilling *a priori* doctrines. But an explanation that goes beyond such historical considerations is needed to explain why the inferential processing of information could not succeed without an exchange of arguments that is public and unforced. Peirce uses the tripartite structure of the sign itself to explain why the sign-mediated cognitive process requires these conditions in order to operate.

A sign can only fulfill its representative function if, along with the relation to the objective world of entities, it simultaneously establishes a relation to the intersubjective world of interpreters. The objectivity of experience is not possible without the intersubjectivity involved in coming to mutual understanding. This argument can be reconstructed in four stages.

• In a distant analogy to Wittgenstein's private-language argument, Peirce emphasizes the internal connection between private experience and public communication. A private aspect is always attached to experience because everyone has privileged access to his own ideas (*Erlebnisse*). At the same time, the sign character of these ideas points beyond the borders of subjectivity. By representing something, a sign expresses something general; therefore, it could not find an interpretant that might remain the exclusive possession of an individual mind. Everybody becomes aware of this supra-subjective partnership in the interpretant at the moment when he confronts the opinion of someone else and, in a flash, an error becomes apparent to him.

• This confrontation of opinions has to take on the rational form of argumentation, because this form of communication merely makes explicit what is already implicit in every proposition. That is, the illocutionary force of the act of assertion indicates that the speaker makes the addressee an offer to support his statement with an argument, if necessary—or, as Peirce says, to develop an argument from the proposition. So rational discourse, in which a proponent defends validity claims against the objections of opponents, is simply the most reflexively developed form of sign processes.

• Because the rules of synthetic inference cannot of themselves generate compelling results, and thus cannot be reproduced on the semantic level as algorithms, the argumentative processing of information has to assume the form of an intersubjective practice. Certainly, in argumentation the "yes" and "no" positions of the participants should be regulated by good reasons. Nonetheless, what may count as a "good reason" in any case has to be decided within argumentation itself. There is no higher court of appeal than the agreement of others that is brought about within discourse and, in this respect, is rationally motivated.

• Of course, the objectivity of experience cannot be made dependent upon the agreement—no matter how rational—of a contingent number of participants, i.e., a contingent agreement within any particular group. Better arguments, which would refute what is here and now held to be true by you and me, might emerge in different contexts or on the basis of further experiences. With the concept of reality, to which every representation necessarily refers, we presuppose something transcendent. As long as we move within a particular linguistic community or a particular form of life, this transcendent relation cannot be supplanted by the rational acceptability of an argument. Since we cannot break out of the sphere of language and argumentation altogether, we can only establish the reference to reality—which is not equivalent to "existence"—by projecting a "transcendence from within." This end is served by the counterfactual concept of a "final opinion," or a consensus reached under ideal conditions. Peirce makes the rational acceptability of an assertion, and thus its truth as well, dependent upon an agreement that could be reached under the communicative conditions for a community of investigators that is extended to ideal limits in social space and historical time. If we understand reality as the conceptual totality of all assertions that are true in this sense, then we are able to do justice to its transcendence without having to surrender the internal connection between the objectivity of experience and the intersubjectivity of reaching mutual understanding:

The real, then, is that which, sooner or later, information and reasoning would finally result in, and which is therefore independent of the vagaries of me and you. Thus, the very origin of the conception of reality shows that this conception essentially involves the notion of a *Community*, without definite limits, and capable of a definite increase of knowledge. (CP 5.311)

III

This semiotic model of knowledge gives rise to an image of a rationally directed process of interpretation in which "men and words reciprocally educate each other." (CE 1:497) The semiotically constituted world of human beings reproduces itself and develops through the medium of signs. At one pole, experience and purposive action secure a contact with reality that is sign-mediated: "The elements of every concept enter into logical thought at the gate of perception and make their exit at the gate of purposive action." (CP 5.212) At the other pole, the exchange of arguments takes place with regard to, and in anticipation of, the counterfactually presupposed conditions of ideal communication. At the former pole, learning processes occur as more or less 'natural' events according to the rules of synthetic inference; at the latter pole, these processes have become reflexive. They come under the direction of a conscious community of investigators that supervises itself. This community is committed to a logic "whose essential end is to test the truth by reasons." (CE 1:329) The relation of experience to argumentation reflects the tension between "private" and "public." Correspondingly, everyday action and argumentation are caught up in the tension between the certainty of common sense and the awareness of radical fallibility.[12]

Both common sense and science operate with the supposition of a reality that is independent of us. In our practices, however, that which we take to be unavoidable and indubitable has the status of an acritical certainty, although it is by no means immune *a priori* against objections. In the realm of argumentatively tested knowledge, on the other hand, we are conscious of the fallibility of every insight. In order to believe that we are capable of the truth nonetheless, we need the compensatory reference point provided by the "final opinion." Only those assertions are true that would always be reaffirmed within the horizon of a community without definite limits. (CP 5.311)

This semiotic model of knowledge, reality and truth, yields consequences for the very concepts of the sign and of interpretation. Up till now we have proceeded from the position that in the mind of an interpreter the sign has the effect of reproducing, as it were, the object which is represented by the sign. Strictly interpreted, this would mean

that a representation is something which produces another representation of the same object, and in this second or interpreting representation the first representation is represented as representing a certain object. This second representation must itself have an interpreting representation and so on ad infinitum, the whole process of representation never reaches a completion. (CE 3:64f.)

Yet, such an infinite regress would only come about if the process of interpretation were to circle within itself, as it were, without continual stimulation from outside, and without discursive processing. But this description is adequate only for the initial phase in which, before any experience, the interpretant relates to the "immediate object" that inheres, as it were, in the sign as its meaning. The actual employment of the sign in a particular situation, however, requires an interpretant that refers in view of collateral experience to the "dynamic object." This object is external to the sign and demands of the interpreter both sensory and practical experience, knowledge of the context, and discursive processing of information. Nor is the interpretation of a sign therein exhausted; because the interpretation aims towards an explicit representation, i.e., one that is capable of being true, it anticipates the possibility of a final interpretant. The latter refers to the object as it would be represented in light of an ideal consensus—that is, to the "final object." Only an orientation toward truth does justice to the role of symbolic expressions that "represent" something, in the sense that interpreters can make use of them *in order to come to an agreement with one another about something in the world.* Understanding, coming to an agreement, and knowledge refer reciprocally to each other.[13]

The interpretation of signs is interwoven with the representation of reality; for this reason, the stream of interpretations takes on a direction. The original text of nature does not go down in the maelstrom of the significant. The telos of a *complete* representation of reality is already inscribed in the structure of the first sign. Nonetheless, one consequence of this disturbed Peirce from the start: because of their semiotic constitution, learning processes are ultimately unable to break away from the circle of the signs that are given interpretations by us. In the end, the limits of our language remain the limits of the world.

This semiotic circle closes itself off all the more inexorably when Peirce's *logical* analysis of language is extended to include *linguistic* aspects. It then becomes apparent that in limit cases successful abduction also requires an innovative modification of language itself—a modification, that is, in the perspective from which we look at the world. In extreme cases, we run up against the limits of our comprehension, and interpretations that labor in vain on resilient problems begin to falter. They only get moving again when, in light of a *new* vocabulary, the familiar facts show themselves in a different light, so that well-worn problems can be posed in a completely new and more promising way. This world-disclosing function of the sign was neglected by Peirce.

This function does not at all imply that the universalizing force of learning processes becomes fragmented whenever it runs up against the borders of a particular language or a concrete form of life. All languages are porous, and every newly disclosed aspect to the world remains an empty projection as long as its fruitfulness does not also *prove its worth* in learning processes that are made possible by the changed perspective on the world. But this interplay between linguistic world-constitution and innerworldly problem solving only highlights the question that disturbed Peirce.

If the limits of semiosis mean the limits of the world, then both the system of signs and the communication among sign-users acquire an almost transcendental status. The structure of reality itself is not what is mirrored in the structure of the language in which subjects give a representation of the world. Peirce stubbornly fought against such nominalistic consequences his entire life; and it seemed to him that they could be avoided if the semiotic circle were not merely to encompass the world of subjects capable of speaking and acting but nature as a whole—to encompass nature and not just our interpretation of nature. Only then would the topos of the "book of nature" shed its metaphorical character, and every natural phenomenon would be transformed—if not into a letter then at least into a sign that determines the series of its interpretants. Moreover, the imaginative generation of conjectures that is at work in all successful abduction would then only have to bring to consciousness what is already prefigured in natural evolution. The synthetic inferences would obtain a *fundamentum in re.* This semiotic idealism[14] requires, of course, a naturalization of semiosis. The price Peirce has to pay for this is the anonymization and depersonalization of the mind in which signs call forth their interpretants. With this metaphysical baggage, however, Peirce overburdens his semiotics.

I see the great achievement of Peircean semiotics in its consistent expansion of the world of symbolic forms beyond the borders of linguistic forms of expression. Peirce did not merely contrast our propositionally differentiated language with signal languages. He did not merely analyze those types of intentionally employed indices and icons that attain independence below the level of linguistic signs. He showed how causal symptoms and spontaneous expressive gestures, as well as preexisting gestalt similarities, can be interpreted on the model of linguistic signs. He thereby opened new realms to semiotic analysis: for example, the extraverbal sign world, in the context of which our linguistic communication is embedded; the aesthetic forms of representation, especially the repertoire of nonpropositional arts; finally, the abductive decoding of a symbolically constructed social world, upon which thrive our everyday communicative practices, as well as characters like Sherlock Holmes or novels like Eco's *Name of the Rose.*[15] Our lifeworld, which is semiotically constructed from bottom up, forms a network of implicit meaning structures that are sedimented in signs that, although nonlinguistic, are nonetheless accessible to interpretation. The situations in which participants to an interaction orient themselves are overflowing with cues, signals, and telltale traces; at the same time, they are marked by stylistic features and expressive characteristics that can be intuitively grasped, and which reflect the "spirit" of a society, the "tincture" of an age, the "physiognomy" of a city or of a social class. If Peirce's semiotics is applied to this sphere, produced by human beings but by no means intentionally *controlled,* then it also becomes clear that the deciphering of implicit meaning structures, i.e., the understanding of meaning, is a mode of experience. Experience *is* communicative experience. Karl-Otto Apel, in particular, has drawn our attention to this.[16]

When we become aware of this wealth of meaning that is not linguistically articulated, but is instead objectivated in presymbolic and even preconventional signs, then one fact emerges all the more clearly: even if natural signs lack authors who give them meaning, still they only have meaning for interpreters who are masters of a language. How should they find their interpretants where there are no interpreters who are able to argue with reasons about their interpretations? Yet, just this is assumed by a semiotic idealism that projects semiosis into speechless nature. Semiotic idealism assumes that the process of habit-formation that is steered by the interpretation of signs extends far beyond the human world to include animal, vegetable, and mineral.

IV

Peirce is convinced

that habit is by no means exclusively a mental fact. Empirically, we find that some plants take habits. The stream of water that wears a bed for itself is forming a habit. (CP 5.492)

A nature that has developed via a semiotic learning process opens its eyes and becomes a virtual participant in the conversation conducted among humans. This venerable idea obtains its appeal from an image of ourselves entering into conversation with nature and unbinding the tongues of the creatures so far excluded from redemption. To the naturalization of humans there would then correspond a humanization of nature, as Marx thought. But a completely different result emerges out of Peirce's semiotic reading of this legacy of Judaic and Protestant mysticism, romantic philosophy of nature, and transcendentalism: by being absorbed into an all-encompassing nexus of communication, the conversation among humans loses just what is specific to it. This becomes apparent in Peirce's concept of the person, in which everything that makes a person into an individual is defined purely negatively, in terms of its difference from what is general—namely, in terms of the distance separating error from the truth and of that dividing the egoist from the community.[17] The individual is something merely subjective and egoistic:

The individual man, since his separate existence is manifested only by ignorance and error, so far as he is anything apart from his fellows, and from what he and they are to be, is only a negation. (CP 5.317)

Thus, the bad legacy of Platonism is reproduced even in the work of the anti-Platonist Peirce. A metaphysical realism in regard to universals that has been set in motion turns the evolution of the cosmos into the bearer of an inexorable tendency towards universalization, a tendency to ever more organization, ever more conscious control. However, the consequence I am examining is not explained by metaphysical realism *per se*. Rather, it only emerges from Peirce's semiotic conception of the universal as a sign-mediated representation together with his interpretation of evolution as a learning process. Both allow communication, in which the tendency to universalization asserts itself, to be seen from only *one* side: communication is not for the sake of reaching mutual understanding between ego and alter about something in the world; rather, interpretation only exists for the sake of the representation and the ever more comprehensive representation of reality. This privileging of the sign's representative relation to the world above the sign's communicative relation to the interpreter causes the full-fledged interpreter to disappear behind the depersonalized interpretant.

This is made all the more feasible because the doctrine of synthetic inferences now finds its foundation in the laws of natural evolution. If the learning processes of the human species merely continue, in reflexive form, those of nature, then argumentation, or what one human being has to say to another, and the power of the better argument to convince, both lose the weight and value that are proper to them. The unforced agreement of individuals who hold one another accountable, and who are faced with opinions that differ from person to person, ought to issue from argumentation by virtue of the latter's specific character. But this specific achievement falls victim to the leveling force of a universalism propelling itself inferentially from within reality itself. The multivocal character of intersubjectivity becomes an epiphenomenon.

It is interesting that in the end Peirce is able to picture one interpreter reaching agreement with another only as an emotional fusion of ego and alter:

> When I communicate my thoughts and my sentiments to a friend with whom I am in full sympathy, so that my feelings pass into him and I am conscious of what he feels, do I not live in his brain as well as in my own—most literally? (CE 1:498)

In this view, the generalization of a consensus not only implies the dissolution of contradictions, but also the extinguishing of the individuality of those who are able to contradict each other—their disappearance within a collective representation. Like Durkheim, Peirce conceives of the identity of the individual as the mirror-image of the mechanical solidarity of a group: "Thus every man's soul is a special determination of the generic soul of the family, the class, the nation, the race to which he belongs." (CE 1:499) George Herbert Mead, a pragmatist of the second generation, was the first to conceive language as a medium that socializes communicative actors only insofar as it simultaneously individualizes them. The collective identities of the family, class, and nation stand in a complementary relation to the unique identity of the individual; the one may not be absorbed by the other. Ego and alter can agree in an interpretation and share the same idea only insofar as they do not violate the conditions of linguistic communication but maintain an intersubjective relationship that requires them to orient themselves toward each other as first person is oriented toward second person. This means, however, that each must distinguish himself from the other in the same way that both in common must distinguish themselves in the first-person plural from others as third persons. Were the dimension of possible contradiction and difference to close, then linguistic communication would contract into a type of communion that no longer needs language as the means of reaching mutual understanding.

Peirce once accused the Hegelians—in just the same sense as Feuerbach had—of neglecting the moment of Secondness, which expresses itself in the external resistance of existing objects. (CP 8.39ff.) He himself neglects that moment of Secondness that we encounter in communication as contradiction and difference, as the *other* individual's "mind of his own" [*Eigensinn*]. To be sure, when it is a matter of a great philosopher, his individuality may also be expressed in his philosophy. In this respect, the participants in this conference will not want to contradict Peirce when he says:

Each man has his own peculiar character. It enters into all he does; but as it enters into all his cognition, it is a cognition of *things in general*. It is therefore the man's philosophy, his way of regarding things,—that constitutes his individuality. (CE 1:501)

Notes

1. References to Peirce's works in this essay and in the footnotes are indicated by CP and CE. CP = *Collected Papers*, 8 vols., ed. C. Hartshorne, et al. (Cambridge, Mass.: Harvard University Press, 1931–58). Citations of this edition are by volume number, followed by a period, followed by the paragraph number. CE = *Writings of Charles S. Peirce. A Chronological Edition,* ed. Max H. Fisch, et al. (Bloomington, Ind.: Indiana University Press, 1982–[1986]). Citations of this edition are by volume number, followed by a colon, followed by the page number.

2. The supposed irrelevance of the intersubjective relationship pointing beyond the structure of the sign-mediated representation is justified as follows: "In every assertion we may distinguish a speaker and a listener. The latter, it is true, need have only a problematical existence, as when during a shipwreck an account of the accident is sealed in a bottle and thrown upon the water. The problematical 'listener' may be within the same person as 'the speaker'; as when we mentally register a judgment independent of any registry . . . we may say that in that case the listener becomes identical with the speaker." (CP 2.334) Additionally, Peirce also doubts whether a judgment could have any logical significance at all if, as presupposed in this thought experiment, it is not structured through the "register" of an internalized proposition, i.e., through a sign. In regard to that it is clear that even the message in a bottle has an addressee, however anonymous.

3. As late as 1891, Peirce defines Tuism as the doctrine "that all thought is addressed to a second person." (Cited from M. H. Fisch, "Introduction," CE 1:XXIX.)

4. For a similar approach, cf. Ernst Cassirer, *The Philosophy of Symbolic Forms,* 3 vols., trans. Ralph Manheim (New Haven: Yale University Press, 1953–57), vol. I, introduction, and vol. III, first and second part.

5. Karl-Otto Apel, *Charles S. Peirce: From Pragmatism to Pragmaticism,* trans. J. M. Krois (Amherst: University of Massachusetts Press, 1981).

6. "It is idle to tell a man to begin by doubting familiar beliefs, unless you say something which shall cause him to really doubt them. It is false to say that reasoning must rest either on first principles or on ultimate facts. For we cannot go behind what we are unable to doubt, but it would be unphilosophical to suppose that any particular fact will never be brought into doubt." (CE 3:14)

7. K. Oehler, "Idee und Grundriß der Peirceschen Semiotik," *Semiotik* 1 (1979): 9ff.

8. Cf. the introduction of the ten classes of signs in: H. Pape, ed., *Phänomen und Logik der Zeichen* (Frankfurt, 1983), 64ff., esp. 121ff. Further: H. Pape, *Erfahrung und Wirklichkeit als Zeichenprozeß* (Frankfurt, 1989).

9. Charles Hookway, *Peirce* (London, 1985), 149ff.

10. Peirce was long of the opinion, "that there is no definite and fixed collection of opinions that are indubitable, but that criticism gradually pushes back each individual's indubitables, modifying the list, yet still leaving him beliefs indubitable for the time being." (CP 5.509)

11. Hookway, 208ff.

12. "*Full belief* is willingness to act upon the proposition in vital crises, *opinion* is willingness to act upon it in relatively insignificant affairs. But pure science has nothing at all to do with action. . . . The scientific man is not in the least wedded to his conclusions. . . . He stands ready to abandon one or all as soon as experience opposes them. Some of them, I grant, he is in the habit of calling *established truths;* but that merely means propositions to which no competent man today demurs." (CP 1.634)

13. D. Savan, "Questions Concerning Certain Classifications Claimed for Signs," *Semiotica* 19 (1977): 179ff.; J. Ransdell, "Some Leading Ideas of Peirce's Semiotic," *Semiotica* 19 (1977): 157ff.

14. J. E. McCarthy, "Semiotic Idealism," *Transactions of the Charles S. Peirce Society* 20 (1984): 395ff.

15. T. A. Sebeok and J. Umiker-Sebeok, *Charles S. Peirce und Sherlock Holmes* (Frankfurt: 1980).

16. Karl-Otto Apel, *Understanding and Explanation: A Transcendental-Pragmatic Perspective,* trans. Georgia Warnke (Cambridge, Mass.: MIT Press, 1984).

17. P. A. Muoio, "Peirce on the Person," *Transactions of the Charles S. Peirce Society* 20 (1984), 169ff.

III

Between Metaphysics and the Critique of Reason

6

The Unity of Reason in the Diversity of Its Voices

"The One and the Many," unity and plurality, designates the theme that has governed metaphysics from its inception. Metaphysics believes it can trace everything back to one. Since Plato, it has presented itself in its definitive forms as the doctrine of universal unity; theory is directed toward the one as the origin and ground of everything. Prior to Plotinus, this one was called the idea of the good or of the first mover; after him, it was called *summum ens,* the unconditioned, or absolute spirit. During the last decade this theme has taken on renewed relevance. One side bemoans the loss of the unitary thinking of metaphysics and is working either on a rehabilitation of pre-Kantian figures of thought or on a return to metaphysics that goes beyond Kant.[1] Conversely, the other side attributes responsibility for the crises of the present to the metaphysical legacy left by unitary thinking within the philosophy of the subject and the philosophy of history. This side invokes plural histories and forms of life in opposition to a singular world history and lifeworld, the alterity of language games and discourses in opposition to the identity of language and dialogue, and scintillating contexts in opposition to univocally fixed meanings. To be sure, this protest against unity made in the name of a suppressed plurality expresses itself in two opposed versions. In the radical contextualism of a Lyotard or a Rorty, the old intention behind the critique of metaphysics lives on: to rescue the moments that had been sacrificed to idealism—the nonidentical and the nonintegrated, the deviant and the heterogeneous, the contradictory and the conflictual, the transitory and the accidental.[2] In *other* contexts, on the other hand, the apologetics of the accidental and the abandonment of the principled lose their subversive traits. In these contexts, all that is retained is the functional significance of shielding the powers of tradition, which are no longer rationally defensible, against unseemly critical claims; the point is to provide cultural protection for the flanks of a process of societal modernization that is spinning out of control.[3]

Thus, the nuanced debate surrounding the one and the many cannot be reduced to a simple for or against. The picture is made even more complex by latent elective affinities. The protest against the overpowering one that is made today in the name of an oppressed plurality allows itself at least a sympathetic detachment vis-a-vis the appearance of unitary thinking in renewed metaphysical form. For the fact is that radical contextualism itself thrives on a negative metaphysics, which ceaselessly circles around that which metaphysical idealism had always intended by the unconditioned but which it had always failed to achieve. But, from the functionalist perspective of a compensation for the burdens of societal modernization, the less radical form of contextualism can also get by with metaphysics, even though this contextualism itself no longer believes in the metaphysical claims to truth. The parties for and against the unitary thinking of metaphysics only form a clear constellation in relation to a third party, in which they detect a common opponent. I am referring to the humanism of those who continue the Kantian tradition by seeking to use the philosophy of language to save a concept of reason that is skeptical and postmetaphysical, yet not defeatist.[4] As seen by the unitary thinking of metaphysics, the procedural concept of communicative reason is too weak because it discharges everything that has to do with content into the realm of the contingent and even allows one to think of reason itself as having contingently arisen. Yet, as seen by contextualism, this concept is too strong because even the borders of allegedly incommensurable worlds prove to be penetrable in the empirical medium of mutual understanding. The metaphysical priority of unity above plurality and the contextualistic priority of plurality above unity are secret accomplices. My reflections point toward the thesis that the unity of reason only remains perceptible in the plurality of its voices—as the possibility in principle of passing from one language into another—a passage that, no matter how occasional, is still comprehensible. This possibility of mutual understanding, which is now guaranteed only procedurally and is realized only transitorily, forms the background for the existing diversity of those who encounter one another—even when they fail to understand each other.

I want to begin (I) by recalling the ambiguous significance of the unitary thinking of metaphysics, which, in emancipating itself from mythological thinking that focuses on origins, still remains tied to the latter. Along the way, I will touch on three topics that have sparked the critique of metaphysics within the very framework of metaphysics: the relationship of identity and difference, the problem of what is ineffably individual, and the discontent with affirmative thinking—above all with the merely privative determinations of matter and evil. Then I would like to retrace (II), in the case of Kant, the turn away from a rational unity derived from the objective order of the world and toward a concept of reason as the subjective faculty of idealizing synthesis; admittedly, the old problem of idealism, how *mundus intelligibilis* and *mundus sensibilis* are to be mediated, returns here in a new form. Hegel, Marx, and Kierkegaard attempt, each in his own way, to lay claim to the medium of history in order to conceive of the unity of a historicized world as process—whether it be the unity of the world as a whole, or of the human world, or of the life history of the individual. Positivism and historicism reply to this with a new turn (III), this time toward the theory of science. As we see today, this turn prepared the way for contextualism in one version or another. The objections to this position draw attention in turn to the impossibility of circumventing the symmetrical structure of perspectives built into every speech situation, a structure that makes possible the intersubjectivity of reaching understanding in language. Thus (IV), a weak and transitory unity of reason, which does not fall under the idealistic spell of a universality that triumphs over the particular and the singular, asserts itself in the medium of language. The theme of the one and the many arises in different ways in the ontological, the mentalistic, and the linguistic paradigms.

I

"The one and the many" is the central topic in the *Enneads* of Plotinus. That work recapitulates the movement of thought within philosophical idealism that began with Parmenides and that led beyond the cognitive limits of the mythological way of seeing the world. *To hen panta* does not mean that everything is absorbed into one but that the many can be traced back to the one and can thereby be conceived as a whole, as totality. Through this powerful abstraction, the human mind gains an extramundane point of reference, a distancing perspective, from which the agitated in-one-another and against-one-another of concrete events and phenomena are joined together in a stable whole that is itself freed from the mutability of occurrences. This distancing view is then able to differentiate between the totality of what is and individual entities, between the world and what occurs within it. In turn, this distinction makes possible a level of explanation that is remarkably different from mythological narratives. The world in the singular refers to *one* origin, and indeed to one that can no longer be of the same sort as the original powers of mythology, which appear in the plural and compete with one another. The latter remained interwoven with the chain of generations and had their beginning *in* time; but as presuppositionless beginning, the one is a first from which time and the temporal first emerge.

Because every phenomenon in need of explanation must now be related in the last instance to the one and the whole, the necessity of disambiguation asserts itself—everything innerworldly must be made univocal as a being that is identical with itself, i.e., as an object that is in each case particular. And the explanation for the phenomena that have become objects cannot be sought at the level of the phenomena themselves but only in something that underlies the phenomena—in essences, ideas, forms, or substances, which, like the one and the whole, are themselves of a conceptual nature or, in the manner of the archetype, at least occupy a middle ground between concepts and images. The one is therefore regarded as the first not only in the sense of the first beginning or origin but also as the first reason or ground, the primordial image, or the concept of the concept. Explanation by principles, which grasps the particular under the universal and derives it from a final axiom, this deductive mode of explanation modeled on geometry, breaks with the concretism of a worldview in which the particular is immediately enmeshed with the particular, one is mirrored in the other, and everything forms an extensive flat weave of oppositions and similarities. One could say, with Nietzsche, that mythology is familiar only with surface, only with appearance and not with essence. In opposition to that, metaphysics delves into the depths.

The world religions, especially the monotheistic ones and Buddhism, attained a conceptual level on a par with philosophical idealism. But when they put the world as a whole at a distance by means of a history of salvation or of a cosmology, the great prophets and founders of religions were led by questions posed *ethically,* whereas the Greek philosophers made the break with the immediacy of the narrative weave of concrete appearances *theoretically.* In this latter case, the advance from mythos to logos had more than socio-cognitive potential. Yet even the act of contemplation had an ethico-religious significance. A manner of living crystalized around the theoretical attitude of one who immerses himself in the intuition of the cosmos. This *bios theoretikos* was laden with expectations similar to those of the privileged paths to salvation of the wandering monk, of the eremite, or of the monastic brother. According to Plotinus, in the medium of thought the soul forms itself into a self, which becomes conscious of itself as a self in the recollective, reflexive intuition of the one. *Henosis,* the uniting of the philosopher with the one, for which discursive thinking prepares the way, is at once ecstatic self-transcendence and reflexive self-reassurance. The dematerializing and de-differentiating recognition of the one in the many, the concentration upon the one itself, and the identification with the source of the limitless light, with the circle of circles—all this does not extinguish the self but intensifies self-consciousness. Philosophy refers to the conscious life as its telos. The identity of the ego forms itself in the contemplative present-ation of the identity of the world. Thus, the thinking of the philosophy of origins did indeed have an emancipatory meaning.

Metaphysics also belongs to the world-historical process described by Max Weber from the perspective of the sociology of religion as rationalization and by Karl Jaspers as the cognitive advance of the 'axial period' (extending from Buddha via Socrates and Jesus up to Mohammed).[5] Of course, that was a process of "rationalization" in an entirely different sense as well. From Freud to Horkheimer and Adorno, the dialectic inherent in metaphysical enlightenment has been retraced.[6] The spell of mythological powers and the enchantment of demons, which were supposed to be broken by the abstraction of universal, eternal, and necessary being, still live on in the idealistic triumph of the one over the many. The fear of uncontrolled dangers that displayed itself in myths and magical practices now lodges within the controlling concepts of metaphysics itself. Negation, which opposed the many to the one as Parmenides opposed nonbeing to being, is also negation in the sense of a defense against deep-seated fears of death and frailty, of isolation and separation, of opposition and contradiction, of surprise and novelty.[7] This same defensiveness still betrays itself in the idealist devaluation of the many to mere appearances. As mere *images* of the Ideas, the surging phenomena become univocal, the surveyable parts of a harmonic order.

The history of metaphysical thinking fuels the materialist suspicion that the power of mythological origins, from which no one can distance himself and go unpunished, is merely extended in idealism in a more sublime and less merciful way. Metaphysics labors in vain on certain key problems that seem to result from the rebellion of a disenfranchised plurality against a unity that is compulsory and, to that extent, illusory. From at least three perspectives, the same question is posed again and again: how are the one and the many, the infinite and the finite, related to each other?

First, How can the one, without endangering its unity, be everything (*Alles*), if the universe (*das All*) is indeed composed of many different things? The question of how the identity of identity and difference can be conceived, which was still the concern of Hegel's *Differenzschrift,* emerges out of the problem of *methexis* in the Platonic doctrine of Ideas. Plotinus had already incisively stated this problem with a paradoxical formulation: "The one is everything and yet not even one (among all things)."[8] The one is everything insofar as it resides in every individual being as its origin; yet, at the same time, insofar as it can preserve its unity only through its distinction from the otherness of each individual being, the one is also nothing among them all. In order to be everything, the one is thus in everything; at the same time, in order to remain the one itself, it is above everything—it both lies beyond and underlies everything innerworldly.

Metaphysics entangles itself in such paradoxical formulations because, thinking ontologically, it vainly tries to subsume the one itself under objectifying categories; but as the origin, ground, and totality of all beings, the one is what first constitutes the perspective that allows the many to be objectivated as the plurality of beings. For this reason, it was still necessary for Heidegger to insist upon the ontological difference between Being and beings, which is supposed to guard against the assimilation of the one to the other.

Plotinus transfers this paradox out of the one itself and into *nous:* only within the human faculty of cognition does the gap open up between discursively grasping the many and intuitively melting together with the one; the former process merely moves toward the latter. Of course, this negative ontological concept of the one as something effusive, which refuses all involvement with discursive reasoning, clears the way for a self-referential critique of reason that continues to hold the thinking of Nietzsche, Heidegger, and Derrida under the influence of metaphysics. Whenever the one is thought of as absolute negativity, as withdrawal and absence, as resistance against propositional speech in general, the ground (*Grund*) of rationality reveals itself as an abyss (*Abgrund*) of the irrational.

Second, there arises the question of whether idealism, which traces everything back to one and thereby devalues innerworldly beings to phenomena or images, can do justice to the integrity of the particular entity in its individuality and uniqueness. Metaphysics uses the concepts of genus and specific difference in order to break the universal down into the particular. Following the genealogical model, the family tree of the Ideas or generic concepts branches off from each level of generality into specific differences, each species of which can in turn constitute a *genus proximum* for further specifications. The particular is a particular only relative to a universal. For the individuation of the particular into single entities there are available the nonconceptual media of space, time, and matter, as well as those accidental features through which the individual deviates from what is appropriate to it by virtue of its membership in genera and its specific differences. Thus, the individual remains accessible only in the accidental husk that clings to the core of the generically and specifically determined being, only as something that is external and contingent. Metaphysical concepts break down in the face of the individual. In the end, this motivates John Duns Scotus to extend the essential all the way down to single entities. He coins the paradoxical concept of *haecceitas,* which stamps individuation itself with the seal of the essential, yet which, as something that is itself like an essence, persists in an indifferent universality vis-a-vis what is truly individual.

From its inception, idealism had hidden from itself the fact that the Ideas inconspicuously include within themselves the merely material and accidental moments of individual things, from which they had indeed only been abstracted.[9] Nominalism exposed this contradiction and demoted substances or *formae rerum* to mere names, to *signa rerum* that, as it were, the knowing subject tacks on to things. When the modern philosophy of consciousness finally dissolved even desubstantialized individual things into the material of sensation, from which the subjects themselves first form their objects, the problem of the ineffability of an individuality that withdraws from conceptual subsumption became even more acute. The critique of the understanding (*Verstandesdenken*) is motivated by the murky constellation joining the universal, the particular, and the individual. After Hegel, this is transformed into the critique of a form of reason that controls and identifies; it terminates in Adorno's attempt to rescue the moment of the nonidentical from the assaults of instrumental reason.[10]

From within the movement of metaphysical thought itself there emerges the third theme in the critique of metaphysics— namely, the suspicion that all its contradictions come together in the venerable concept of matter; the latter constitutes the dross, as it were, of affirmative thinking. Should matter, to which innerworldly beings owe their finitude, their concretion in space and time, and their resistance, be determined purely negatively as nonbeing? Must not matter, in which the Ideas are supposed to be deluded and to wane into mere phenomena, be conceived as a principle that not only contrasts with the intelligible but *contradicts* it—not merely as privation, as a residue that is left over after the removal of all determinate being and all good, but as an active power of negation that first generates the world of appearance and evil? This question has been insistently repeated from a genetic perspective. Once the primacy of the one, which precedes and underlies everything, is posited—why then are there any beings at all, rather than nothing? The question of theodicy is simply a moral-practical variant of this: given the primacy of the good, from which everything is derived, how then does anything evil come into the world in the first place? Schelling still labored away on this question in 1804 and again in 1809 (in his treatise on human freedom). He set himself against the Platonic tradition, in which what is material or evil is represented as a mere shading, weakening, or diminishing of the intelligible and the good, and not as the principle of negating and of egoity, of closing off, of actively striving back into the depths. In his remarkable polemic against the bias toward the affirmative, against the purification and the harmonization of the unruly and the negative, of what refuses itself, there also stirs an impulse to resist the danger of idealist apotheosis—the same impulse that directly provides the impetus for the critique of ideology that extends all the way up to the pessimistic materialism of the early Horkheimer and to the optimistic materialism of Bloch.[11]

II

Schelling's reflections already presuppose the premises of a philosophy of consciousness that no longer thinks of the unity of the many as an objective whole prior to the human mind but conceives of it as a result of the synthesis executed by mind itself. Beyond this, Schelling's *System des transzendentalen Idealismus* (1800) already contains a first, partially elaborated construction of world history. Both of these elements—reason as the source of *world-constituting* ideas, and history as the medium through which mind carries out its synthesis—revolutionize the basic concepts of metaphysics and give rise to the resulting problems that, with the Young Hegelians, set postmetaphysical thinking in motion.

It is well known that Kant connected the concept of knowledge with the synthetic accomplishments of the productive imagination and of the understanding, through which the manifold of sensations and representations are organized into a unity of experiences and judgments. Apprehension within intuition, reproduction within imagination, and recognition within the concept are spontaneous actions that run through the manifold, take up its elements, and combine them into a unity. Kant uses the construction of simple geometric forms and number series to elucidate the operation of *producing* unity in a previously unordered multiplicity. In doing this, the independently acting subject proceeds according to fundamental rules, for the representation of unity cannot emerge out of the act of combination itself. And for their part, these synthetic connections in the understanding are unified by the higher-level synthesis of pure apperception. With this title Kant refers to the formal "I think," which must be capable of accompanying all of my representations if the egological unity of a constantly identical self-consciousness is to be preserved in the manifold of representations. If the subject is not to forget itself and submerge in the stream of its lived experiences, it must hold itself fast as the same subject. Only this identity, which is produced in apprehending self-consciousness, and which is by no means empirically given but is instead transcendentally presupposed—only this identity permits the self-attribution of all of my representations. Only through the transcendental unity of apperception does the manifold of my representations take on the general connectedness of representations that are my own, that *belong* precisely to me as the knowing subject.

The *Critique of Pure Reason* thus reaches the point from which, in its own way, it connects with that metaphysical figure of thought, universal unity. That is, the transcendental unity of the knowing subject who relates itself to itself requires, on the side of what is known, a symmetrical concept of everything that stands over and against the subject, a transcendental concept of the world as the totality of all appearances. Kant calls this world-concept a cosmological idea, i.e., a concept of reason by means of which we make the totality of conditions in the world into an object. A new type of synthesis thereby comes into play. Cosmological ideas generate the "unconditioned synthetic unity of all conditions in general"; by aiming at the whole of possible experience and at the unconditioned, they follow principles of completeness and perfection that transcend all experience. This idealizing surplus distinguishes the *world-constituting* synthesis of reason from the synthetic accomplishments of the understanding, which allow us to know something *in the world*. Because the ideas are concepts that project a world, nothing that looks in any way like an object of experience could correspond to them. In relation to the world of appearances, they are suitable only as principles that regulate the use of the understanding and obligate it to the goal of systematic knowledge, that is, to theory formation that is as unitary and complete as possible. They have heuristic value for the progress of knowledge.

By taking the totality of beings and making it dependent upon the synthetic accomplishments of the subject, Kant downgrades the cosmos into the object domain of the nomological natural sciences. The world of appearances is no longer a "whole organized according to ends." Thus, although the transcendental concept of the world traces everything back to one, it differs from the old metaphysical concept of the world in that it can no longer also satisfy the need for establishing a meaningful organization, an organization that would absorb contingencies, neutralize what is negative, and calm the fear of death, of isolation, and of what is simply new. In exchange, Kant now offers the compensation of another world, namely the intelligible. True, the latter remains closed off to theoretical knowledge, but its rational core, the moral world, is nonetheless attested to by the fact of the "ought." That is, unlike the cosmological idea, the idea of freedom finds support in the moral law; it not only regulates but determines moral action: "Reason is here, indeed, exercising causality, as actually bringing about that which its concept contains."[12] It is only the affiliated concept of a "world of rational beings" that is regulative, a world in which each acts as if, through his maxims, he were at all times a legislating member in the universal kingdom of ends. In this way like theoretical reason, practical reason also projects an unconditioned unity of all conditions in general—but this time the whole to which it is directed is that of an "ethical-civic" commonwealth. The latter would come about by systematically connecting all humans through shared objective laws. The world-constituting synthesis of reason once again comes into play, but this time its idealizing surplus does not have a merely heuristic meaning that guides cognition but a moral-practical meaning that obligates us.

Through this doubling of the transcendentally redirected concept of the world, Kant solves two of the three problems mentioned above, upon which metaphysics had labored in vain. The question of how the identity of the one and the many is to be conceived was only an unsolvable problem under the constraints imposed by the conceptual strategy of an ontologically objectifying thinking, which mixes up the world and beings in the world. But the transcendental illusion that the one and the whole must correspond to objects vanishes as soon as world-concepts are seen through as ideas of reason, that is, as the result of an idealizing synthesis. The problem of matter, too, is dissolved, because synthetic accomplishments are attributed to a subject that must be *given* its material, both in cognition and in action. Of course, the initial metaphysical question—how the one and the many or the infinite and the finite are related to each other—now reappears in a transcendentally modified form. The murky side-by-side status of the intelligible and the sensible worlds translates the old problem into many new questions, questions about the relationship between practical and pure reason, between the causality of freedom and the causality of nature, between morality and legality, etc. Kant is unable to overcome this dualism of worlds even by introducing a third kind of Idea of Reason, one that places the consideration of nature and history under teleological perspectives. For, without the solid empirical foundation provided by the judgments of the understanding, Ideas of this kind do not have even heuristic significance. Rather, they form the *focus imaginarius* for a way of viewing nature and history that treats them *as if* they *were* capable of constituting a kingdom of ends.

In any case, the inherited problem of the ineffability of the individual remains unsolved.[13] The scientific activity of the understanding subsumes what is particular under universal laws without having to worry about what is individual. No place remains for the ego *qua* individual person between the ego as something universal and the ego as something particular, i.e., between the transcendental ego as one over and against everything and the empirical ego as one among many. To the extent that knowledge of myself is transcendental, it encounters the naked identity of the ego as the formal condition for the connectedness of my representations. To the extent that this self-knowledge is empirical, my inner nature appears as foreign to me as outer nature.

As long as a redemptive significance for the individual soul extended to philosophical theory as a form of life, the subject who devoted himself to theory did not need, *within* theory itself, to reassure himself of his unique existence; he could be satisfied by the promise of the salvation that was to be obtained through participation in the theoretical life. It was secularized confessional literature, for which Rousseau provided the great example, that recalled that the basic concepts of rational psychology had never gotten a hold on the fundamental experience of the Judeo-Christian tradition, despite the kinship of metaphysics with theology. The experience to which I am referring is the individuating gaze of that transcendent God, simultaneously judging and merciful, before whom every individual, alone and irreplaceable, must answer for his life as a whole. This individuating power of the consciousness of sin, which could not be captured by the concepts of philosophy, sought for itself a different, literary form of expression in the autobiographical revelation of one's life story, as the published documentation of an existence that has always to answer for itself. In addition, the theme of ineffable individuality takes on new relevance as historical thinking comes on the scene.

Both romanticism and the cultural sciences that arose in its spirit filled the transcendental concept of the world with new unities in the temporal, social, and spatial dimensions: with (the one) history, (the one) culture, and (the one) language. These new singulars introduced a synthetic unity into the plurality of histories, cultures, and languages, which had until then been seen as products of natural growth. Herder, Humboldt, and Schleiermacher assumed straightaway that this synthetic unity resulted from an underlying mental or spiritual productivity. And yet *this* synthesis must be conceived according to a model *different* from that of the construction of a straight line or of a number series, because in the spheres disclosed by the cultural sciences, the particular can no longer be subsumed under the universal while the individual is disregarded. It is, in an emphatic sense, individuals who are enmeshed in their histories, their forms of life, and their conversations, and who for their part convey something of their individuality to these engulfing, intersubjectively shared, yet concrete contexts. The particular of a specific history, culture or language stands, as an individual type, between the universal and the singular. It was with groping concepts such as these that the old historical school operated.[14]

It was to this stage of the debate, which had been transformed equally by Kant's critique of metaphysics and by post-Kantian historical consciousness, that Hegel responded. The ambivalence that was only incipient in Kant emerges openly in Hegel's philosophy: by taking up and radically developing the theme of self-critique that had issued from the movement of metaphysical thought, Hegel renews the unitary thinking of metaphysics for the last time. In demolishing Platonic idealism, he adds the last imposing link to the chain of tradition that extended through Plotinus and Augustine, Thomas, Cusanus and Pico, Spinoza and Leibniz; but he does this only by revitalizing the concept of universal unity in a distinctive way. Hegel sees his philosophy of reconciliation as an answer to the historical need for overcoming the diremptions of modernity in modernity's own spirit. The same idealism that had denied any philosophical interest to the merely historical *qua* nonbeing is thereby placed under the historical conditions of the new era. That explains *first* why Hegel conceives of the one as absolute subject, thereby annexing the metaphysical figures of thought to that concept of autonomously acting subjectivity from which modernity draws its consciousness of freedom and, indeed, the whole of its characteristic normative content consisting of self-consciousness, self-determination, and self-realization. And it explains *secondly* why he lays claim to history as the only medium for the mediation of the one and the many, the infinite and the finite.[15]

These two aspects of his conceptual strategy compel Hegel to revise a premise that had remained in force from Plotinus to Schelling's *Jenaer Identitätsphilosophie*. Conceived in the terms of first philosophy, the one, as the ground of everything, could not be equated with the totality of beings. And the absolute had been held fast as the one itself, prior to and higher than everything. To this relationship between the one and the many, the infinite and the finite, there corresponded a subordinate position for a human spirit that was reflected into itself and already divided within itself. Characteristically, *nous* formed the first hypostasis in Plotinus: in the discursive mind, the one had already stepped outside itself. In place of this, Hegel now makes reflection itself absolute—reflection as the self-reference of a spirit that works its way up out of its substantiality to self-consciousness and which bears within itself the unity as well as the difference of the finite and the infinite. What had still been true for Schelling is inverted: the absolute subject is precisely not supposed to *precede* the world process. Rather, it exists only in the relationship of the finite and the infinite to each other, in the consuming activity of reflection itself. The absolute is the mediating process of a self-reference that produces itself unconditionally. One and all no longer stand over and against each other as relata; instead, it is now the relation itself, set in motion historically, which establishes the unity of its relata.

With this innovation, Hegel confronts both problems that Kant had bequeathed to his successors. As soon as history is placed on the level of metaphysics and the self-mediation of absolute spirit takes on the grammatical form, so to speak, of the historical progressive, the fractured continuity of a single self-formative process generates itself. This self-formative process sublates the dualisms of the sensible world and the moral world, of the constitutive and the regulative use of the Ideas of Reason, of form and content. Moreover, each particular is granted the solid form of a concrete universal by syntheses that have congealed to shapes of spirit, and for which nothing provides the material other than the preceding shapes of spirit themselves. The concrete universal is supposed to allow each conceptually grasped individual to receive its due in exactly the same way that it allows history to be glimpsed as a self-formative process. Adorno's negative dialectics can only sue for the recovery of the nonidentical from Hegel because the nonidentical was already on Hegel's programme.

But in the present context I am merely interested in the thesis that spirit falls within history. Until Hegel, metaphysical thinking was cosmologically oriented; nature was identical with the totality of beings. Now, the sphere of history is supposed to be integrated into this totality. Moreover, the synthetic labor of spirit is supposed to be performed through the medium of history and assimilated to the progressive form of the latter. Along with history, however, contingencies and uncertainties break into the circular, closed-off structure of unifying reason, and in the end these contingencies and uncertainties cannot be absorbed, even by a supple dialectic of reconciliation. With historical consciousness Hegel brought a force into play whose subversive power also set his own construction teetering. A history that takes the self-formative processes of nature and spirit up into itself, and that has to follow the logical forms of the self-explication of this spirit, becomes sublimated into the opposite of history. To bring it to a simple point that had already irritated Hegel's contemporaries: a history with an established past, a predecided future, and a condemned present, is no longer *history.*

III

Marx and Kierkegaard drew the moral from this. Along with the primacy of practice and of existence, the participant perspective of the "for us" and the "for me" also takes the lead theoretically. Historical consciousness thereby recognizes its provinciality in relation to the future. The synthesis of the process of world history or of a life history, whether it be executed through social labor and revolutionary practice or through Christian consciousness of sin and radical choice, follows the Kantian rather than the Hegelian model. But the stages run through by social formations or by one's own existence still obey a teleology, even if it is only to be carried to its end practically or existentially. A foundationalist residue adheres to Marx's social theory and to Kierkegaard's existential-dialectical writing. Since their day, it has become ever harder to ignore the way in which history intrudes into the structures of unifying reason with the contingencies of what is unforeseeably new and other, and these contingencies belie all rash syntheses and limiting constructions. For the later nineteenth century, this experience made the scientistic renunciation of metaphysics and the withdrawal into the theory of science seem advisable.

With Newton's physics in view, Kant had already set phenomenal (which primarily means scientifically objectified) nature free from metaphysical structures of meaning; he watered the unity of the cosmos down to the heuristic goal of unified theory construction. Why, then, should history not be similarly released from the burden of unitary thinking in the philosophy of history, which was a substitute for metaphysics, and be left to the human sciences that had since been established? Indeed, unlike the nomological sciences, the hermeneutic appropriation and narrative representation of tradition no longer seemed to obey even the heuristic imperative of a unified description of reality. Historicism, in any case, declared the context-dependent knowledge of the interpreter and of the narrator to be the domain of a plurality that escapes the claims of objectivity and unity for knowledge. In dualistic conceptions of science, which arose above all in Germany, the unity of reason was removed not only from the cosmos but from subjectivity as well. Unity evaporates into a methodological ideal that is now supposed to be valid only for the natural sciences, whereas according to historicist self-understanding, a plurality set free from all syntheses makes relativism inevitable in the human sciences. In the latter arena, then, histories triumph over the philosophy of history, cultures and forms of life triumph over culture as such, and the histories of national languages triumph over the rational grammar of language in general. Interpretation and narration supercede argumentation, multivalent (*vieldeutig*) meaning emancipates itself from simple validity, local significance is freed from the universalist claim to truth.

Philosophers have seldom been satisfied with such dichotomies; every dualism prods them to an explanation. Joachim Ritter's compensation theory represents such an attempt to come to terms with the historicist dichotomization of the scientific world.[16] Ritter begins by placing the natural sciences, which are committed to unity and universality, in relation to civil society, and the human sciences, which are committed to plurality and individuality, in relation to personal life. Then, by way of these contexts of employment, he brings the two types of science into a complementary relationship with one another. The natural sciences develop the productive forces of an industrial society undergoing modernization; the human sciences look after the powers of tradition in a lifeworld threatened in its historical substance. The natural world and the historical world are said to form a rational and dynamic whole only as long as the human sciences, which specialize in narrative re-presentation, compensate for those losses in the lifeworld that are unavoidably brought about by the depersonalization and modernization of life conditions induced by the natural sciences.

I refer to this familiar thesis because today it serves to limit the human sciences to the business of narration and, in the name of a culture of multivalence, to release them from cognitive claims of the kind connected with theory construction and, indeed, with argumentation in general. This moderate variety of contextualism includes the further thesis that the lifeworld can only be protected from disintegration and civil war, from "hermeneutical manslaughter," when reason, in the sense of an orientation toward agreement based on reasons, is no longer imputed to it.[17] The text of the lifeworld must be made up of contexts alone. I do not want to dwell on the fact that the explanatory social sciences, together with linguistics and other reconstructive human sciences, find no place in the model of science thus established (which, incidently, Schelsky already noted in his own day[18]). More important in the present context is the fact that the compensation theory itself operates with a concept of reason that it fails to identify. Without saying so, this theory relies on an anthropology that would have to explain why human beings require an equilibrium between modernization and historicization. Such an anthropology would have to indicate *why* a deficit of compensatory enchantment, refamiliarization, and transmission of meaning comes about in the first place; *when* the deficit grows into a "loss unbearable for humans"; and *how* it can be balanced out through the production of narratives by the human sciences.[19] There is no such anthropology. And if one has any idea how difficult it is to come by universal statements about *the* human being, one is almost tempted to consider a theory that is at least available in draft form, one which tries to use the structures of the type of action that is oriented to mutual understanding in order to explain why and when lifeworlds are in danger of becoming deformed under the pressure of system imperatives.

Praising the many, difference, and the other may be able to count on acceptance today, but a mood is no substitute for arguments.[20] Of course, postempirical theory of science has indeed used arguments to change the image we have of the sciences.[21] In the wake of Kuhn, Feyerabend, Elkana, and others, unifying reason has been deprived of its last domain, physics. Richard Rorty[22] had only to draw the consequences from this to deconstruct the picture of the "mirror of nature" that had been derived from the philosophy of the subject and to relieve the natural sciences as well as epistemology from the requirement of unitary theory construction and the need for "some permanent neutral framework of all possible inquiry."[23]

Finally, then, even the weakest of the Kantian ideas of reason has been retracted. Without the spur of an idealizing world projection and a transcendent truth claim, objectifying science is swallowed up by its contingent contexts in the very same way as everyday practices are. In the laboratory as in life, the *same* culture of multivalence prevails once all standards of rationality and practices of justification claim to be nothing more than actually exercised conventions—nothing more "than just such practices."[24]

Having arrived at the threshold of the present, I want to end my retrospective in the history of ideas. As it is, the impression of a history of ideas might have been given only because an elaborate development of the arguments wrapped up in the ideas has been unnecessary for an audience of philosophical experts who are informed about the subject. However, in the matter of radical contextualism I have to become explicit. But first, one more comment about the shift in paradigms from the philosophy of consciousness to the philosophy of language.

Of course this linguistic turn had various motives. I will name one: the conviction that language forms the medium for the historical and cultural embodiments of the human mind, and that a methodologically reliable analysis of mental activity must therefore begin with the linguistic expressions of intentional phenomena, instead of immediately with the latter. Now it is not accidental that this realm of objective spirit came into view from two angles, on the one side from the angle of language, culture, and history in general, and on the other side from the angle of individual national languages, cultures, and histories. Hence the old theme of unity and plurality comes up once again in the question of how these two aspects are to be brought into relation to each other. As before, nothing would stand in the way of the concept of *one* reason today if philosophy and science were able to reach through the thicket of natural languages to the logical grammar of a single language that describes the world, or could at least come close to this ideal in a promising way. In contrast, if even the reflexive activity of mind always remained caught in the grammatical limits of various particular worlds that were linguistically constituted, reason would necessarily disintegrate kaleidoscopically into a multiplicity of incommensurable embodiments.

The question of how objective knowledge is possible has been answered by some theorists in an objectivistic and by others in a relativistic sense. Members of the first group reckon on an independent reality, toward which our interpretations finally converge, in the sense intended by a correspondence theory of truth. This group leaves intact the idea of reason that holds that in the long run exactly one true and complete theory would have to correspond to the objective world. On the other hand, the relativists hold a socialization theory of truth. They are of the opinion that every possible description only mirrors a particular construction of reality that inheres grammatically in one of various linguistic worldviews. There are no standards of rationality that point beyond the local commitments of the various universes of discourse. Both these positions are however confronted with insurmountable difficulties. The objectivists are faced with the problem of having to take up a standpoint between language and reality in order to defend their thesis; but they can only argue for such a null-context from within the context of the language they themselves use. On the other hand, the relativistic thesis, which concedes a perspectival right to every linguistically constituted view of the world, also cannot be put forth without a performative self-contradiction. So whoever absolutizes one of the two aspects of the linguistic medium of reason, be it its universality or its particularity, gets caught in aporias. Both Richard Rorty and Hilary Putnam want to find a way out of this situation, and I will link up with their discussion here.[25]

Rorty represents a contextualism that avoids the relativistic consequence of equal status for incommensurable standards and perspectives. If he did not, he would have to explain how a kind of truth extending beyond the perspective of our Western traditions could be thought to accrue to the perspectivistic thesis itself. Rorty recognizes that contextualism must be *cautiously* formulated in order to be radical. The contextualist must exercise caution in order not to take that which he may assert as a participant within a specific historical linguistic community and a corresponding cultural form of life and translate it into a statement made from the third-person perspective of an observer. The radical contextualist claims only that it is pointless to uphold the distinction, going back to Plato, between knowledge and opinion. "True" denotes what we hold to be justified according to our standards in a given case. And these standards of rationality are simply not to be distinguished in type from any other standards used in our culture. Practices of justification, like all other social conduct, are dependent upon our language, our traditions, and our form of life. "Truth" does not signify the correspondence between statements and some X prior to all interpretations; "truth" is simply an expression of commendation, with which we advise those who speak our language to accept the conceptions that we hold to be justified. Rorty explains the objectivity of knowledge in terms of the intersubjectivity of an agreement based, in good Wittgensteinian manner, on agreement in our language, our factually shared form of life. He replaces the aspiration to objectivity with the aspiration to solidarity within the linguistic community to which he contingently belongs. The cautious contextualist is not going to extend his lifeworld into the abstract; he must not dream of an ideal community of all those who communicate (Apel), freed from their provinciality, as Peirce and Mead dreamed of the ultimate community. He must rigorously avoid every idealization, and it would be for the best if he did without the concept of rationality altogether. For "rationality" is a limit concept with normative content, one which passes beyond the borders of every local community and moves in the direction of a universal one.[26]

An idealization of this sort, which conceives of truth as acceptability grounded in reasons under certain demanding conditions, would constitute a perspective that would in turn point beyond the practices of justification that are contingently established among us, one that would distance us from these practices. According to Rorty, that is not possible without a backslide into objectivism. The contextualist should not let himself be lured out of his participant perspective—even when the price he has to pay for this is admitted ethnocentrism. He admits that we have to privilege the interpretive horizon of our own linguistic community, although there can be no noncircular justification for this. But this ethnocentric standpoint only means that we have to test all alien conceptions in light of our own standards.[27] Confronting this position, Hilary Putnam shows that an idealizing concept of truth or of validity in general is both necessary and possible without objectivistic fallacies.

Putnam establishes the unavoidability of an idealizing conceptual construction with the following argument. If the distinction between a conception that is held to be true here and now and a conception that is true, i.e., one that is acceptable under idealized conditions, collapses, then we cannot explain why we are able to learn reflexively, that is, are able also to *improve* our own standards of rationality. The dimension in which self-distancing and self-critique are possible, and in which our well-worn practices of justification can thereby be transcended and reformed, is closed off as soon as that which is rationally valid collapses into that which is socially current. To this Rorty would reply that of course someone could at any time come up with new evidence, better ideas, or a novel vocabulary; in order to take that into account, however, we should not hold our conceptions, which are always only locally justified, to be "true" in an objectivistic sense. But the objectivistic alternative invoked by Rorty does not pose itself for Putnam. Rorty once said that for him the aspiration to objectivity is not the desire to flee from one's own linguistic community but simply the desire for as much intersubjective agreement as possible, namely, the desire to expand the referent of "for us" to the greatest possible extent.[28] In light of this intuition, I would reformulate Putnam's objection as follows: can we explain the possibility of the critique and self-critique of established practices of justification at all if we do not take the idea of the expansion of our interpretive horizon seriously *as an idea,* and if we do not connect this idea with the intersubjectivity of an agreement that allows precisely for the distinction between what is current "for us" and what is current "for them"?

Putnam and (in a penetrating contribution to the relativism controversy) Thomas McCarthy rightfully insist upon the existence of a *symmetrical* relationship between "us" and "them" in the exemplary cases of intercultural or historical understanding, in which rival conceptions collide not only with each other but with conflicting standards of rationality as well.[29] The cautious contextualist's ethnocentrism, admitted by Rorty, cannot but fail to capture the symmetry among the claims and perspectives of *all* participants in a dialogue because it describes the process of understanding as an assimilative incorporation of what is alien into our (expanded) interpretive horizon. But in a situation of profound disagreement, it is not only necessary for "them" to try to understand things from "our" perspective, "we" have to try in the same manner to grasp things from "their" perspective. They would never seriously get a chance to learn from us if we did not have the chance to learn from them, and we only become aware of the limits of "our" knowledge through the faltering of "their" learning processes. The merging of interpretive horizons, which according to Gadamer is the goal of every process of reaching understanding, does not signify an assimilation to "us"; rather, it must mean a convergence, steered through learning, of "our" perspective *and* "their" perspective—no matter whether "they" or "we" or both sides have to reformulate established practices of justification to a greater or lesser extent. For learning itself belongs neither to us nor to them; both sides are caught up in it in this same way. Even in the most difficult processes of reaching understanding, all parties appeal to the common reference point of a possible consensus, even if this reference point is projected in each case from within their own contexts. For, although they may be interpreted in various ways and applied according to different criteria, concepts like truth, rationality, or justification play the *same* grammatical role in *every* linguistic community.

Certainly, some cultures have had more practice than others at distancing themselves from themselves.[30] But all languages offer the possibility of distinguishing between what is true and what we hold to be true. The *supposition* of a common objective world is built into the pragmatics of every single linguistic usage. And the dialogue roles of every speech situation enforce a symmetry in participant perspectives. They open up both the possibility for ego to adopt the perspective of alter and vice versa, and the exchangeability of the participant's and the observer's perspectives. By no means do these universal pragmatic presuppositions of communicative action suggest the objectivistic fallacy according to which we could take up the extramundane standpoint of a subject removed from the world, help ourselves to an ideal language that is context-free and appears in the singular, and thereby make infallible, exhaustive, and thus definitive statements which, having neither the capacity nor the need for a commentary, would pull the plug on their own effective history. From the possibility of reaching understanding linguistically, we can read off a concept of situated reason that is given voice in validity claims that are both context-dependent and transcendent: "Reason is, in this sense, both immanent (not to be found outside of concrete language games and institutions) and transcendent (a regulative idea that we use to criticize the conduct of all activities and institutions)."[31] To put it into my own words: the validity claimed for propositions and norms transcends spaces and times, but in each actual case the claim is raised here and now, in a specific context, and accepted or rejected with real implications for social interaction.[32]

IV

The linguistic turn did transform reason and unitary thinking, but it did not drive them out of the philosophical discussion, as is shown by the outcome of the controversy surrounding both versions of contextualism. All the same, contextualism has become a manifestation of the spirit of the times. Transcendental thinking once concerned itself with a stable stock of forms for which there were no recognizable alternatives. Today, in contrast, the experience of contingency is a whirlpool into which everything is pulled: everything could also be otherwise, the categories of the understanding, the principles of socialization and of morals, the constitution of subjectivity, the foundation of rationality itself. There are good reasons for this. Communicative reason, too, treats almost everything as contingent, even the conditions for the emergence of its own linguistic medium. But for everything that claims validity *within* linguistically structured forms of life, the structures of possible mutual understanding in language constitute something that cannot be gotten around.

All the same, the postmodern mood is making its mark, all the way into the detective novel and onto the back-cover blurb. The publisher extols Enzensberger's new book with the notice that he enlists what is irregular against the project of homogenization, the margins against the center of power, living from difference against unity—Derrida's jargon migrates into commodity aesthetics. And a well-known author of detective stories has the thematic thread of his fable unravel in the confusion of a rich variety of contexts, to the extent that the genre-specific distinction between perpetrator and victim becomes unrecognizable in the weave of many small differences—after a sympathetic talk with the likeable murderer, who is finally caught, the police neither report him nor prosecute him.[33] Repulsion towards the One and veneration of difference and the Other obscures the dialectical connection between them. For the transitory unity that is generated in the porous and refracted intersubjectivity of a linguistically mediated consensus not only supports but furthers and accelerates the pluralization of forms of life and the individualization of lifestyles. More discourse means more contradiction and difference. The more abstract the agreements become, the more diverse the disagreements with which we can *nonviolently* live. And yet in the consciousness of the public, the idea of unity is still linked to the consequence of a forced integration of the many. Greater universalism is still treated as the enemy of individualism, not as what makes it possible. The attribution of identical meanings is still treated as the injury of metaphorical multivalence, not as its necessary condition. The unity of reason is still treated as repression, not as the source of the diversity of its voices. The background for this anxiety is still formed by the false suggestions of a unitary thinking that was left behind one-hundred-fifty years ago— just as if it were necessary today, as it was for the first generation of Hegel's students, to defend ourselves against the predominance of the great masters of metaphysics.

The reasons for this attitude appear to reside in society rather than in philosophy itself. For society has indeed become so complex that it can hardly still be made transparent from within as the dynamic whole of a structural organization. The functionally differentiated society is decentered; the state no longer forms the political apex in which the functions relevant to the whole of society could be united; *everything* appears to have become part of the periphery. The economy and public administration have in fact expanded beyond the horizons of the lifeworld. These media-steered subsystems have congealed into a second nature. As depersonalized networks of communication, they recede from the intuitive knowledge of members, who are shunted aside into the environment of these systems. It thus seems plausible to treat society, which can no longer be grasped through narratives, in a way similar to that in which nature has been treated, to entrust it to an objectifying social science—now, of course, with the result that our self-understanding is immediately affected. That is, to the extent that the objectifying descriptions of society migrate into the lifeworld, we become alienated from ourselves as communicatively acting subjects. It is this self-objectification that transforms the perception of heightened societal complexity into the experience of being delivered over to sheer contingencies. All referents for coping with these contingencies have been lost—both the societal subject and transcendental consciousness have long since slipped away from us, the anxious members of the high-risk society.

The resulting discouragement is expressed in the radically contextualist processing of paralyzing experiences with contingency. But this discouragement will shed its character of being unavoidable if it is possible to defend and make fruitful for social theory a concept of reason that attends to the phenomenon of the lifeworld and permits the outmoded concept of the "consciousness of society as a whole" (which comes from the philosophy of the subject and finds no foothold in modern societies) to be reformulated on the basis of a theory of intersubjectivity. Even the decentered society cannot do without the reference point provided by the projected unity of an intersubjectively formed common will. I cannot pursue this thought further here. It signals, however, the practical implications resulting from the transformation of the unitary thinking of metaphysics and from the controversy surrounding contextualism. I have gone into this controversy with the intention of rendering plausible a weak but not defeatistic concept of linguistically embodied reason. I want to close with a few brief theses relating to (1) the transformed status of the debate, and to (2) the question of what still remains of the normative content of metaphysics "at the moment of its downfall" (Adorno).

(1) The concept of reason that is identified in the presuppositions of action oriented toward mutual understanding frees us from the dilemma of having to choose between Kant and Hegel. Communicative reason is neither incorporeal, like the spontaneity of a subjectivity that is world-constituting yet itself without a world (*weltlos*), nor does it twist history into a circular teleology for the sake of the absolute self-mediation of a historicized spirit. The transcendental gap between the intelligible and the empirical worlds no longer has to be overcome through the philosophy of nature and the philosophy of history. It has instead been reduced to a tension transferred into the lifeworld of the communicative actors themselves, a tension between the unconditional character of context-bursting, transcendent validity claims on the one hand and, on the other hand, the factual character of the context-dependent "yes" and "no" positions that create social facts *in situ*. Kant's irreconcilable worlds, the objective world of appearances and the moral world of autonomous action, shed their transcendental-ontological dignity. Together with the inner world of the empirical subject, they return in everyday communicative practice as more or less trivial suppositions of commonality that make possible the cognitive, the regulative, and the expressive uses of language, and thus the relation to "something in the world."

Yet, beyond this, communicatively acting subjects are freed from the work of world-constituting syntheses. They already find themselves within the context of a lifeworld that makes their communicative actions possible, just as it is in turn maintained through the medium of these processes of reaching understanding. This background, which is presupposed in communicative action, constitutes a totality that is implicit and that comes along prereflexively—one that crumbles the moment it is thematized; it remains a totality only in the form of implicit, intuitively presupposed background knowledge. Taking the unity of the lifeworld, which is only known subconsciously, and projecting it in an objectifying manner onto the level of explicit knowledge is the operation that has been responsible for mythological, religious, and also of course metaphysical worldviews. With criticizable validity claims, and with the ability to orient oneself toward validity claims, everyday practice becomes permeated with idealizations that nevertheless set the stage for social facts. The ideas of meaning-identity, truth, justice, sincerity, and accountability leave their marks here. Yet they retain world-constituting power only as heuristic ideas of reason; they lend unity and organization to the situation interpretations that participants negotiate with each other. A transcendental illusion arises therefrom only when the totality of the lifeworld, presupposed as a background in everyday practice, is hypostatized as the speculative idea of the One and All, or as the transcendental idea of a mental spontaneity that brings everything forth out of itself.

The concept of pragmatic, yet unavoidable and idealizing presuppositions of action oriented toward reaching understanding must be differentiated according to the various burdens it has to bear. Those acting communicatively presuppose the lifeworld behind them in a different manner than the validity basis of their speech. In yet another way, understanding a thematically uttered propositional content presupposes understanding the associated illocutionary act, whose meaning 'comes along' unthematically in the performance of the complete speech act.

The philosophical tradition, as we have seen, has always held only privative concepts or negatively encircling formulas ready for what is individual because it has privileged the being of entities, the knowledge of objects, and the assertoric sentence or propositional content and has *equated* these with the comprehensible. But if we assume that the only thing we can understand is the propositional contents of assertions, then the individual essence—the very expression is paradoxical—unavoidably eludes the infinitely many (falsely objectifying) specifications. Since Kierkegaard we have been in a position to know that individuality can only be read from the traces of an authentic life that has been existentially drawn together into some sort of an appropriated totality. The significance of individuality discloses itself from the autobiographical perspective, as it were, of the first-person—I alone can performatively lay claim to being recognized as an individual in my uniqueness. If we liberate this idea from the capsule of absolute inwardness and follow Humboldt and George Herbert Mead in grafting it onto the medium of a language that crosses processes of socialization and individuation with each other, then we will find the key to the solution of this final and most difficult of the problems left behind by metaphysics.[34] The performative attitude we have to take up if we want to reach an understanding with one another about something gives every speaker the possibility (which certainly has not always been put to use) of employing the "I" of the illocutionary act in such a way that it becomes linked to the comprehensible claim that I should be recognized as an individual person who cannot be replaced in taking responsibility for my own life history.

(2) The concept of communicative reason is still accompanied by the shadow of a transcendental illusion. Because the idealizing presuppositions of communicative action must not be hypostatized into the ideal of a future condition in which a definitive understanding has been reached, this concept must be approached in a sufficiently skeptical manner.[35] A theory that leads us to believe in the attainability of a rational ideal would fall back behind the level of argumentation reached by Kant. It would also abandon the materialistic legacy of the critique of metaphysics. The moment of unconditionality that is preserved in the discursive concepts of a fallibilistic truth and morality is not an absolute, or it is at most an absolute that has become fluid as a critical procedure. Only with this residue of metaphysics can we do battle against the transfiguration of the world through metaphysical truths—the last trace of "*Nihil contra Deum nisi Deus ipse.*" Communicative reason is of course a rocking hull—but it does not go under in the sea of contingencies, even if shuddering in high seas is the only mode in which it 'copes' with these contingencies.

This foundation is not even stable enough for a negative metaphysics. The latter after all continues to offer an equivalent for the extramundane perspective of a God's-eye view: a perspective radically different from the lines of sight belonging to innerworldly participants and observers. That is, negative metaphysics uses the perspective of the radical outsider, in which one who is mad, existentially isolated, or aesthetically enraptured distances himself from the world, and indeed from the lifeworld as a whole. These outsiders no longer have a language, at least no speech based on reasons, for spreading the message of that which they have seen. Their speechlessness finds words only in the empty negation of everything that metaphysics once affirmed with the concept of the universal One. In contrast, communicative reason cannot withdraw from the determinate negations in language, discursive as linguistic communication in fact is. It must therefore refrain from the paradoxical statements of negative metaphysics: that the whole is the false, that everything is contingent, that there is no consolation whatsoever. Communicative reason does not make its appearance in an aestheticized theory as the colorless negative of a religion that provides consolation. It neither announces the absence of consolation in a world forsaken by God, nor does it take it upon itself to provide any consolation. It does without exclusivity as well. As long as no better words for what religion can say are found in the medium of rational discourse, it will even coexist abstemiously with the former, neither supporting it nor combatting it.

There is also something more in being able to do less and in wanting to do less than negative metaphysics entrusts to itself. The analysis of the necessary conditions for mutual understanding in general at least allows us to develop the idea of an intact intersubjectivity, which makes possible both a mutual and constraint-free understanding among individuals in their dealings with one another and the identity of individuals who come to a compulsion-free understanding with themselves. This intact intersubjectivity is a glimmer of symmetrical relations marked by free, reciprocal recognition. But this idea must not be filled in as the totality of a reconciled form of life and projected into the future as a utopia. It contains no more, but also no less, than the formal characterization of the necessary conditions for the unforeseeable forms adopted by a life that is not misspent. No prospect of such forms of life can be given to us, not even in the abstract, this side of prophetic teachings. All we know of them is that if they could be realized at all, they would have to be produced through our own combined effort and be marked by solidarity, though they need not necessarily be free of conflict. Of course, "producing" does not mean manufacturing according to the model of realizing intended ends. Rather, it signifies a type of emergence that cannot be intended, an emergence out of a cooperative endeavor to moderate, abolish, or prevent the suffering of vulnerable creatures. This endeavor is fallible, and it does fail over and over again. This type of producing or self-bringing-forth places the responsibility on our shoulders without making us less dependent upon the "the luck of the moment." Connected with this is the modern meaning of humanism, long expressed in the ideas of a self-conscious life, of authentic self-realization, and of autonomy—a humanism that is not bent on self-assertion. This project, like the communicative reason that inspires it, is historically situated. It has not been made, it has taken shape—and it can be pursued further, or be abandoned out of discouragement. Above all, the project is not the property of philosophy. Philosophy, working together with the reconstructive sciences, can only throw light on the situations in which we find ourselves. It can contribute to our learning to understand the ambivalences that we come up against as just so many appeals to increasing responsibilities within a diminishing range of options.

Notes

1. Robert Spaemann, "Natur," in *Philosophische Essays* (Stuttgart: Reclam, 1983), 19ff.; idem, *Das Natürliche und das Vernünftige* (Munich, 1987); Dieter Henrich, *Fluchtlinien* (Frankfurt: Suhrkamp, 1982); idem, "Dunkelheit und Vergewisserung," in *All-Einheit, Wege eines Gedankens in Ost und West,* ed. D. Henrich (Stuttgart: Klett-Cotta, 1985), 33ff.

2. Jean-Francois Lyotard, *The Differend,* trans. Georges van den Abbeele (Minneapolis: University of Minnesota Press, 1988); and generally: Jonathan Culler, *On Deconstruction* (Ithaca: Cornell University Press, 1983).

3. Odo Marquard, *Farewell to Matters of Principle,* trans. Robert M. Wallace (Oxford: Oxford University Press, 1989).

4. Hilary Putnam, *Reason, Truth, and History* (Cambridge: Cambridge University Press, 1981).

5. Cf. Max Weber, *The Sociology of Religion*, trans. Ephraim Fischoff (Boston: Beacon Press, 1963); and Karl Jaspers, *The Great Philosophers*, vol. 1, trans. Ralph Manheim (New York: Harcourt, Brace and World, 1962).

6. Max Horkheimer and Theodor Adorno, *The Dialectic of Enlightenment*, trans. John Cumming (New York: Continuum, 1972).

7. Klaus Heinrich, *Dahlemer Vorlesungen*, vol. 1 (Frankfurt, 1981).

8. Werner Beierwaltes, *Denken des Einen* (Frankfurt: Klostermann, 1985), 31ff.

9. Karl Heinz Haag, *Der Fortschritt in der Philosophie* (Frankfurt: Suhrkamp, 1983), 33.

10. Theodor Adorno, *Negative Dialectics*, trans. E. B. Ashton (New York: Seabury Press, 1973).

11. H. Brunkhorst, "Dialektischer Positivismus des Glücks," *Zeitschrift für Philosophische Forschung* 39 (1985): 353ff.; M. Korthals, "Die kritische Gesellschaftstheorie des frühen Horkheimer," *Zeitschrift für Soziologie* 14 (1985): 315ff.

12. Immanuel Kant, *Critique of Pure Reason*, trans. Norman Kemp Smith (New York: St. Martin's Press, 1965), B-385.

13. Cf. below, "Individuation through Socialization," section VIII.

14. E. Rothacker, "Die dogmatische Denkform in den Geisteswissenschaften und das Problem des Historismus," *Abhandlungen der Akademie der Wissenschaft und der Literatur* (Mainz, 1954).

15. Jürgen Habermas, *The Philosophical Discourse of Modernity*, trans. Frederick Lawrence (Cambridge, Mass.: MIT Press, 1987), 7ff.

16. Joachim Ritter, "Die Aufgabe des Geisteswissenschaften in der modernen Gesellschaft" (1963), in *Subjektivität* (Frankfurt: Suhrkamp, 1974), 105ff; cf. my critique in: J. Habermas, *On the Logic of the Social Sciences*, trans. Shierry Weber Nicholsen and Jerry Stark (Cambridge, Mass.: MIT Press, 1988), 16ff.

17. Odo Marquard, "Über die Unvermeidlichkeit der Geisteswissenschaften," in *Apologie des Zufälligen* (1986), 98ff.; idem, "Verspätete Moralistik," *Frankfurter Allgemeine Zeitung* (March 18, 1987).

18. Helmut Schelsky, *Einsamkeit und Freiheit* (Reinbeck bei Hamburg: Rowohlt, 1963), 222ff.

19. Odo Marquard, "In Praise of Polytheism," in *Farewell to Matters of Principle*, 87ff.

20. The compensation theory does not become more plausible when its political meaning is revealed to us. Marquard's "In Praise of Polytheism" is based on the following narrative. There are wholesome myths; they are the ones that we normally call myths and that always appear in the plural. What is harmful is monomythology, because it always lays claim to exclusivity; monomythology first appears in the doctrines of universal unity in monotheism and the philosophy of origins. Due to a paucity of safeguarded non-identity among the circle of their followers, these doctrines generate

an unfree ego-identity. In the wake of the disintegration of this religious-metaphysical unitary thinking, a vacuum arises, which in the course of the eighteenth century is filled by the most harmful monomythology of all, namely that of progress. The absolute autarchic mythology is the philosophy of history, which takes the power of the one over the human many and intensifies it into open terror. The only thing that could help counter this would be a *disenchanted* return of polytheism, in the form of *Geistes-wissenschaften* that are no longer bewitched by the universalism of reason. I am amazed by the explanatory burden that this story is expected to bear. Why should the thinking of the philosophy of history, which has always entertained arguments, be vanquished by an anti-philosophy-of-history that is offered narratively, that is, without arguments? I also have no idea who, today, still thinks in terms of the philosophy of history at all, if that means "defining history as the long march into the universal and as the dissolution of the individual in the species." ("Universalgeschichte und Multiversal-geschichte," in *Apologie des Zufälligen*, 70.) Only the political meaning of the whole undertaking is clear: the continuation of a very German tradition, namely the vener-able struggle against the ideas of the French Revolution.

21. Richard Bernstein, *Beyond Objectivism and Relativism* (Philadelphia: University of Pennsylvania Press, 1983).

22. Richard Rorty, *Consequences of Pragmatism* (Minneapolis: University of Minnesota Press, 1982).

23. Richard Rorty, *Philosophy and the Mirror of Nature* (Princeton: Princeton University Press, 1979), 211.

24. Ibid., 390.

25. Richard Rorty, "Solidarity or Objectivity?," in *Post-Analytic Philosophy*, ed. John Rajchman and Cornel West (New York: Columbia University Press, 1985), 3ff.; Hilary Putnam, "Why Reason Can't Be Naturalized," *Synthese* 52 (1982): 1ff. (Reprinted in *After Philosophy—End or Transformation?*, ed. K. Baynes, J. Bohman, and T. McCarthy [Cambridge, Mass.: MIT Press, 1987], 222ff.)

26. Richard Rorty, "Pragmatism, Davidson, and Truth," in *Truth and Interpretation*, ed. E. LePore (Oxford: Blackwell, 1986), 333ff.

27. Richard Rorty, "Solidarity or Objectivity?," 12f.

28. Ibid., 8.

29. Thomas McCarthy, "Contra Relativism: A Thought Experiment," in Michael Krausz, ed., *Relativism: Interpretation and Confrontation* (Notre Dame, 1989), 256–271.

30. Martin Hollis and Steven Lukes, eds., *Rationality and Relativism* (Oxford: Blackwell, 1982).

31. H. Putnam, "Why Reason Can't Be Naturalized," 228.

32. Jürgen Habermas, *Philosophical Discourse of Modernity*, 322f.

33. Jan van de Wetering, *Rattenfang* (Hamburg, 1986).

34. Cf. below, "Individuation through Socialization," section IX.

35. Albrecht Wellmer, *The Persistence of Modernity* (Cambridge, Mass.: MIT Press, 1991).

7

Individuation through Socialization: On George Herbert Mead's Theory of Subjectivity

I

Durkheim was the first to observe the connection between societal differentiation, or what he calls the "division of labor," and progressive individuation: "no one today contests the obligatory character of the rule which orders us to be more and more of a person."[1] This formulation harbors an ambiguity that reappears in the expression chosen by Parsons, "institutionalized individualism."[2] On the one hand, the person is supposed to achieve greater freedom of choice and autonomy in proportion to his individuation; on the other hand, this extension of the degree of freedom is described deterministically: even liberation from the stereotyping dictates of institutionalized behavioral expectations is described as a new normative expectation—as an institution. This flipside is conceptualized by Arnold Gehlen ironically: an individual—that's an institution in one instance.[3] This emphatic formulation is supposed to indicate that the very process through which the individual is emancipated from the power of the universal is itself directed toward the subsumption of the individual under the universal. With this Gehlen wanted to denounce the idea of individuation as mere illusion; like Foucault, he wanted to convict modernity of an illusory self-understanding.[4] What is in fact at issue, however, is a dilemma arising from a lack of appropriate basic concepts.

Sociological interpreters lack the concepts that would enable them to capture descriptively a specific experience of modernity, one that is present to them intuitively. The individual is supposed to be distinguished as what is essential, yet it can only be defined as the accidental, namely, as that which deviates from the exemplary embodiment of a generic universal: "To be a person is to be an autonomous source of action. Man acquires this quality only insofar as there is something in him which . . . individualizes him, as he is something more than a simple incarnation of the generic type of his race and his group."[5] Durkheim understands social individualization as a growth in the spontaneous forces that enable the individual to be himself; but he can only describe these forces in terms of the particularities through which the individual *deviates* from the more general determinations of his social milieu. In the course of time, these deviations from the normative givens of a relatively homogeneous group give rise to the normative plurality of a group that is differentiated within itself. However, these new norms do not shed the character of being pregiven general determinations simply in virtue of their pluralization; the individual is now subordinated to them in just the same way as he was previously subordinated to the behavior patterns of a less differentiated form of life. What was once accidental has now merely become the essence; individualism itself has become a further institution. This description, however, conceals the specific thing that Durkheim himself actually intended with the expression "individualization"—the increase in singularity, personality, or the capacity for being oneself. Whether we have need of a greater or a lesser number of social roles for characterizing a socialized subject, every combination of roles, no matter how complex, has to be expressed in the form of a conjunction of general determinations. These predicates *remain* general determinations, even when they admit relatively many different combinations, and even when every individual combination applies to only a few members of a collectivity.

Differences in the extent of individuation are elucidated by Hegel in the following manner:

The star is exhausted by its simple law and brings this law into appearance; a few specific traits characterize the configuration of the world of rocks; but already in the nature of plants there arises an infinite copiousness of the most diversified forms, transitions, hybrids, and anomolies; animal organisms display a still greater range of difference and of interaction with the surroundings to which they are related; and if, finally, we rise to the spiritual and its appearance, we find a still infinitely wider many-sidedness of inner and outer existence.[6]

Staying entirely within the spirit of scholasticism, Hegel conceives of degrees of "being" as also being gradations of individuality. Of course, unlike Thomas Aquinas, Hegel also finds the tendency toward the progressive individuation of beings in the process of world history; just like the forms of nature, the historical formations of spirit are characterized by greater individuality the more highly they are organized. The passage just cited stems from the point in the *Aesthetics* at which Greek art is introduced; this new type of art is supposed to be distinguished from the symbolic art forms of the Old Empires through "concentrated individuality," or the complete interpenetration of the universal and the particular. For Hegel the idea of individuality obtains its most perfect palpable embodiment when the gods of Greek mythology are formed into sculptural works of art. He makes use of the concept of the "individual totality" in order to explain why the mere diversity of predicative determinations does not exhaust the essence of individuality. But the sociologist, who finds himself faced with similar problems on his own terrain, lacks an equivalent concept; he lacks the reference point that could prevent him from confusing processes of individualization with processes of differentiation.

The only promising attempt to grasp the entire significance of social individualization in concepts is, I believe, initiated in the social psychology of George Herbert Mead. Mead makes the connection between differentiation within the structure of roles, on the one hand, and the formation of conscience and gain in autonomy by individuals who are socialized in increasingly differentiated conditions, on the other hand. Just as, for Hegel, individuation depends upon the progressive subjectivization of spirit, for Mead it depends upon the internalization of the agencies that monitor behavior, which migrate, as it were, from without to within. In the process of socialization, the growing subject takes what the reference person expects of him and first makes it his own, so that thereafter he can universalize and integrate the diverse and even contradictory expectations by means of abstraction; and to the extent that this occurs, there arises an internal center for the self-steering of individually accountable conduct. Such an agency of conscience implies

a degree of individuation, which in turn requires a detachment from roles, a distance from the expectations others exact when we play these roles. Such detachment and individuation come about when there are conflicting expectations exacted, along the sequence of our careers and currently among our circles of significant others. Individuation of the self results from the variety and scope of voluntary actions [imputed to us] which we undertake. It involves the reality of individual decisions and being held responsible for personal choices.[7]

In this formulation by Gerth and Mills, various aspects of social individualization are combined that are in need of a more precise analysis. What appears historically as societal *differentiation* is mirrored ontogenetically in the course of an ever more differentiated perception of, and confrontation with, diversified and tension-filled normative expectations. The internalizing processing of these conflicts leads to an *autonomization* of the self: to a certain extent the individual itself must first posit itself as a spontaneously acting (*selbsttätig*) subject. To this extent, individuality is not conceived primarily as singularity, nor as an ascriptive feature, but as one's own achievement—and *individuation* is conceived as the self-realization of the individual (*des Einzelnen*).[8] Admittedly, by themselves these features merely recapitulate the reinterpretation of the concept of individuality that had already been made possible when the basic concepts of metaphysics turned toward the philosophy of the subject. I see the more far-reaching contribution of Mead in his having taken up themes that can be found in Humboldt and Kierkegaard: individuation is pictured not as the self-realization of an independently acting subject carried out in isolation and freedom but as a linguistically mediated process of socialization and the simultaneous constitution of a life-history that is conscious of itself. The identity of socialized individuals forms itself simultaneously in the medium of coming to an understanding with others in language and in the medium of coming to a life-historical and intrasubjective understanding with oneself. Individuality forms itself in relations of intersubjective acknowledgement and of intersubjectively mediated self-understanding.

Here as elsewhere, the decisive innovation relative to the philosophy of the subject was made possible through a turn to the pragmatics of language, a turn that concedes primacy to world-disclosing language—as the medium for the possibility of reaching understanding, for social cooperation, and for self-controlled learning processes—over world-generating subjectivity. For the first time, this frees up the basic concepts needed to capture an intuition that has long been enunciated in religious speech. From the structure of language comes the explanation of why the human spirit is condemned to an odyssey—why it first finds its way to itself only on a detour via a complete externalization in other things and in other humans. Only at the greatest distance from itself does it become conscious of itself in its irreplaceable singularity as an individuated being (*Wesen*).

Before I go into Mead's conception, I would like to take a look at the history of the concept in order to recall how the "individual essence" (*Wesen*)—the very expression betrays the paradox—eludes the basic concepts of metaphysics, even in the form that these take on in the philosophy of consciousness.

II

In the specialized language of philosophy, "individual" is the translation of the Greek *atomon;* in logic it designates an object about which something can be stated, and in ontology it designates a single thing or a determinate being.[9] The expression "individuality" primarily means the singularity or particularity of a numerical individual, and not what is atomic or indivisible. In this sense we call every object "individual" that can be picked out and recognized again among the set of possible objects as being this particular one, i.e., every object that can be identified. Since William of Occam, terms such as proper names, demonstratives, designations, etc., with whose aid we identify individual objects, have been called singular terms. In the empiricist tradition space and time are regarded as principles of individuation: every object can be identified through space-time coordinates. The singularity of an object is determined according to the spatio-temporal identity of the relevant body. For instance a human being can in this way be *numerically* identified through the spatio-temporal segment that his body occupies. In contrast, we speak of *qualitative* identification when we denote the same human being through a determinate gene combination, through a social role constellation, or through a biographical pattern.

Although the *singularity* of an object can be explicated in terms of a numerically ascertainable identity, I would like henceforth to speak of the *individuality* of a being only when this being can be distinguished from all (or at least most) other things through qualitative determinations. Now in the metaphysical tradition the properties that can be asserted or denied of an object have always been understood in both a logical and an ontological sense. Predicative determinations reflect ideal essences, forms, or substances, which individuate themselves into single things through their conjunction with material substrates. Individual chairs are thus more or less exemplary embodiments of the same idea or form, which determines the end for which chairs generally are supposed to be good. No matter how the relationship of universals to individuals is conceived, this idealistic conceptual approach predetermines a peculiar primacy of the universal over the individual. From the beginning there clings to the individual something of that dubious obstinacy (*Eigensinn*) that separates the concrete individual from what is universal. In German usage, especially in the older etymological strata, "individual" still retains something of the pejorative connotations relating to what is lower and peripheral in an existence that is dull and isolated and closed in on itself.

This devaluation of what is individual gives expression not only to a socially conditioned ideology but to a philosophical embarrassment as well. If matter is regarded as the only principle of individuation, and if matter qua nonbeing is determinate solely because it can be determined by formal substances, then the individuality of the single thing must remain *underdetermined*. The qualitative determinations that distinguish each individual from other things are derived from essences or forms that are themselves by nature universal and cannot mark out the individual as unique.[10] As early as late antiquity, this dilemma led to attempts to bestow at least the appearance of substantiality upon the individual by means of the determination of its being atomic, thus of being indivisible, whole, independent, etc.;[11] but above all it led, with the doctrine of accidental qualities, to the introduction of the category of the particular into the realm of the formal substances themselves: the *substantia universalis* and the *substantia particularis* were augmented by the *accidens universale* and the *accidens particulare*. The individual was now not only thought to be *numerically* identifiable through its connection with matter but also *qualitatively* identifiable through various distinctions in form. This path led in the end to Duns Scotus, who elevated to a formal determination that which makes an individual into one such as this, Socrates into Socrates. He completes the chain of genera and species with a final, purely individuating determination— *haecceitas*. In this paradox of an essential determination that extends to every being qua individual, the universal triumphs, against all intentions, over the individual, which in its uniqueness and irreplaceability eludes the basic metaphysical concepts of form and matter.

Although he does not surrender the metaphysical problematic, Leibniz bestows a positive sense upon the ineffability of the individual. He finds a ready support for this in the concept of a subjectivity that represents the world as a whole to itself; at the same time, he can make use of an idea derived from the infinitesimal calculus, namely, that of an infinite analytic convergence toward an ideal limit value. Every individual is a mirror of the world as a whole; it can in principle be defined by the conjunction of all the predicates that apply to it. Such a characterization constitutes the complete concept of the individual, but because it would have to contain infinitely many propositions, it is never actually available to us; rather, as Kant will say, it only represents an Idea of Reason. Of course, unlike Kant, Leibniz still insists on the ontological significance of this Idea of Reason. He conceives of the infinitesimally characterized total individual as an individual substance in which the gap between *infima species* and underlying matter is closed: the material substrate disappears into the encompassing network of formal determinations, which penetrate and organize, consume and at the same time sublimate everything. Hence individuals are no longer set within a spatio-temporally extended universe and no longer stand in external contact with each other. Each instead forms a totality for itself, which encloses everything within itself by representing as a whole the world from its perspective. Monads exist as individual representations of the entire universe. Individuating force is no longer possessed by matter but by the transcendental circumstance that every representing subjectivity is centered in itself and in each case represents the world as a whole in a way peculiar to it. Thus it is not true, as it was for Plotinus, that everything is in One; instead, everything is mirrored in a different manner in every individual:

Indeed, each Monad must be different from every other. For in nature there are never two beings which are perfectly alike and in which it is not possible to find an internal difference, or at least a difference founded upon an intrinsic quality.[12]

Here Leibniz introduces an ontological model for a concept of individual substance, a concept which, as a discursively unredeemable program of exhaustive characterizations, resists complete explication. Hegel's dialectical logic can be understood as the promise to redeem this program nonetheless. Hegel finds support for this already prepared: the statically reflecting monads have undergone both a transcendental-philosophical and an aesthetic-expressive reinterpretation as creative individual totalities that are caught up in self-formation. It is now no longer the organism that serves as a model but the genial setting-to-work of the organic work of art. In the work of art, the totally organized matter has entirely become form; that is, it is so thoroughly formulated that it merges as a work of art with its organic form. The individual totality derives from transcendental subjectivity the power of spontaneously generating a world, and from aesthetic productivity it derives the motion of a formative process from which something new is always emerging. Hegel is aware that he is indebted for this concept to Schiller, who had taken the productive artist as his model for conceiving of the individuated being.[13] Just as the artist playfully reconciles form and matter in his work, so too does every figure (*Gestalt*) that has matured to individuality: the human being "is to turn everything that is mere form into world, and realize all his potentialities"; at the same time, he "is to eradicate in himself everything that is merely world, and produce harmony in all its mutations; . . . he is to turn outward everything internal, and give form to everything external."[14]

As before, what is individuated is here apprehended using the basic concepts of metaphysics; the play impulse, which seamlessly mediates form and matter, admittedly stands in for an ontological model that has yet to be conceived. In order to conceptualize the individual totality, which has so far only been circumscribed, and thereby to make the individual accessible to rigorous knowledge, Hegel has to explicate the connection among the different monads. He cannot be satisfied with the "intercession" of the Leibnizian God, who places the coexisting monads into a timelessly harmonious order. For Hegel, the individual totalities that are themselves already caught up in formative processes must also be joined together at a higher level through a formative process that reaches right through them to form a super-totality. But this absolute spirit, which appears in the singular, can acquire the individuality that it claims for itself only at the expense of the individual figures of spirit encased in it—just as the world spirit contests the individuality of world-historical individuals, whom it merely utilizes as means to its ends. Hegel's philosophy of history and his philosophy of right merely illustrate in a drastic way something that is generally valid: as long as the problematic of metaphysical unitary thinking remains in force, and as long as idealist modes of thought remain in use, the universal will triumph over the individual, which is banished to ineffability. Along the course of metaphysical thinking, the endangered individual reveals itself at best *ironically* as the nonidentical—as the marginal that is pressed to the side and drops out of the running at every attempt to identify an individual as itself and distinguish it from *all* other individuals.[15]

III

In the meantime, the philosophy of consciousness had taken on a new configuration with Kant, one which opened up a different route to that in the concept of individuality which had eluded thought. With the relationship of the knowing subject to itself, Descartes had disclosed the realm of conscious phenomena and equated this self-consciousness in turn with the *ego cogito*. Thenceforth, the concept of individuality, insofar as it has meant more than singularity, has been associated with the ego as the spontaneous source of cognition and action. Since Kant, the transcendentally revaluated ego has been conceived simultaneously as a *world-generating* and *autonomously acting subject*. For the concept of individuality, however, this combination initially provides only the notion of a spontaneously acting subjectivity. In Kantian philosophy the individuated ego falls through the cracks, as it were, between the transcendental ego, which stands over and against the world as a whole, and the empirical ego, which finds itself already in the world as one among many.[16] What distinguishes the individual from all other individuals, i.e., uniqueness and irreplaceability in the emphatic sense, can at best apply to the intelligible ego; but as the addressee of the moral law, this latter is oriented precisely toward maxims that have universal validity. Furthermore, the ego qua a subject capable of moral action is a thing-in-itself and thus eludes cognition, even if it could be thought of as completely individuated.

Fichte is the first to hone the Kantian concepts for the problem of individuality by reducing the transcendental accomplishments of the knowing ego and the practical ego, world-constitution and self-determination, to the common denominator of spontaneous activity, and by radicalizing them to the primordial act of *self-positing*. Fichte answers the question, Who am I really?, with a program: I am the one into whom I make myself.

Who am I, in truth? That is to say, what individual am I? And what is the ground, why I am *this* individual and none other? I reply: From the moment that I have arrived at consciousness I am that individual which I make myself to be with freedom, and I am it because I make myself it.[17]

With this phrasing Fichte interprets the ontological process of individuation, which is now concentrated into the genesis of the ego, as an act that is *practically executed* (*vollzogen*) and at the same time *reflexively recapitulable* (*nachvollziehbar*); he understands it as a process of self-constitution that has gone before yet is comprehensible after the fact—a process that the individual, insofar as it comes upon itself as a spontaneously acting ego, must be able to attribute to itself. Kierkegaard will take up these ideas with his concept of self-choice (*Selbstwahl*). Fichte himself carries his thoughts a step in the direction of a theory of intersubjectivity. But it is Humboldt who first transfers the latter to the premises of the philosophy of language.

Fichte wants to demonstrate that the ego can posit itself only as something individual; he wants to explain why the consciousness of individuality belongs *a priori* to my self-understanding as ego.[18] In the first act of self-consciousness, I come upon myself as an object, which is nonetheless supposed to be an ego—a free, spontaneously active subject: "As sure, therefore, as I am to find myself as natural product, I must also find myself as freely active (*freitätig*). . . . [M]y self-determination exists without my assistance."[19] This paradoxical experience can be elucidated by the fact that I first confront the concept of my freedom through an expectation or demand that is directed to me by another subject:

This requirement, or appeal, addressed to me to be spontaneously active, I cannot comprehend without ascribing it to an actual being outside of me, which intended to communicate to me such a conception; and which is therefore capable of a conception of the conception. But such a being is a rational being, a being positing itself as Ego. . . .[20]

Because the Other confronts me with a demand that can only be satisfied by virtue of a free will, I experience myself as a being capable of spontaneous activity: "Namely, my Egohood and self-sufficiency generally is conditioned through the freedom of the other individual. . . ."[21] This intersubjective relationship between intelligent beings, who oppose and respect each other as free beings, requires exactly the kind of limitation and self-restriction that makes the one ego as well as the other into an individual; for through the reciprocal relation there arises "a sphere of freedom, which these many separate beings divide amongst themselves."[22] I must oppose (*entgegensetzen*) myself as an individual to another individual and oppose this individual in turn to me. It is thereby shown that "a rational being can not self-consciously posit (*setzen*) itself as such, without positing itself as an *individual,* or as one of many rational beings, which many it assumes outside of it by assuming itself."[23]

In all of his constructions, in the *Wissenschaftslehre* as in the *Sittenlehre,* Fichte takes his starting point from the circle inherent in every philosophy of consciousness: in consciously assuring itself of itself, the knowing subject unavoidably makes itself into an object, and it thereby falls short of itself as the antecedent source of all accomplishments of consciousness, a source that precedes all objectification and is absolutely subjective. In its spontaneous activity the ego is supposed to make itself into an object. Even the resolution that Fichte proposes for the deduction of the concept of law remains caught up in this initial circle. Namely, the individuation of egos, which makes possible an intersubjective relationship among several individuals, and therewith the encounter with an alien freedom as well—this individuation of egos proves in the continuation of the construction to be purely illusory. That is, using the concepts of the philosophy of the subject, Fichte can only define individuality as the restriction of oneself (*Selbsteinschränkung*), as renunciation of the possibility of realizing one's own freedom—not as the productive cultivation of one's own essential powers. Subjects can only be objects for one another, so that even in the reciprocally limiting influence they have on each other, their individuality does not reach beyond the objectivistic determinations of the strategic freedom of choice whose paradigm is the arbitrary will of privately autonomous legal subjects. As soon as the restrictions on subjective freedom are deduced as legal in character, even the individuality of the legal subjects forfeits all significance. Like the world-generating transcendental ego, Fichte's original *ego* comes on the scene in the singular, as one over and against everything; thus, "freely active" subjectivity, of which I want to reassure myself without illusion in the consciousness of myself, unveils itself in every individual consciousness as something universal after all—as Egohood in general. Since it is

accidental to Egohood in general, that *I*, the individual A, am precisely this A, and since the impulse of self-sufficiency is to be an impulse of Egohood in general, *as such*, this impulse certainly does not crave the self-sufficiency of the particular individual A, but of reason in general. . . .[I]f *this* self-sufficiency can only be represented *in* the individuals A, B, C, etc., and *through* them; then it is necessarily altogether indifferent to me whether A, or B, or C represents it; . . . it is always reason in general which is represented, and hence my impulse is always satisfied.[24]

Fichte is unable to exhaust the explanatory potential of his proposed solution because he is forced to resolve the intersubjective relationship, through which the ego is able to individuate itself to several individuals in the first place, into a subject-object relationship. The problem of intersubjectivity cannot be solved within the limits of the philosophy of the subject; instead it arises ever more intractably from Husserl's Fifth Cartesian Meditation through Sartre's construction of Being-for-another. But Fichte himself already addresses this problem, namely the dynamic of reciprocal objectification that falls short of what is specific both to an intersubjectively shared understanding of language and to a communicative relationship between first person and second person.[25] With his central argument Fichte does, it is true, lay claim to language as a medium through which one is able to *demand* independent activity of the other and to confront him with one's expectation. But like all philosophers of consciousness, he peers right through language as though it were a glassy medium without properties.

Fichte opened up a new route to the concept of individuality. To be sure, before his intuitions could be made fruitful, they had to be detached from the architectonic of his *Wissenschaftslehre*. The connection between individuality and intersubjectivity would be investigated by Wilhelm von Humboldt with reference to the noncoercive synthesis that is carried out in the process of coming to an understanding in language. And the idea that each individual must first make itself into that which it is would be honed by Kierkegaard into the act of taking responsibility for one's own life history. Finally, the fusion of world-constitution and self-determination that Fichte aimed at with his concept of spontaneous activity proves to be fruitful for the concept of an ego-identity that is *claimed* by me for me. Admittedly, before the emphatic sense of individuality can be completely transferred to the performative use of the personal pronoun in the first person, Fichte's peculiar linkage of reflection with the performance of an action in the act of self-positing, in which as it were an eye is inserted, must be disencumbered of theoretical pretensions. G. H. Mead will carry through these thoughts by downgrading the agency of the ego in the philosophy of consciousness into a "me," into a self that first emerges in contexts of interaction before the eyes of an alter ego—and, in doing so, Mead will shift all fundamental philosophical concepts from the basis of consciousness to that of language.

IV

For Humboldt, language is the whole comprising the system of grammatical rules and speech. Itself subjectless, language makes possible the linguistic practice among subjects who belong to a linguistic community, while at the same time it renews and maintains itself as a linguistic system through this practice. Humboldt's interest is devoted above all to one phenomenon: in the process of linguistic communication, a synthetic force is at work that generates unity within plurality in a *different* manner than by way of subsuming what is manifold under a general rule. The construction of a number series had served Kant as a model for the generation of unity. This constructivistic concept of synthesis is replaced by Humboldt with the concept of unforced agreement (*Einigung*) in conversation. In place of one unifying perspective, which the generative subject brings first to the material of sensation with its forms of intuition and categories and then to the stream of its own lived experiences with the "I think" of transcendental apperception, there now appears the unrelinquished difference between the perspectives from which the participants in communication reach understanding with each other about the same thing. These speaker and hearer perspectives no longer converge at the focal point of a subjectivity centered in itself; they instead intersect at the focal point of language—and as this focal point Humboldt designates the "reciprocal conversation in which ideas and feelings are sincerely exchanged." In this conversation the "irrevocable dualism" of speech and reply, question and answer, utterance and response, reactivates itself each time anew. The smallest analytic unit is therefore the relationship between ego's speech-act and alter's taking a position. Humboldt expends great effort in analyzing the use of the personal pronouns; he surmises that the specific conditions for the unforced synthesis of linguistically reached understanding, which simultaneously socializes and individuates the participants, are to be found in the I-you and you-me relation, which is distinguished from the I-s/he and I-it relations.

Mead will be the first to make use of the performative attitude of the first person toward the second person—and above all of the symmetrical you-me relationship—as the key for his critique of the mirror-model of the self-objectifying subject and its relationship to itself. Already, however, Humboldt takes his start here in order to illuminate the basic experience of every interpreter—the experience, that is, that language only appears in the plural of particular languages, which present themselves as individual totalities and yet are porous to one another. On the one hand, languages impress their own stamp on worldviews and forms of life and thus make translations from one language into others more difficult; nonetheless, they are directed like converging rays toward the common goal of reaching universal understanding:

Individuality fragments, but in such a wondrous way that it awakens, precisely through separation, the feeling of unity, and even appears as a means of establishing the latter, at least in the idea. . . . For, struggling deep inside for that unity and universality, the human being seeks to overcome the dividing barriers of his individuality, yet must . . . heighten his individuality precisely through this struggling. He thus makes ever increasing advances in a striving that is in itself impossible. Now language comes to his aid in a truly wondrous way here—language, which binds together even as it distinguishes (*verein-zelt*), and which contains within the hull of the most individual of expressions the possibility of universal understanding.[26]

Yet, Humboldt himself never came up with a plausible explanation for the fact that language is a mechanism that distinguishes and unifies *at the same time*.

Fichte had derived the individual ego from the fact that a distinct subject must oppose itself to the other in an intersubjective relationship. The necessity of an encounter between ego and alter ego was supposed to result from the fact that an ego, which, paradoxically, has *itself* posited itself, is able to become conscious of itself only in the mode of active subjectivity. Soren Kierkegaard now makes this singular figure of thought—self-positing—so much his own that he interprets self-relation (*Selbstbeziehung*) as a relating-to-oneself (*Zusichselbstverhalten*), wherein I relate myself at the same time to an antecedent Other on whom this relation depends.[27] To be sure, Kierkegaard no longer identifies this Other with the absolute ego qua the subject of the original act of self-positing. But that means the problem is posed all the more acutely: how, under the contingent circumstances of a life history that he cannot himself choose, is a subject nonetheless supposed to be able to encounter himself as a spontaneously acting subject, conscious of being the one into which he has made himself? The act of self-positing must now be shifted to an individual who is entangled in history; the historicized, situated self must return to itself from out of the facticity of a life that has developed naturally.

That is only possible if the individual *critically* appropriates his own life history: in a paradoxical act, I must choose myself as the one who I am and want to be. *Life history* becomes the principle of individuation, but only if it is transposed by such an act of self-choice into an existential form for which the self is responsible. This extraordinary decision to posit oneself, which as it were retroactively places the historicized self under one's own direction, results in the claim of the individual to be identical with himself in ethical life: "Now he discovers that the self he chooses has a boundless multiplicity within itself inasmuch as it has a history, a history in which he acknowledges identity with himself."[28] The authentic individual has himself to thank for his individuation; as this determinate product of determinate historical surroundings, he has made himself responsible for himself: "in choosing himself as product he can just as well be said to produce himself."[29] For Kierkegaard, spontaneous activity is tied up with the "avowal" ("*Bekenntnis*") of individuality because it must prove itself in the recalcitrant material of one's own life history:

To a certain degree, the person who lives ethically cancels the distinction between the accidental and the essential, for he takes responsibility for all of himself as equally essential; but it comes back again, for after he has done that, he makes a distinction, but in such a manner that he takes an essential responsibility for excluding what he excludes as accidental.[30]

In the performative attitude of the subject who chooses himself, the metaphysical opposition between what applies to the individual essentially and what applies to him accidentally loses all significance.

Fichte had placed two topics on the agenda: first, individuality and linguistic intersubjectivity, second, individuality and life-historical identity. Humboldt and Kierkegaard took these topics up from a perspective that had been transformed by the historical mode of thinking. The one topic is linked to the other through the thought that the call, the demand, or the expectation of an Other is needed in order to awaken the consciousness of spontaneous activity in me. Kierkegaard's Either-Or poses itself ineluctably in the conversation of the lone soul with God. The ethical stage of life is only the gateway to the religious stage, where the dialogue with oneself proves to be a mask behind which has been concealed the prayer, the dialogue with God. The Christian consciousness of sin and the Protestant hunger for grace therefore form the real spur for the return to a life that takes on form and coherence only in relation to the justification, due at the Last Judgment, of an irreplaceable and unique existence. From Augustine to Kierkegaard, the structure of a prayer was imposed on the inner monologues of the missionary author setting down his confessions. But already in the middle of the eighteenth century, Jean-Jacques Rousseau secularized the confession of sin set before the judging God into a self-confession, which the private man circulated before the reading audience of the bourgeois public. The prayer was deflated to a public conversation.[31]

In January 1762 Rousseau writes M. de Malesherbes four letters in which he presents and projects himself as the one who he is and who, with the will to authenticity, he wants to be. With growing intensity and desperation, he continues this existential presentation of self in his *Confessions,* later in the *Dialogues,* and lastly in the *Reveries of a Solitary Walker.* But those initial letters already name the communicative presuppositions for the public process of mercilessly reaching self-understanding and of assuring oneself of one's own identity. Rousseau turns to Malesherbes with his revelations in order to justify himself before him: "You will pass judgment when I have said everything."[32] Of course, the addressee is only the representative of an omnipresent public. The form of the letter does indeed indicate the private character of the contents; but the claim to radical sincerity with which Rousseau writes these letters requires unrestricted publicity. The real addressee extends beyond the contemporary audience; it is the universal public of a justly judging posterity: "Whether it is to my advantage or my disadvantage, I am not afraid of being seen as I am."[33]

The religious background is indeed present, but it lingers only as a metaphor for an innerworldly scene, robbed of all transcendence, in which no one knows the author better than he knows himself. He alone possesses privileged access to his inwardness. The experience of conversion, datable according to time and place, is no more missing than is the thematic of the consciousness of sin and·the hope for redemption. But the profane equivalents twist the meaning of religious justification into the desire to be recognized before the forum of all fellow human beings as the one who one is and who one wants to be: "I know my great faults and vividly feel all of my vices. With all of that, I will die without despairing in God Supreme, quite persuaded that of all the men whom I have known in my life, none has been better than I."[34] In truth Rousseau knows that he is dependent on the judgment of the public. He wants to win its recognition, without which radical self-choice would lack confirmation. Once the vertical axis of the prayer has tipped into the horizontal axis of interhuman communication, the individual can no longer redeem the emphatic claim to individuality solely through the reconstructive appropriation of his life history; now the positions taken by others decide whether this reconstruction succeeds.

From this secularized perspective, the *performatively employed* concept of individuality has been completely detached from its descriptive use. A totally different meaning is invested in the claim to individuality that is put forth by a first person in dialogue with a second person. Justificatory confessions, through which the performatively raised claim to one's own identity can be authenticated, are not to be confused with the description, always selective, of an individual. The literary genre of the letter, the confession, the diary, the autobiography, the *Bildungsroman,* and the didactically recited self-reflection, which authors such as Rousseau and Kierkegaard favor, testifies to the transformed illocutionary mode: it is not a matter of *reports* and descriptions from the perspective of an observer, not even of *self-observations;* rather, it is a matter of interested *presentations of self,* with which a complex claim presented to second persons is justified—a claim to recognition of the irreplaceable identity of an ego manifesting itself in a conscious way of life. This claim is brought to bear in the performative attitude, and the attempt to make it plausible by means of a totalizing draft of one's life will always remain fragmentary; but this attempt must not be confused with the never completed descriptive endeavor of characterizing a subject through the totality of all statements that could apply to it. Rousseau's confessions can be most properly understood as an encompassing ethical self-understanding with justificatory intent, put before the public in order for the public to take a position on it. These confessions belong to a different genre than the description that a historian could give of Rousseau's life. They are not measured against the truth of historical statements, but against the authenticity of the presentation of self. They are exposed, as Rousseau knows, to accusations of *mauvaise foi* and of self-deception, not simply to that of being untrue.

V

Leibniz had preserved a descriptive sense for the meaning content of individuality that extends beyond singularity—with the reservation, of course, that it is not possible to completely explicate the individual concept of any being. Fichte had brought Kant's theoretical and practical philosophy together in the highest point of the originary act; hence, in Fichte the moments of cognition and of the performance of an action fuse together in the spontaneous activity of the subject that itself posits itself. Further discussion has shown that the semantic content of "individuality" can be salvaged only if we reserve this expression for performative usage and, in all descriptive contexts, employ it only with the sense of singularity. Our examination of the conceptual history therefore ends with the recommendation that we explain the meaning of the expression "individuality" with reference to the self-understanding of a subject who is capable of speech and action, one who in the face of other dialogue participants presents and, if necessary, justifies himself as an irreplaceable and distinctive person. However diffuse it may remain, this self-understanding grounds the identity of the ego. In it, self-consciousness is articulated not as the self-relation of a knowing subject but as the *ethical self-reassurance (Selbstvergewisserung)* of an accountable person. Standing within an intersubjectively shared lifeworld horizon, the individual projects himself as someone who *vouches* for the more or less clearly established continuity of a more or less consciously appropriated life history; in light of the individuality he has attained, he would like to be identified, even in the future, as the one into whom he has made himself. In short, the meaning of "individuality" should be explicated in terms of the ethical self-understanding of a first person in relation to a second person. A concept of individuality that points beyond mere singularity can only be possessed by one who knows, before himself and others, who he is and who he wants to be.

To be sure, it is not entirely unproblematic to concede the status of *knowledge* to this self-understanding, when this "knowledge" is not analyzable into a finite number of propositions but, as a claim demanding acknowledgment, can only be illustrated in the form of provisional confessions or presentations of self that can be extended *ad hoc*. What is at issue is a performative knowledge that is *sui generis*. Even the performative knowledge that a speaker expresses with the help of a performative clause in carrying out an illocutionary act, for example, only accompanies the explicit knowledge expressed in the propositional component as something that comes along with it; it can, however, be made fully into the object of a *further* constative speech act and thereby transformed into propositional knowledge. The totalizing self-understanding of an individual eludes such an effortless explication. Every attempt at the reassurance and justification of one's own identity must remain fragmentary. In Rousseau's case there were at first letters, then confessions, then commentaries on the confessions which took the form of dialogues, of diary entries, of books. It would be false to look on these exemplary attempts as substitutes for a *descriptive* explication of the ineffable individual that can never be completed. For the identity-bestowing self-understanding of a person has no *descriptive* sense whatsoever; its sense is that of a guarantee; and the meaning of this guarantee has been *completely* grasped by the addressee as soon as he knows that the other is vouching for his ability to be himself. The latter *shows* itself in turn through the continuity of a more or less consciously assumed life-history.

This also explains why such a self-understanding, articulated in the totality of a life project, stands in need of confirmation by others, whether they be concrete or possible participants in interaction. The circumstance that Rousseau and Kierkegaard remained so very dependent on the positions taken toward them by their audiences points beyond the specific reasons that lay in their persons. Phenomenologically it is easy to show that unendangered identity structures must be anchored in relations of intersubjective recognition if they are to be somewhat secure. The explanation for this clinical fact is that the structure for which someone assumes the guarantee with his claim to individuality is by no means absolutely that person's own (*das Eigenste einer Person*)—as is suggested by the decisionistic conceptual framework extending from Fichte to Kierkegaard (and Tugendhat).[35] No one can dispose over his identity as property. The guarantee under discussion must not be conceived according to the model of a promise through which an autonomous speaker binds his will; no one is able *in this way* to obligate himself to remain identical with himself or to be himself. A simple circumstance explains why this does not lie solely within his power. The self of an ethical self-understanding is not the absolutely inward possession of the individual. The impression that it is arises from the possessive individualism of a philosophy of consciousness that begins with the abstract self-relation of the knowing subject, instead of conceiving the latter as result. The self of an ethical self-understanding is dependent upon recognition by addressees because it generates itself as a response to the demands of an other in the first place. Because others attribute accountability to me, I gradually make myself into the one who I have become in living together with others. The ego, which seems to me to be given in my self-consciousness as what is purely my own, cannot be maintained by me solely through my own power, as it were for me alone—it does not "belong" to me. Rather, this ego always retains an intersubjective core because the process of individuation from which it emerges runs through the network of linguistically mediated interactions.

G. H. Mead was the first to have thought through this intersubjective model of the socially produced ego. He leaves behind the reflection-model of self-consciousness, according to which the knowing subject relates to itself as an object in order to lay hold of and thereby become conscious of itself. Fichte's *Wissenschaftslehre* already *began* with the aporias of the philosophy of reflection—but Mead is the first to lead the way out of them via an analysis of interaction, which had, however, at least been initiated in Fichte's *Sittenlehre*.

VI

Mead takes up the program of the philosophy of consciousness once again, albeit under the naturalistic presuppositions of John Dewey's functionalist psychology. His interest in the explanation of subjectivity and self-consciousness is at first epistemological, seen namely from the angle of a psychologist who is giving an account of the constitution of his object domain. That is the problematic of the early essay "The Definition of the Psychical" (1903). The question of the subjective world's accessibility for the psychologist is joined straightaway by the genetic question of the conditions under which self-conscious life emerges. An exploratory answer is to be found in the essay on "Social Consciousness and the Consciousness of Meaning" (1910). In rapid succession further articles appear in which Mead works out the solution to the twofold problem of the self-reflexive access to consciousness and of the genesis of self-consciousness.[36] The last essay in this series, "The Social Self" (1913), begins with the circle of reflection from which Fichte had taken his start: the "I," which is the aspect in which the knowing subject comes upon itself in its self-reflection, has always already been objectified into a "me" that is merely observed. The self that is made into an object must indeed presuppose the spontaneous I or the self of self-reflection, but the latter is not given in conscious experience:

For the moment it is presented it has passed into the objective case, presuming . . . an "I" that observes—but an "I" that can disclose himself only by ceasing to be the subject for whom the object "me" exists.[37]

The idea that lets Mead break out of this circle of self-objectifying reflection requires the transition to the paradigm of symbolically mediated interaction.[38] As long as subjectivity is thought of as the inward space of one's own representations, a space that is disclosed when the object-representing subject bends back, as if in a mirror, upon its activity of representing, everything subjective will be accessible only in the form of objects of self-observation or introspection—and the subject itself only as a "me" objectified under this gaze. The "me" casts off the reifying gaze, however, as soon as the subject appears not in the role of an *observer* but in that of a *speaker* and, from the *social perspective* of a *hearer* encountering him in dialogue, learns to see and to understand himself as the alter ego of another ego: "The self which consciously stands over against other selves thus becomes an object, an other to himself, through the very fact that he hears himself talk, and replies."[39]

It is intuitively plausible that the manner in which I objectify myself as a first person in a self-relation that is mediated through my relation to a second person is not the same as the way in which I objectify myself in introspection. While introspection requires the objectifying attitude of an observer who confronts himself in the third person, the performative attitude of the speaker and hearer requires the differentiation between "you," as the alter ego on my level *with whom* I seek to reach an understanding, and the "something" *about which* I want to reach an understanding with "you." As Mead explains it, the actor comes upon himself as a social object in communicative action when he orients himself to the current I-you relationship and thereby encounters himself as the alter ego of his alter ego; Mead explicates the self of self-consciousness as this *social* object. In the first person of his performative attitude, the actor encounters himself as a second person. In this way there arises an entirely different "me." Even this "me" is not, however, identical with the spontaneously acting "I," which now, as before, withdraws from every direct experience; but the "me" that is accessible in the performative attitude *does* present itself as the exact memory of a spontaneous state of the "I," which can, moreover, be authentically read from the reaction of the second person. The self that is given for me through the mediation of the gaze of the other upon me is the "memory image" of my ego, such as it has just acted in the sight of an alter ego and face to face with it.

Admittedly, this construction exposes itself to the objection that it only applies to the reflected self-relation of a subject speaking with itself, but does not apply to *originary* self-consciousness, which must already be *presupposed* for the utterance of simple experiential sentences. According to Wittgenstein, utterances such as:

(1) I have a toothache.
(2) I am ashamed.
(3) I am afraid of you.

still retain, in spite of their propositional structure, something of the symptomatic character possessed by those body-bound expressive gestures for which they are occasionally the substitute. Even gestures, when they are employed with communicative intent *as* linguistic expressions, betray an intentional relation of the subject to itself, even though we cannot already attribute the reflected self-relation of "an inner conversation" to such a subject.[40] The "me" that is supposed to have emerged from the adoption of the perspective of an alter ego could explain self-consciousness as an originary phenomenon only if it were inserted deeper, beneath the level of a linguistic competence that has already been acquired and used for inner monologues.[41] In fact, Mead does presume that we have already to presuppose self-consciousness even for the employment of symbols with identical meaning. Let us briefly look back at his starting point.

In his earliest works, Mead had followed up on ideas from Dewey in order to expose the "I" as the source of spontaneous accomplishments behind the introspectively reified "me" of positivistic psychology. Mead at first sought access to the subjective world through a pragmatistic concept that had been previously introduced by Peirce, namely the problematization of a conventional situation interpretation. A "problem" disturbs the execution of a plan of action that is being undertaken, removes the basis for the acceptance of a hitherto tried-and-true expectation, and gives rise to a conflict of impulses. In this phase of disintegration, what had been regarded by us as objective collapses in on itself: "the result . . . is . . . to dislodge our objects from their objective position and relegate them to a subjective world. . . ."[42] Within a world-horizon that remains intact, the segment of the world that has become problematic is robbed of its familiarity and validity; it remains behind as the material of the *merely subjective* representations and constitutes the matter from which "the psychical" is made. Thus, the actor becomes conscious of his subjectivity at the moment when his habitualized performance of an action is disturbed, since he must form better hypotheses through abduction out of the rubble of the invalidated representations, that is, he must reconstruct a collapsed interpretation of the situation. In this way, functionalist psychology locates its object, the psychical itself, precisely from within the perspective of an actor who in the performative attitude becomes aware of his performance— which has been interrupted by being problematized:

For this functional psychology an explicit definition of its subject matter . . . is as follows: that phase of experience within which we are immediately conscious of conflicting impulses which rob the object of its character as object-stimulus, leaving us insofar in an attitude of subjectivity; but during which a new object-stimulus appears due to the reconstructive activity which is identified with the subject "I". . . .[43]

This "definition of the psychical" is supposed to provide information about the phenomenon in need of elucidation, namely, about the subjective world of a subject who forms hypotheses and engages in abductive activity. Mead soon realizes that this attempt at an explanation fails, for he cannot in this way make plausible how the subject catches sight of himself in the actual performance of his problem-solving accomplishment. In the moment when he notices, for example, that the ball is too heavy, the ditch too wide, or the weather too uncertain for risking the throw, the jump, or the stroll, the actor does no doubt see himself entangled in a problem, which may bring to consciousness the invalidation of those *action premises* that have foundered on reality; but how the *problem-solving process* itself, which leads to new action premises, could become *conscious*, remains unilluminated. Thus, Mead can explain the phenomenon and emergence of conscious life only after he has given up Dewey's model of an isolated actor's instrumental dealings with things and events and has made the transition to the model of several actors' interactive dealings with each other.

Mead expands the familiar ethological approach, which privileges the individual organism in its species-specific environment, with a social dimension. He concentrates on the relationship between several organisms (of the same species) because problem-solving behavior in such interactions stands under conditions of double contingency. Unlike physical circumstances such as gathering clouds, the behavioral reactions of a social object can also be influenced by my own behavior. This constellation implies, on the one hand, a perpetuation of the danger that my habitualized behavioral expectations might be problematized by the unpredictable reactions of the opposing side; on the other hand, it promises a selective advantage to the side that could calculate the effects of its own behavioral reactions and react to the other, in an elementary sense, *self-consciously:* "A man's reaction toward weather conditions has no influence upon the weather itself. . . . Successful social conduct [however] brings one into a field within which a consciousness of one's own attitudes helps toward the control of the conduct of others."[44] This functionalistic argument directs attention to the situation of interaction as a place where particular advantages of adaptation are to be expected for the emergence of self-consciousness. Yet, as before, the real problem remains the following: How can a self-relation that is rewarded in this way arise under conditions of interaction *in the first place, before* there has developed a linguistic medium with speaker-hearer perspectives that would allow ego to adopt the role of an alter ego toward himself? The competence to speak with oneself already presupposes for its part an elementary form of self-relation. That is the reason why Mead believes he must redirect his analysis to the prelinguistic level of gestural communication.

Nonetheless, an internal reconstruction of the conditions that make original self-consciousness possible can be based upon a prior understanding of linguistic communication. One organism can understand another organism's behavioral reaction that is triggered by the first's gesture *as if it were* an interpretation of this gesture. This idea of recognizing-oneself-in-the-other serves Mead as the key to his explanation, according to which the elementary form of self-relation is made possible by the interpretive accomplishment of another participant in the interaction. In order to understand Mead's thoughts correctly (perhaps somewhat better than he did himself), one must pay heed to the premise that gesture-mediated interaction is still steered by instinct. Thus, in the functional circle of behavior steered by instinct, what are expressed are objective meanings that are assigned from the perspective of the observing ethologist, such as flight, defense, caring for others, propagation, etc.[45] The interpretation that any of one's own behavior receives through the reaction of the other organism is then to be understood in this objective sense. At first, then, this is not an interpretation in the strict sense for either organism. Mead must recur to a further circumstance, already identified by Herder, in order to explain when the objective process of interpreting one's own behavior through the behavioral reaction of another can be understood *as* interpretation by the actor who meets with this reaction—under the condition, namely, that the gesture interpreted by the other is a vocal gesture.

With the vocal gesture, which both organisms perceive simultaneously, the actor affects himself at the same time and in the same way as he affects his opposite number. This coincidence is supposed to make it possible for the one organism to have an effect upon itself in the same way as it does upon the other and thereby to learn to perceive itself exactly as it is perceived from the view of the other, as a social object. It learns to understand its own behavior from the perspective of the other and, specifically, in the light of the other's interpreting behavioral reaction. The antecedent objective meaning of this interpretation of my behavior—e.g., as an emission to which a member of our species reacts with aggression, defensiveness, or submission—now becomes accessible to me as the subject of this emission. My vocal gesture obtains a meaning *for me* taken from the perspective of the other who reacts to it. The character of the vocal gesture is thereby transformed. In the effect it has on oneself, one's vocal gesture stands in for the behavioral reaction of one's opposite number; it takes its provisionally objective meaning from the interpreting force of this behavioral reaction; in that this meaning becomes accessible 'for me,' however, the vocal gesture transforms itself from a segment of behavior into a sign substrate—the stimulus turns into a bearer of meaning.

These considerations explain why the issue covertly shifts for Mead, that is, how the emergence of an originary self-relation is connected with the transition to an evolutionarily new stage of communication. The actor takes the perspective toward himself of another participant in interaction and becomes visible to himself as a social object only when he adopts as his own the objective meaning of his vocal gesture, which stimulates both sides equally. With this self-relation, the actor doubles himself in the instance of a "me," which follows the performative "I" as a shadow—a shadow, because "I," as the author of a spontaneous gesture, am given to "me" only in memory: "If you ask, then, where directly in your own experience the 'I' comes in, the answer is that it comes in as a historical figure. It is what you were a second ago that is the 'I' of the 'me.'"[46] The self of self-consciousness is not the spontaneously acting "I"; the latter is given only in the refraction of the symbolically captured meaning that it took on for its interaction partner "a second ago" in the role of the alter ego: "The observer who accompanies all our self-conscious conduct is then not the actual 'I' who is responsible for the conduct in *propria persona*—he is rather the response which one makes to his own conduct."[47] The expression "observer" in this context is however misleading. For the self of the originary self-relation is a "me" constituted from the performative attitude of a second person and not one objectified from the observer perspective of a third person. For this reason, original self-consciousness is not a phenomenon inherent in the subject but one that is communicatively generated.

VII

Until now the topic has been the epistemic self-relation, the relation of the problem-solving, i.e., knowing subject to itself. The turn to an intersubjectivistic way of looking at things leads in the matter of "subjectivity" to a surprising result: the consciousness that is centered, as it seems, in the ego is not something immediate or purely inward. Rather, self-consciousness forms itself on the path from without to within, through the symbolically mediated relationship to a partner in interaction.

To this extent it possesses an intersubjective core; its eccentric position attests to the tenacious dependence of subjectivity upon language as the medium through which one recognizes oneself in the other in a nonobjectifying manner. As in Fichte, self-consciousness first arises out of the encounter with another ego confronting (*entgegengesetzten*) me. To this extent, the "posited" (*gesetzte*) ego is comparable to the "me." But in the naturalistic view of pragmatism, this "me" appears as the form of mind that is higher or reflected and not as the product of an antecedent ego ("itself positing itself") which withdraws from consciousness. Admittedly, Mead neglects the distinction between an originary self-relation, which first makes the transition from communication that is mediated through vocal gestures to communication that is genuinely linguistic, and the reflected self-relation that is only established in the conversation with oneself, and that thus already presupposes linguistic communication. Only the latter discloses the domain of representations attributable to me, a domain from which the philosophy of the subject has, since Descartes, proceeded as something apparently ultimate. This lack of clarity may be connected with weaknesses in Mead's philosophy of language, which I have discussed elsewhere.[48]

Equally unclear remains the important distinction between the *epistemic* self-relation (*Selbstbeziehung*) of the knowing subject and the *practical* relation-to-self (*Selbstverhältnis*) of the acting subject.[49] Presumably, Mead blurs this difference in his lectures because from the start he comprehends "knowing" as problem-solving practice and conceives of the cognitive self-relation as a function of action.[50] Nonetheless, the meaning of the central conceptual pair "I" and "me" is surreptitiously altered as soon as the motivational dimension of the practical relation-to-self comes into play. To be sure, Mead explains the practical relation-to-self just as he does the epistemic self-relation, on the basis of a reorganization of the stage of prelinguistic, instinct-steered interaction. Just as the epistemic self-relation emerges from a transition to another mode of communication, the practical relation-to-self emerges from the transition to another mechanism of behavioral control. But along with these transitions, two aspects of behavioral coordination are differentiated that had still coincided in the model of an instinctual reaction triggered by species-specific stimuli. Symbolically mediated interaction allows one to *monitor and control one's own behavior* through self-referential cognition; this cannot, however, replace the *coordinative accomplishments* that had previously been secured through a common instinctual repertoire and the corresponding behavior patterns that made the actions of the one actor 'fit' those of the other. This void is now filled by normatively generalized behavioral expectations, which take the place of instinctual regulation; however, these norms need to be anchored within the acting subject through more or less internalized social controls.

This correspondence between social institutions and behavioral controls within the personality system is also explained by Mead with the aid of the familiar mechanism of taking the perspective of an other who, in an interactive relationship, takes up a performative attitude toward ego. Now, however, taking the other's perspective is extended into *role-taking:* Ego takes over alter's *normative,* not his *cognitive* expectations. To be sure, the process retains the same structure. Through the fact that I perceive myself as the social object of an other, a new reflexive agency is formed through which ego makes the behavioral expectations of others into his own. To the normative character of these expectations, however, there corresponds a transmuted structure of this second "me" as well as a different function of the self-relation. The "me" of the *practical* relation-to-self is no longer the seat of an originary or reflected self-*consciousness* but an agency of self-*control*. Self-reflection here takes on the specific tasks of mobilizing motives for action and of internally controlling one's own modes of behavior.

The stages of development leading to a conventional moral consciousness, which is dependent upon the forms of life and institutions existing at a given time, need not occupy us here.[51] Mead conceives of this "me" as the "generalized other," i.e., as the behavioral expectations of one's social surroundings that have, as it were, migrated into the person. The "I" in turn relates to this agency as a spontaneity that eludes consciousness. But unlike the epistemic "I," the practical "I" forms an unconscious that makes itself noticed in *two* ways: as the onrush of impulses that are subjected to control and as the source of innovations that break up and renew conventionally rigidified controls. The epistemic self-relation had been made possible by a "me" that fixed in memory the spontaneously acting "I," such as it presented itself in the performative attitude of a second person. The practical relation-to-self is made possible by a "me" that places limits, from the intersubjective perspective of a social "we," on the impulsiveness and the creativity of a resistant and productive "I." From this perspective, the "I" appears on the one hand as the pressure of presocial, natural drives, and on the other hand as the impulse of creative fantasy—or as the impetus for the innovative transformation of a way of seeing. This distinction should account for the experience we have of the *difference* between the way in which institutionalized forms of social intercourse are placed in question by the revolt of split-off motives and repressed interests, and the way in which they are placed in question by the intrusion of a revolutionarily renewed language that allows us to see the world with new eyes.

In both cases, the "me" of the practical relation-to-self proves to be a conservative force. This agency is closely united with what already exists. It mirrors the forms of life and the institutions that are practiced and recognized in a particular society. It functions in the consciousness of the socialized individual as society's agent and drives everything that spontaneously deviates out of the individual's consciousness. At first glance it is counterintuitive that Mead attributes the unconscious powers of spontaneous deviation to an "I"—instead of to an id (or it), as Freud does—and that he conceives of the self of the practical relation-to-self, or the identity of the person, the consciousness of concrete duties, as the anonymous result of socializing interactions. This irritation does not disappear completely, even when one realizes that it is by no means a matter of arbitrary usage, but involves the point of the entire approach.

The self of the epistemic self-relation does not coincide with the "I" as the author of spontaneous performances, but it does cling to the latter as closely as possible because it is held fast (in memory) from the perspective of a coacting, not an objectifying, alter ego. The *terminus ad quem* here is the *recording* of the subject in the performance of its spontaneous accomplishments. In the practical relation-to-self, on the other hand, the acting subject does not want to *recognize* (*erkennen*) itself; rather, it wants to *reassure* (*vergewissern*) itself about itself as the initiator of an action that is attributable solely to it—in short, to become sure of itself as a free will. It is thus plausible to approach this reassurance from the perspective of the generalized other or the community will that we find already embodied, so to speak, in the intersubjectively recognized and autonomous norms and forms of life of our society. Only to the extent that we grow into these social surroundings do we constitute ourselves as accountably acting individuals; by internalizing social controls, we develop for *ourselves*, in our own right, the capacity either to follow or also to violate the expectations that are held to be legitimate.

This interpretation has not yet explained, however, why Mead maintains the difference between the "me" and the "I" at all, instead of letting one be absorbed by the other. The socially constituted free will seems in the act of reassurance to be *completely* captured by the self of the practical relation-to-self. The unconscious elements of the personality that both withdraw from and force themselves upon this self can hardly lay claim to the title of an "I" as the subject of accountable action: "It is only by taking the roles of others that we have been able to come back to ourselves."[52] This insight, which is already valid for the epistemic self-relation, takes on a particular nuance for the practical relation-to-self. For the self of the practical relation-to-self is not a memory shadow trailing an antecedent spontaneity; it is a will that, solely as a result of socialization, constitutes itself as an "I will," as an "I can posit a new beginning, for the results of which I am responsible." Mead also says: "this generalized other in his experience . . . provides him with a self."[53]

But the clarification that Mead provides for the way this self or this ego-identity functions already hints at why it is not equated with the "I":

We approve of ourselves and condemn ourselves. We pat ourselves upon the back and in blind fury attack ourselves. We assume the generalized attitude of the group, in the censor that stands at the door of our imagery and inner conversations, and in the affirmation of the laws and axioms of the universe of discourse.[54]

The "me" is the bearer of a moral consciousness that adheres to the conventions and practices of a specific group. It represents the power of a *particular* collective will over an individual will that has not yet come into its own. The latter is *not completely* able to recognize itself in its own identity, generated through socialization, as long as this identity requires us to "attack ourselves in blind fury." The "me" characterizes an identity formation that makes responsible action possible only at the price of blind subjugation to external social controls, which remain external in spite of the internalizing effect of role-taking. The conventional ego-identity is at best a steward for the true one. And in virtue of this difference, the difference between the "I" and the "me" may not be retracted, even for the practical relation-to-self.

At this crucial juncture Mead recurs both to processes of societal differentiation and to experiences of emancipation from narrowly circumscribed, tradition-bound and standardized forms of life; these experiences typically accompany the transition to and integration of expanded reference groups and forms of intercourse, or those which are both more comprehensive and functionally differentiated. In this context Mead speaks of the process of "civilizing" society, which signifies a step forward in the individuation of the individual:

In primitive society, to a far greater extent than in civilized society, individuality is constituted by the more or less perfect achievement of a given social type. . . . [I]n civilized society individuality is constituted rather by the individual's departure from, or modified realization of, any given social type . . . and tends to be something much more distinctive and singular. . . .[55]

This is in accord with Durkheim's descriptions and those of the other sociological classics. Mead's originality reveals itself in the fact that he is in the position to provide, from the reconstructive perspective of his independently developed theory of communication, a more precise meaning for these basic sociological concepts.

VIII

From the point of view of the individuals affected by it, the process of social individualization has two different aspects. To a growing degree, both *autonomy* and a *conscious conduct of life* are culturally imputed to and institutionally demanded from them. Moreover, the cultural paradigms and social expectations of *self-determination* and *self-realization* become differentiated from each other, depending upon the degree to which the accents are placed on the subject's own achievements. In the "me," to the extent that we have examined it thus far, there are layed down the concrete forms of life and institutions of a particular collective; however, to the degree that this conventional identity formation disintegrates under the pressure of societal differentiation, or the diversification of conflicting role expectations, the moral and the ethical dimensions (in the language of psychoanalysis: the agency of conscience and the ego-ideal) become separated from each other. "Turning away from rigid conventions," which is socially enforced, burdens the individual, on the one hand, with moral decisions of his own and, on the other hand, with an individual life project arising from the process of ethical self-understanding.

However, the self from which these independent achievements are expected is socially constituted through and through; it is not able, by detaching itself from particular life contexts, to step outside of society altogether and settle down in a space of abstract isolation and freedom. Rather, the abstraction that is expected of it lies *in the same direction* in which the civilization process is already pointed. The individual projects himself in the direction of a "larger society":

one appeals to others on the assumption that there is a group of organized others that answer to one's own appeal—even if the appeal be made to posterity. In that case there is the attitude of the "I" as over against the "me."[56]

We are already familiar with the appeal to posterity from Rousseau, who regards the process in which he reaches self-understanding as being subjected to similar conditions of communication, conditions for a universal discourse that is counterfactually directed into the future. In modern societies it is ever more common for moral decisions to overtax a merely conventional moral consciousness; these decisions must now also be made under the conditions of a universal discourse. The transition to a postconventional morality becomes unavoidable. Mead interprets it thus:

> In logical terms there is established a universe of discourse which transcends the specific order [and] within which the members of the community may, in a specific conflict, place themselves outside of the community order as it exists, and agree upon changed habits of action and a restatement of values.[57]

The formation of moral judgments (like reaching ethical self-understanding) is referred to a forum of reason that simultaneously *socializes* and *temporalizes* practical reason. Rousseau's universalized public and Kant's intelligible world are rendered socially concrete and temporally dynamic by Mead; in this way, the anticipation of an idealized form of communication is supposed to preserve a moment of unconditionality for the discursive procedure of will formation.

The Peircean concept of a consensus achieved in an unlimited communication community, or an "ultimate opinion," returns in Mead. In practical discourse we erect

> an ideal world, not of substantive things but of proper method. Its claim is that all the conditions of conduct and all the values which are involved in the conflict must be taken into account in abstraction from the fixed forms of habits and goods which have clashed with each other.[58]

Social individualization means, for the individuals, that the self-determination and the self-realization that are expected of them presuppose a nonconventional sort of ego-identity. Even this identity formation can, however, only be *conceived* as socially constituted; it must therefore be stabilized in relationships of reciprocal recognition that are at least *anticipated*.

This is confirmed by those extreme cases in which the self of the practical relation-to-self, in grappling with its moral or ethical problems, is thrown back entirely upon itself: "A person may reach a point of going against the whole world about him. . . ."[59] But as a person he will not be able to sustain himself as a solitary being *in vacuo,* even in this extreme isolation, "except as he constitutes himself [as] a member of this wider commonwealth of rational beings."[60] This wider commonwealth is not, however, an ideal in the Kantian sense, severed from the empirical world: "It is a *social* order, for its function is a common action on the basis of commonly recognized conditions of conduct and common ends."[61] Kant's Kingdom of Ends must be *supposed* here and now as a context of interaction and as a communication community in which everyone is capable of taking up the perspective of everyone else and is willing to do so. Whoever is thrown back entirely upon himself and wants to speak to himself with the voice of reason

has to comprehend the voices of the past and of the future. That is the only way in which the self can get a voice which is more than the voice of the [presently existing] community. As a rule we assume that this general voice of the community is identical with the larger community of the past and the future. . . .[62]

Mead carries the approach of moral theory further than that of ethics. The latter would have to give the concept of self-realization a communication-theoretical formulation, similar to that given the concept of self-determination by moral theory. Progressive individuation is measured just as much against the *differentiation of unique identities* as it is against the *growth of personal autonomy.* In this respect, too, Mead insists upon the interlacing of individuation and socialization:

The fact that all selves are constituted by . . . the social process, and are individual reflections of it . . . is not in the least incompatible with, or destructive of, the fact that every individual self has its own peculiar individuality . . . because each individual self within that process, while it reflects in its organized structure the behavior pattern of that process as a whole, does so from its own particular and unique standpoint within that process . . . (just as every monad in the Leibnizian universe mirrors that universe from a different point of view . . .).[63]

Here Mead repeats his earlier conclusion,

that each individual . . . slices the events of the community life that are common to all from a different angle from that of any other individual. In Whitehead's phrase, each individual stratifies the common life in a different manner, and the life of the community is the sum of all these stratifications. . . .[64]

Both of these passages do a good job of presenting the intuition that Mead wants to express; but the ontologizing connections with Leibniz and Whitehead distort its adequate explication, toward which Mead's own thoughts are pointing.

Not only as an *autonomous* being but also as an *individuated* being, the self of the practical relation-to-self cannot reassure itself about itself through direct reflection but only via the perspective of others. In this case I have to rely not on others' *agreement* with my judgments and actions but on their *recognition* of my claim to uniqueness and irreplaceability. Since an ego-identity that no longer merely adheres to the "social type," that is, one that is postconventional, articulates itself in an unconditional claim to uniqueness and irreplaceability, a moment of idealization comes into play this time as well. But this moment of idealization no longer concerns only the circle of addressees, which virtually encompasses *everyone,* or the unlimited communication community; rather, it concerns the claim to individuality itself, which relates to the guarantee that I consciously give, in light of a considered individual life project, for the continuity of my life history. The idealizing supposition of a universalistic form of life, in which everyone can take up the perspective of everyone else and can count on reciprocal recognition by everybody, makes it possible for individuated beings to exist within a community—individualism as the flipside of universalism. Taking up a relationship to a projected form of society is what first makes it possible for me to take my own life history seriously as a principle of individuation—to regard it *as if it were* the product of decisions for which I am responsible. The self-critical appropriation and reflexive continuation of my life history would have to remain a nonbinding or even an indeterminate idea as long as I could not encounter myself before the eyes of all, i.e., before the forum of an unlimited communication community. Here "myself" means: my existence as a whole—in the full concretion and breadth of the life contexts and formative processes that shape identity.

Here, too, the ego finds its way to itself only along a detour by way of others, by way of the counterfactually supposed universal discourse. Once again, the self of the practical relation-to-self can only assure itself of itself if it is able to return to itself from the perspective of others as their alter ego. But this time it does not return to itself as the alter ego of some other alter ego from among its own concrete group (as the "me"). It now comes upon itself as the alter ego of *all* others in every community—specifically, as a free will in moral self-reflection and as a fully individuated being in existential self-reflection. Thus, the relationship between the "I" and the "me" *remains* the key even for an analysis of the socially imputed postconventional ego-identity. But at this stage the relationship between the two is reversed.

Previously, the "me" was supposed to capture a spontaneously acting "I," which eludes direct seizure, in a nonobjectifying manner in mediated acts of self-knowledge or self-reassurance. Now, however, the anticipatory establishment of interactive relations to a circle of addressees is imputed to the "I" itself; for it is from their perspective that the "I" is able to return to itself and assure itself of itself as an autonomous will and an individuated being. The "me," which in a way follows the "I," is now no longer made possible through an *antecedent* interactive relationship. The "I" itself *projects* the context of interaction that first makes the reconstruction of a shattered conventional identity possible on a higher level. This reconstruction is made necessary by processes of societal differentiation. That is, the latter have set in motion a generalization of values and, especially in the system of rights, a universalization of norms, and these processes demand a specific kind of independent accomplishment from the the socialized individuals.[65] The onus of these decisions requires a nonconventional ego-identity. Although the latter can only be thought of as socially constituted, still a social formation corresponding to it in any way does not yet exist. This paradox is resolved in the temporal dimension.

Among the characteristic experiences of modernity are an acceleration of the historical process and a constant expansion of the future horizon, with the result that present situations are ever more plainly interpreted in the light of pasts made present and, above all, future presents. One function of this transformed and reflexive consciousness of time is the imputation that present action will be placed under premises that anticipate future presents. This applies to systemic processes (such as long-term political commitments, debt-financing, etc.) as well as to simple interactions. The consciousness of crisis that is becoming more and more prevalent in modern societies is the underside of this now-endemic utopian current. Yet, this current also encompasses the mode of anticipation that is imputed to the free will in moral self-reflection and to the fully individuated being in existential self-reflection, a mode of anticipation that is now socially expected. A postconventional ego-identity can only stabilize itself in the anticipation of symmetrical relations of unforced reciprocal recognition. That may explain tendencies toward a certain existential burdening and moralizing of public issues or, more generally, the increasing normative congestion within the political culture of developed societies, which is so lamented in the neoconservative critique of the present.[66] Yet, it is also the source from which the radically democratic perspectives of Mead and Dewey derive their own internal consistency.[67]

IX

The projection of the unlimited communication community is backed up by the structure of language itself. Just as the "I" of the "I think" occupies a key role for the philosophy of the subject, so the first person singular also occupies a key role in the successor to this philosophy, communication theory. Admittedly, up till now linguistic analysis has busied itself above all with two grammatical roles of the personal pronoun "I" that only indirectly touch on our problem. One debate concerns "I" as a self-referential expression, with which the speaker numerically identifies himself before a hearer as a particular entity from among the set of all possible objects.[68] Another debate concerns the grammatical role of the first person in experiential sentences, in which this expression signals the privileged access of the speaker to his own subjective world. The issue there is the epistemic self-relation in expressive speech acts.[69] In contrast, the self of the practical relation-to-self first comes under scrutiny when we investigate the grammatical role that the first person takes on as the subject expression in performative sentences. The "I" then stands for the actor of a speech act, who in a performative attitude enters into an interpersonal relationship (which is more specifically determined by the mode of communication) with a second person. In this respect, the personal pronoun in the first person neither fulfills the function of self-reference, which must however be presupposed as fulfilled, nor is it a matter of the mode-specific meaning of the 'self' in the presentation of self, to whom an audience attributes experiences that are unveiled before its eyes—since this concerns only one out of several classes of speech acts. The meaning of the "I" that is employed performatively is a function of *any* illocutionary act. Here the expression relates to the speaker at the moment at which he performs an illocutionary act and encounters a second person as his alter ego. In this attitude toward a second person, the speaker can relate to himself as a speaker *in actu* only by taking up the perspective of the other and becoming visible to himself as the alter ego of his opposite number, as the second person of a second person. The performative meaning of the "I" is thus Mead's "me," which must be capable of accompanying all my speech acts.

Mead always insisted that the relation to a second person is unavoidable—and to this extent fundamental—for every self-relation, including one that is epistemic. However, with the development of different modes of communication (which, like the illocutionary-propositional double structure of speech, Mead did not investigate),[70] the epistemic self-relation is restricted to the class of expressive speech acts, while a practical relation-to-self in a narrower sense differentiates itself from the latter. The meaning of the subject expression of performative sentences also specifies itself thereby, and indeed in the sense of the "me" that Mead conceived social-psychologically as the 'identity' of a person capable of speaking and acting.[71]

The self of the practical relation-to-self reassures itself about itself through the recognition that its claims receive from an alter ego. But these identity claims aiming at intersubjective recognition must not be confused with the validity claims that the actor raises with his speech acts. For the "no" with which the addressee rejects a speech-act offer concerns the validity of a particular utterance, not the identity of the speaker. The speaker certainly could not count on the acceptance of his speech acts if he did not already *presuppose* that the addressee took him seriously as someone who could orient his action with validity claims. The one must have recognized the other as an accountable actor whenever he expects him to take a position with "yes" or "no" to his speech-act offers. In communicative action everyone thus recognizes in the other his own autonomy.

However, the performative use of the personal pronoun in the first person comprehends not only the self-interpretation of the speaker as a free will but also his self-understanding as an individual who distinguishes himself from all others. The performative meaning of the "I" also interprets the role of the speaker in relation to his own irreplaceable position in the weave of social relations.[72]

Normative contexts establish the set of all interpersonal relationships that are held to be legitimate in a given intersubjectively shared lifeworld. Whenever the speaker enters into an interpersonal relationship with a hearer, he also relates himself as an actor to a network of normative expectations. Nevertheless, as long as interactions are linguistically structured, filling social roles can never imply their mere reproduction. The interwoven perspectives of the first and the second person are indeed exchangeable, but the one participant can adopt the perspective of the other only *in the first person;* that is, never as a mere representative, but always *in propria persona.* Thus, the communicative actor is encouraged by the bare structure of linguistic intersubjectivity to remain *himself,* even in behavior conforming to norms. In action guided by norms, the initiative to realize oneself cannot in principle be taken away from any one—and no one can give up this initiative. For this reason, Mead never tires of emphasizing the moment of unpredictability and spontaneity in the *manner* in which the actor interactively plays his roles. The individuation effected by the linguistically mediated process of socialization is explained by the linguistic medium itself. It belongs to the logic of the use of the personal pronouns, and especially to the perspective of a speaker who orients himself to a second person, that this speaker cannot *in actu* rid himself of his irreplaceability, cannot take refuge in the anonymity of a third person, but must lay claim to recognition as an individuated being.

These brief formal-pragmatic considerations confirm the result that Mead arrived at by another route and that is also in harmony with our recapitulation of the conceptual history. Among the universal and unavoidable presuppositions of action oriented to reaching understanding is the presupposition that the speaker qua actor lays claim to recognition both as an autonomous will and as an individuated being. And indeed the self, which is able to assure itself of itself through the recognition of this identity by others, shows up in language as the meaning of the performatively employed personal pronoun in the first person. To be sure, the extent to which this meaning, with its two aspects of self-determination and self-realization, either emerges articulated, remains implicit, or is even neutralized in any concrete case, depends upon the action situation and the further context. The universal pragmatic presuppositions of communicative action constitute semantic resources from which historical societies create and articulate, each in its own way, representations of mind and soul, concepts of the person and of action, consciousness of morality, and so on.

The actor's claim to recognition as an accountable subject receives *different* interpretations depending on whether the framework is provided by a conventional morality, by a religious ethic of conviction, by a principled morality that has become autonomous, or by a completely secularized procedural ethics. Like the concept of the autonomous will, that of an individual being can also be radicalized. We have seen that in our tradition it is only since the eighteenth century that the idea of a completely individuated being has shed the connotations associated with an interpretation of history in terms of religious salvation. But even at a level of social development in which most people generally dispose over a radicalized understanding of autonomy and of conscious life conduct, and in which they allow themselves to be guided by these intuitions in communicative action, this self-understanding still varies according to the action situation and the action system. Wherever relations are more or less formalized, be it in markets, in the firm, or in dealings with administrative authorities, legal norms relieve one of responsibilities of a moral kind; at the same time, anonymous and stereotyped behavior patterns leave little room for individual characterizations. Exceptions, such as the conflict engendered by compulsory orders in cases of legally sanctioned human rights violations, confirm this rule. However, the reciprocally raised claims to recognition for one's own identity are not completely neutralized, even in rigorously formalized relationships, as long as recourse to legal norms is possible; the two moments are preserved (*aufgehoben*) in the concept of the legal person as the bearer of subjective rights.

In communicative action, the suppositions of self-determination and self-realization retain a rigorously intersubjective sense: whoever judges and acts morally must be capable of anticipating the agreement of an unlimited communication community, and whoever realizes himself in a responsibly accepted life history must be capable of anticipating recognition from this unlimited community. Accordingly, an identity that always remains mine, namely, my self-understanding as an autonomously acting and individuated being, can stabilize itself only if I find recognition as a person, and as this person. Under conditions of strategic action, the self of self-determination and of self-realization slips out of intersubjective relations. The strategic actor no longer draws from an intersubjectively shared lifeworld; having himself become worldless, as it were, he stands over and against the objective world and makes decisions solely according to standards of subjective preference. He does not rely therein upon recognition by others. Autonomy is then transformed into freedom of choice (*Willkürfreiheit*), and the individuation of the socialized subject is transformed into the isolation of a liberated subject who possesses himself.

Mead examined social individualization solely from the point of view of progressive individuation: modern societies burden the individual with decisions that require a postconventional ego-identity and thus also necessitate a radicalization of the actor's practical self-understanding, which is always already implicitly presupposed in the use of language that is oriented toward reaching understanding. But reality looks different. By no means do processes of social individualization occur in a linear fashion. The complex processes appear with confusing, contradictory aspects. However, in order to distinguish *these* aspects appropriately, we must reinterpret the basic concepts of conventional sociology in light of the theory of communication that Mead developed, from the outset, in a different methodological attitude.[73]

X

In sociology it is customary to describe processes of societal modernization from two different angles: as the functional differentiation of the social system and as the detraditionalization of the lifeworld. The complementary differentiation of an economic system that is steered by labor, capital, and commodity markets and of a bureaucratic system of public administration that has a monopoly on force and is thus steered by power, serves as the great historical example of a line of development along which modern societies are gradually absorbed by their functionally specified subsystems. The dissolution of traditional lifeworlds, on the other hand, is reflected in the decomposition of religious worldviews, of stratified orders of domination, and of those institutions which, by combining various functions, continue to characterize the society as a whole.

From the point of view of the socialized individuals, both the loss of conventional supports and the emancipation from quasi-natural dependencies are linked up with this. This dual significance is echoed, for example, in Marx when he ironically speaks of "free" wage labor. The status of productive wage labor is characteristically bound up with the *ambiguous* experience of being released (*Freisetzung*) from life conditions that are socially integrating but also marked by dependencies, that orient and protect yet restrict and oppress at the same time.[74] This multilayered complex of experiences forms the background for what the sociological classics have called social individualization. They have emphasized the gains that correspond to the integrative losses, without having the concepts at hand that might have allowed them to free this intuition from the suspicion that it is an arbitrary evaluation of social facts. Now Mead, with his intersubjectivistically formulated concept of 'identity,' offers a means for drawing a finely tuned distinction between contrary aspects of social individualization.

It is possible to speak in a descriptive sense of the progressive individuation of socialized subjects, but only if this is not interpreted simply as being an expansion of the range of options for putative purposive-rational decisions. This kind of interpretation traces the individualization that is effected by societal modernization back to an exchange in which ligatures are traded against expanded opportunities for making choices.[75] Detraditionalization, which is experienced as ambiguous by those who are affected by it, can be described in this way only if the dissolution of traditional lifeworlds is treated exclusively as a function of societal differentiation. This picture suggests that the lifeworld should be viewed systems-theoretically as the substrate and form of a traditional society that is to be absorbed into functionally differentiated subsystems without, so to speak, any residue. The functional systems relegate the socialized individuals to their 'environments' and then lay claim only to functionally specific performances from them. From the point of view of subsystems that are steered by their own codes and are reflexively encapsulated within themselves, social individualization appears as the functional inclusion of personality systems that are at the same time left out, i.e., released and isolated.

What Parsons called 'inclusion' is explicated by Luhmann in the following way:

The phenomenon designated as inclusion . . . first arises with the dissolution of the society of Old Europe, which was stratified by estates. This society had assigned each person (more precisely, each family) to one and only one stratum. With the transition to a type of differentiation oriented primarily by functions, this order had to be given up. Its place is taken by access regulations. The human being lives as an individual outside of functional systems, but every individual must obtain access to every functional system. . . . Every functional system takes in the entire population, but only with the segments of its members' life conduct that are functionally relevant in a given case.[76]

Ullrich Beck has portrayed the same processes from the point of view of the affected individuals. These individuals are *excluded* by the reified subsystems, yet they are at the same time *integrated* into them in a functionally specific manner as laborers and consumers, as social-insurance contributors and as the insured, as voters, as school-age children, etc.

For the individuals, the detraditionalization of their lifeworld at first presents itself as a fatalistically experienced differentiation of diversified life situations and conflicting behavioral expectations, which burden them with new coordinative and integrative performances. In past generations birth, family, marital partner, career, and political position formed a constellation that was specific to one's social stratum and largely determined the pattern of one's biography; but now life situations and life plans that had been normatively bundled are becoming ever more splintered. The need for individually processed decisions grows with the expanded range of options. The individual's milieu no longer relieves him even of those decisions that have the greatest consequences for his biography: which school one attends, which career one chooses, which relationships one enters into, whether and when one marries, has children, joins a party, whether one changes one's spouse or one's career, adopts a new city or country, etc.:

In the individualized society, the individual has to . . . learn to conceive of himself as a center of actions, as a planning bureau in relation to his life, his capabilities, his partnerships, etc. 'Society' has to be handled individually as a variable under conditions of the biography that is to be produced. . . . The societal determinants that intrude into one's own life have to be conceived in this way as 'environmental variables,' which . . . can be gotten around or suspended by means of 'imaginative measures.'[77]

The systems-theoretic mirror-image of inclusion is therefore the released and isolated individual, who finds himself in diversified roles confronting multiplying opportunities; of course, he must make the requisite decisions under system conditions that are not under his control. As a member of organizations, as a participant in systems, the individual who is seized by inclusion is simply subjected to *another kind* of dependence. One who is integrated must orient himself toward steering media such as money and administrative power. These media exercise a behavioral control that, on the one hand, *individualizes* because it is tailored to choices of the individual that are steered by preferences; but on the other hand it also *standardizes* because it only allows options in prestructured dimensions (having or not having, commanding or obeying). Moreover, the very first decision entangles the individual in a network of further dependencies. But if the individual is turned more and more into a "reproduction unit of the social," his release and isolation must not be equated "with successful emancipation":

The individuals who are released become dependent on the market, and dependent *thereby* on education, on consumption, on social-policy regulations and entitlements, on transportation planning, on consumer goods, on possibilities and fads in medical, psychological and pedagogical consultation and care.[78]

Progressive inclusion in increasing numbers of functional systems does not imply any increase in autonomy, but at most a transformation in the mode of social control:

The place of traditional bonds and social forms (social class, nuclear family) is taken by secondary instances that mold the biography of the individual and, running contrary to the individual control which asserts itself as a form of consciousness, turn him into the plaything of fads, relations, conjunctures and markets.[79]

According to this reading, social individualization is bound up with the conversion of the social integration that had been carried out through values, norms, and understandings over to steering media such as money or power, which refer to the preferences of isolated actors who reach decisions rationally. Whoever conceives of the dissolution of traditional lifeworlds in this way, i.e., *only* as the flipside of the functionally specific inclusion of excluded individuals in subsystems that have become independent, must arrive at the conclusion that social individualization isolates or *singularizes* but does not *individuate* in the emphatic sense. Beck definitely has a feel for the latter sense of individuation, which is not captured by the basic concepts of conventional sociology. Resigned, he observes: "With 'individualization' many associate individuation, which equals becoming a person, which equals uniqueness, which equals emancipation. That might be right. But so might the contrary."[80] Beck sees that detachment from ascribed social forms and the loss of traditional certainties, that is, release and disenchantment, can provide the impetus not only for the singularization of individuals who have been socialized elsewhere, but *also* for "a new kind of social integration."[81]

This new kind of social integration would have to be conceived as the individual's *own achievement*. As Mead has shown, however, a conventional identity formation does not suffice for this. Just as inadequate is an ego conceived as the center of a prudent, egocentric selection among systemically prestructured options. For this simultaneously released and isolated individual disposes over no criteria other than his own preferences for processing the growing number of decisions required from him, and these preferences are regulated by the quasi-natural imperative of self-maintenance. An ego-instance shorn of all normative dimensions and reduced to cognitive achievements of adaptation does indeed form a functional complement to the subsystems that are steered by media; but it cannot replace the individuals' own socially integrative accomplishments, which a rationalized lifeworld expects of them. Only a postconventional ego-identity could satisfy these demands. And such an ego-identity can only develop in the course of progressive individuation.

Beck himself illustrates the empirical content of this consideration in terms of the dynamic through which the labor market, via the mobilization of female labor power, influences the sphere of socialization in the nuclear family. He interprets the statistically verified trends (which vary in intensity according to social stratum) toward a reduction in marriages and births and toward an increase in divorces, one-person households, single parents, changes in partners, etc., as symptoms of the problems that result from the growing employment of women and of the resolution of these problems in conformance with the demands of the labor market:

With the decisive question of career mobility there are associated other decisive questions: timing, number and care of children; the abiding problem of everyday chores that are never to be equally divided; the 'onesidedness' of contraceptive methods; the nightmare question of terminating pregnancies; differences in type and frequency of sexuality; not to mention the sensitivity of an optics that senses sexism even in an advertisement for margarine.

Moreover, these themes of conflict have different weights in the unsynchronized life cycles of men and women. Beck offers a dramatic view:

What here descends upon the family as the lifting of taboos and as new technical possibilities . . . takes the [personal] situations that were once unified in it and divides them up piece by piece: wife against husband, mother against child, child against father. The traditional unit breaks apart in the decisions that are demanded from it.[82]

Of course, this proposition leaves open whether the familial lifeworld is crumbling under the growing pressure of decisions or whether it will transform itself *as* a lifeworld. If one regards the detraditionalization process only from the perspective of the labor market and the occupational system, only as the flipside of 'inclusion,' then it is to be expected that the drifting apart of individualized life situations will inevitably result in the singularization of the released family members and in the transformation of socially integrated relationships into contractual connections. The legal institutionalization of marriage and of the family in terms of civil law is then transformed into a juridification of familial relationships that becomes transparent and is held perpetually present. The end point of this tendency would be the dissolution of the family altogether:

The existential form of the single person is not a deviant case along the path to modernity. It is the prototype for the triumphant labor-market society. The negation of social bonds that asserts itself in the logic of the market even begins in its final stage of progress to dissolve the presuppositions for the enduring togetherness of two people.[83]

One senses that such a systems-theoretic description misstates things in a peculiar way—and yet does not misstate things entirely. It is only in the pathological peripheral zones, however, that the states of affairs that it describes are not completely distorted. The irritation that it arouses is not of a moral nature; it has empirical grounds. The decision structure required by media-steered subsystems misses the mark when it encroaches on the private and public core domains of the lifeworld. The independent performances that are here demanded from the subjects consist of something *different* than rational choices steered by one's own preferences; what these subjects must perform is the kind of moral and existential self-reflection that is not possible without the one taking up the perspective of the other. Only thus can there emerge a new kind of social integration among individuals who are individualized and not merely manipulated. The participants must themselves generate their socially integrated forms of life by recognizing each other as autonomous subjects capable of action and, beyond this, as individuated beings who vouch for the continuity of the life histories for which they have taken responsibility.

Beck pursues the plausible hypothesis that

the lifeworld norms, value orientations, and lifestyles that characterize people in developing industrial capitalism are, in terms of their genealogy, not so much the products of the formation of industrial classes, but are often the relics of precapitalistic and preindustrial traditions.[84]

From this point of view one can understand why the task of reconstructing premodern forms of social integration (which must be performed by the affected individuals themselves) is only coming upon us with full force today. Social individualization, which has long since been gotten underway by systems differentiation, is an objectively ambiguous phenomenon; a description is therefore needed that does not reduce it to only one of its aspects. Only to the extent that the lifeworld is *rationalized* can this process imply something other than the singularizing release of self-reflexively steered personality systems—namely, the *individuation* of socialized subjects. Mead exposed the intersubjective core of the ego. Using it, he can explain why a postconventional ego-identity does not develop without at least the anticipation of transformed structures of communication; but once this becomes a part of social reality, it cannot leave the traditional forms of social integration untouched.

Notes

1. Emile Durkheim, *The Division of Labor in Society*, trans. George Simpson (Glencoe: Free Press, 1933), 405.

2. Talcott Parsons, "Religion in Postindustrial America," in *Action Theory and the Human Condition* (New York: Free Press, 1978), 321.

3. Arnold Gehlen, *Man in the Age of Technology*, trans. Patricia Lipscomb (New York: Columbia University Press, 1980), 166.

4. Cf. Jürgen Habermas, *The Philosophical Discourse of Modernity*, trans. Frederick Lawrence (Cambridge, Mass.: MIT Press, 1987), 238ff.

5. E. Durkheim, *Division of Labor*, 403.

6. G. W. F. Hegel, *Aesthetics*, 2 vols., trans. T. M. Knox (Oxford: Clarendon Press, 1975), 1: 490. (German: *Theorie-Werkausgabe*, 20 vols. [Frankfurt: Suhrkamp] 14: 92f.)

7. Hans Gerth and C. Wright Mills, *Character and Social Structure* (New York: Harcourt, Brace & World, 1953), 100. [Translator's note: The interpolation is by Habermas, who also writes "autonomous actions" (*autonomen Handlungen*) in place of Gerth and Mills' "voluntary actions."]

8. A. Piper, "Individuum," in *Handbuch philosophischer Grundbegriffe*, 3 vols., ed. H. Krings, H. M. Baumgartner and C. Wild (Munich: Kösel-Verlag) 2: 728–737.

9. "Individuum," in *Enzyklopädie Philosophie und Wissenschaftstheorie*, ed. J. Mittelstraß (Mannheim, Vienna & Zurich: Bibliographisches Institut) 2: 229ff.

10. The expression "*einzigartig*" ["unique" or "singular"—from '*einzig*,' which means 'sole' or 'only,' and '*Art*,' which means 'kind' or 'species.'—Trans.] itself attests to the tradition that differentiates genera in terms of species (*Arten*).

11. "Individuum, Individualität," in *Historisches Wörterbuch der Philosophie*, ed. Joachim Ritter and Karlfried Gründer (Basel & Stuttgart: Schwabe & Co., 1976), 300ff.

12. G. W. von Leibniz, *The Monadology*, trans. Robert Latta (Oxford: Oxford University Press, 1898), §9, p. 222.

13. G. W. F. Hegel, *Aesthetics* 1: 61. (German: *Theorie-Werkausgabe* 13: 89.)

14. Friedrich Schiller, *On the Aesthetic Education of Man*, trans. Reginald Snell (New York: Ungar, 1965), eleventh letter, pp. 63–64.

15. Theodor Adorno, *Negative Dialectics*, trans. E. B. Ashton (New York: Seabury Press, 1973), 351.

16. Dieter Henrich, *Fluchtlinien* (Frankfurt: Suhrkamp, 1982), 20.

17. Johann Gottlieb Fichte, *The Science of Ethics*, trans. A. E. Kroeger (London: Kegan Paul, Tranch, Trübner & Co., 1907), 233–234. (German: *System der Sittenlehre*, in *Fichtes Werke*, ed. Fritz Medicus [Leipzig: Meiner] 2: 616.)

18. For what follows cf. ibid. 6ff. (German: 2: 395ff.)

19. Ibid., 231, translation altered. (German: 2: 614.)

20. Ibid., 232, translation altered. (German: 2: 614–615.)

21. Ibid., 232f. (German: 2: 615)

22. J. G. Fichte, *Science of Rights*, trans. A. E. Kroeger (Philadelphia: Lippincott, 1869), 18. (German: *Grundlage des Naturrechts*, in *Fichtes Werke* 2: 12.)

23. Ibid., 17. (German: 2: 12.)

24. J. G. Fichte, *Science of Ethics*, 243–244, translation altered. (German: 2: 625–626.)

25. Michael Theunissen, *The Other*, trans. Christopher Macann (Cambridge, Mass.: MIT Press, 1984), 187ff.

26. Wilhelm von Humboldt, "Über die Verschiedenheiten des menschlichen Sprachbaus (1827–1829)," in *Werke*, ed. Andreas Flintner and Klaus Giel (Darmstadt: Wissenschaftliche Buchgesellschaft, 1963), 3: 160–161.

27. Soren Kierkegaard, *The Sickness Unto Death*, trans. Howard V. Hong and Edna H. Hong (Princeton: Princeton University Press, 1980), 13–21.

28. Soren Kierkegaard, *Either/Or*, 2 vols., trans. Howard V. Hong and Edna H. Hong (Princeton: Princeton University Press, 1987), 2: 216.

29. Ibid. 2: 251.

30. Ibid. 2: 250–251.

31. For the following cf. Hans Robert Jauss, *Aesthetic Experience and Literary Hermeneutics*, trans. Michael Shaw (Minneapolis: University of Minnesota Press, 1982), 142ff.

32. Jean-Jacques Rousseau, "Lettres à Malesherbes," in *Oeuvres Complètes*, Pleiade Edition (Geneva: Gallimard, 1959) 1: 1133. (German: "Vier Briefe," in *Schriften*, ed. J. Ritter, 1: 480.)

33. Ibid.

34. Ibid. (German: 1: 481.)

35. Ernst Tugendhat, *Self-Consciousness and Self-Determination*, trans. Paul Stern (Cambridge, Mass.: MIT Press, 1986).

36. George Herbert Mead, "Social Consciousness and the Consciousness of Meaning," in *Selected Writings*, ed. Andrew Reck (Chicago: University of Chicago Press, 1964), 123ff.; "What Social Objects Must Psychology Presuppose?," *Selected Writings*, 105ff.;

"The Mechanism of Social Consciousness," *Selected Writings,* 134ff.; "The Social Self," *Selected Writings,* 142ff.

37. G. H. Mead, "The Social Self," 142.

38. Cf. Hans Joas, *G. H. Mead, A Contemporary Re-examination of His Thought,* trans. Raymond Meyer (Cambridge, Mass.: MIT Press, 1986).

39. G. H. Mead, "The Social Self," 146.

40. Ibid.

41. Otherwise, one would not be able to take the reservation into account which Dieter Henrich presents in "Was ist Metaphysik—was Moderne?," in *Konzepte* (Frankfurt, 1987), 34ff.

42. G. H. Mead, "The Definition of the Psychical," in *Selected Writings,* 40. [The original, unabridged version of this article appears in *Decennial Publications of the University of Chicago,* first series, vol. III (Chicago: University of Chicago Press, 1903), 77ff.]

43. Ibid., 55.

44. G. H. Mead, "Social Consciousness and the Consciousness of Meaning," 131.

45. Mead refers to McDougall here: "Social Psychology as Counterpart to Physiological Psychology," in *Selected Writings,* 97–98.

46. G. H. Mead, *Mind, Self and Society* (Chicago: University of Chicago Press, 1934), 174.

47. G. H. Mead, "The Social Self," 145.

48. Jürgen Habermas, *Theory of Communicative Action,* 2 vols., trans. Thomas McCarthy (Boston: Beacon Press, 1984, 1987), 2: 15–21.

49. [Translator's note: Although the German terms *"Selbstbeziehung"* and *"Selbstverhältnis"* would usually be synonymous, in this essay Habermas uses them to distinguish between the two different ways in which the subject can take up a relation to itself— the first cognitive, the second practical. To mark this distinction in English, in this essay I have translated *"Selbstbeziehung"* with "self-relation" and *"Selbstverhältnis"* with "relation-to-self." Unfortunately, this translation does not preserve certain connotations of the German terms that are relevant to the distinction being drawn by Habermas. The reflexive verb *"sich beziehen,"* for example, also means "to refer," giving *"Selbstbeziehung"* the cognitive overtones of "self-reference." The reflexive verb *"sich verhalten,"* on the other hand, often means to "behave" or "conduct oneself," and this practical connotation still resonates in *"Selbstverhältnis."*]

50. G. H. Mead, *Mind, Self, and Society,* 173ff.

51. J. Habermas, *Theory of Communicative Action* 2: 31–39.

52. G. H. Mead, "The Genesis of the Self and Social Control," in *Selected Writings,* 284.

53. Ibid., 285. [Translator's note: The German has "ego-identity" (*Ich-Identität*) in place of Mead's "self."]

54. Ibid., 288. [Translator's note: The German has "of our communication community" (*unserer Kommunikationsgemeinschaft*) in place of Mead's "of the universe of discourse."]

55. G. H. Mead, *Mind, Self, and Society*, 221.

56. Ibid., 199.

57. G. H. Mead, "Philanthropy from the Point of View of Ethics," in *Selected Writings*, 404. [Translator's note: The German has "unbounded communication community" (*unbegrenzte Kommunikationsgemeinschaft*) in place of Mead's "universe of discourse."]

58. Ibid., 404–405.

59. G. H. Mead, *Mind, Self, and Society*, 168.

60. G. H. Mead, "Philanthropy from the Point of View of Ethics," 405.

61. Ibid., 404. [Emphasis by Habermas.]

62. G. H. Mead, *Mind, Self, and Society*, 168. [Interpolation by Habermas.]

63. Ibid., 201.

64. G. H. Mead, "The Genesis of the Self and Social Control," 276.

65. G. H. Mead, "Natural Rights and the Theory of the Political Institution," in *Selected Writings*, 150ff.

66. H. Brunkhorst, *Der Intellektuelle im Land der Mandarine* (Frankfurt, 1987).

67. G. H. Mead, *Gesammelte Aufsätze*, ed. Hans Joas (Frankfurt: Suhrkamp, 1980), vol. 2, part III. [Contains the following articles: "The Working Hypothesis in Social Reform," in *Selected Writings*, 3ff.; "Review of G. LeBon: 'The Psychology of Socialism'," *American Journal of Sociology*, 5 (1899): 404ff.; "Review of Jane Addams: 'The Newer Ideal of Peace'," *American Journal of Sociology*, 13 (1907): 121ff.; "The Social Settlement: Its Basis and Function," *The University Record* (Chicago), 12 (1908): 108ff.; "Review of B. M. Anderson: 'Social Value, A Study in Economic Theory'," *Psychological Bulletin*, 8 (1911): 432ff.; "Natural Rights and the Theory of the Political Institution," op. cit.; "The Psychological Bases of Internationalism," *Survey*, 33 (1913–14): 443–444; "Review of Thorstein Veblen: 'The Nature of Peace and the Terms of its Perpetuation'," *Journal of Political Economy*, 26 (1918): 752ff.; "Review of William A. White: 'Thoughts of a Psychiatrist on the War and After'" (unpublished in English); and "National-Mindedness and International-Mindedness," in *Selected Writings*, 355ff.]

68. P. F. Strawson, *Individuals* (London: Methuen, 1959).

69. Ernst Tugendhat, *Self-Consciousness and Self-Determination*.

70. Jürgen Habermas, "What is Universal Pragmatics?," in *Communication and the Evolution of Society*, trans. Thomas McCarthy (Boston: Beacon Press, 1979), 1–68.

71. [Translator's note: "Identity" (*Identität*) is the term used to render Mead's "self" throughout the German translation of *Mind, Self, and Society (Geist, Identität und Gesellschaft*).]

72. J. Habermas, *Theory of Communicative Action* 2: 59–60.

73. The reconstructive analysis of language use can no more be undertaken from the perspective of the observer than can a transcendental-philosophical investigation of cognitive achievements. Just as the transcendental philosopher carries out his investigation in the attitude of a first person who relates himself to himself, so Mead carries out his linguistic pragmatics in the attitude of a participant in interaction who relates himself to himself from the perspective of a second person.

74. [Translator's note: *Freisetzen* means to emancipate, liberate, or set free—but also to "release" or to "lay off" a person from employment. "Release" best captures this ambiguity, which is central to Habermas's argument; I thus use this term to translate "*freisetzen*" and its derivatives in the remainder of this text.]

75. Claus Offe, "Die Utopie der Null-Option," in *Die Moderne*, ed. J. Berger, *Soziale Welt*, Sonderheft 4 (1986).

76. Niklas Luhmann, *Politische Theorie im Wohlfahrtsstaat* (Munich, 1981), 25–26.

77. Ullrich Beck, *Risikogesellschaft. Auf dem Weg in eine andere Moderne* (Frankfurt, 1986), 216.

78. Ibid., 219.

79. Ibid., 211.

80. Ibid., 207.

81. Ibid., 206.

82. Ibid., 192.

83. Ibid., 200.

84. Ibid., 136.

8

Philosophy and Science as Literature?

I

Jurists like Savigny, historians like Burckhardt, psychologists like Freud, philosophers like Adorno, were also important writers. Every year a German literary academy gives a prize for scientific prose. Kant and Hegel could not have given suitable expression to their thoughts if they had not given a completely new form to the inherited language of their discipline. In philosophy and the human sciences, even more than in physics, the propositional content of statements cannot be separated from the rhetorical form of its presentation. And even in physics, theory (as Mary Hesse has shown) is not free of metaphors, which are necessary if new models, new ways of seeing things and new problematics are to be made plausible (with intuitive recourse to the preunderstanding established in ordinary language). No innovative break with tried-and-true cognitive forms and scientific habits is possible without linguistic innovation: this connection is hardly controversial.

Freud was *also* a great writer. When we say that, however, we do not mean that his scientific genius expresses itself in the creative power of his flawless prose. It was not his eminent literary ability that enabled him to discover a new continent but rather unbiased clinical vision, speculative power, sensitivity and fearlessness in dealing skeptically with himself, persistence, curiosity—that is to say, the virtues of the productive scientist. Nobody regards it as inappropriate to treat Freud's texts as literature, too—but are they that alone or in the first place? Until recently we were certain of the answer; now the voices are multiplying that respond with questions of their own. Is the orientation toward truth really a sufficient criterion for the traditional demarcation between science and literature? The influential school of deconstructionism places the usual distinctions between genres in question. The later Heidegger still distinguishes between thinkers and poets. But he treats texts by Anaximander and Aristotle no differently than texts by Hölderlin and Trakl. Paul de Man reads Rousseau no differently than Proust and Rilke. Derrida works on Husserl and Saussure no differently than on Artaud. Is it not an illusion to believe that texts by Freud and texts by Joyce can be sorted according to characteristics that definitively identify them as theory on the one hand and as fiction on the other?

In our newspapers and cultural periodicals, the two are still separated—nonfiction and literature. There are different headings: first the fiction, then the search for truth; in front the products of poets and writers, in back the works of philosophers and scientists (to the extent that they are of general interest). It was meant as a demonstration when the *Frankfurter Allgemeine Zeitung* dedicated the first page of a literary supplement to the book of a philosopher, not indeed to one of his excellent studies in the history of ideas but to a manageable collection with meditations and sketches. The reviewer did not beat around the bush for long before giving an explanation of the demonstration: "In the future when we speak of the leading writers of the land, we will also have to mention the name Blumenberg. He collects glosses, anecdotes, philosophical tales; in short, the ongoing stories of a world-historical disillusionment, which in their best parts can be compared with the paradoxical essays of Jorge Luis Borges."[1] What interests me is not the orotund evaluation, but the liquidation of the distinction between genres.[2] The blurb on the cover had already suggested it: the author is confident "of the indeterminacy of the genre in which his texts could be placed."

Tempora mutantur. When Adorno's *Minima Moralia* appeared a generation ago, neither the author nor the reader had problems with the genre. The fact that an important philosopher who was also a brilliant writer had published a volume of maxims and meditations did not in those days prevent the reviewers from recommending that this collection of aphorisms be read as if it were a major philosophical work. For no one doubted that in each of the polished fragments the theory appeared in its entirety. Is the issue here one of two incomparable cases—or only one of a changed understanding of the *same* thing?

II

The leveling of the distinction between the genres of philosophy and science on the one hand and that of literature on the other hand is the expression of an understanding of literature that is derived from philosophical discussions. The context of these discussions is the turn from the philosophy of consciousness to the philosophy of language, specifically that variation of the linguistic turn that does away with the legacy of the philosophy of consciousness in a particularly relentless way. Every connotation of self-consciousness, self-determination, and self-realization has to have been exorcised from the basic concepts of philosophy before language (instead of subjectivity) can declare its independence in this way—whether as an epochal destining of Being, as the frenzy of signifiers, or as a shoving match between discourses, the borders between literal and metaphorical meaning, between logic and rhetoric, and between serious and fictional speech are washed away in the flow of a universal textual occurrence (which is presided over indiscriminately by thinkers and poets). To the genealogy of this thought there belong, roughly speaking, the early Heidegger, structuralism, and the later Heidegger.

The circle in which a subject who aims at self-knowledge becomes trapped was already noted by Fichte; by referring itself to itself, the subject makes itself into an object and thus fails to attain itself as spontaneously generative subjectivity. Heidegger breaks out of this circle with his analysis of Being-in-the-world in *Being and Time*. He conceives of theoretical or objectifying thinking as a derivative mode of a more primordial practical loss of world, and, later, he interprets the tendency to objectivism as the flipside of a subjectivity that is set on self-assertion. Thought that represents and disposes over things receives a place within the history of metaphysics between Descartes and Nietzsche. We can think of this critique as the idealist counterpart to a materialist critique of reification that goes back to Marx and Max Weber. Attempts to break the basic conceptual spell cast by the subject-centered thinking of the philosophy of consciousness *always* take advantage of the transition to the paradigm of language, a transition that was, however, also made in analytic philosophy without any connection to a critique of instrumental reason. But the directions differ in terms of the concept of language that is set down in each case; this in turn determines whether each merely transforms the normative content of the concept of reason that had been developed from Kant to Hegel—or whether it more or less radically rejects it.

The *communications-theoretic* approach follows Humboldt's lead and begins with the model of mutual understanding in language; it overcomes the philosophy of the subject by uncovering the *intersubjective structure* of reciprocal recognition and the interlocking perspectives within the 'self' of self-consciousness, self-determination, and self-realization. The epistemic self-relation and the practical relation-to-self are deconstructed, but in such a way that the received concepts of the philosophy of reflection *are transformed* into intersubjective knowledge, communicative freedom, and individuation through socialization.

The *structuralist* approach follows Saussure's lead and begins with the model provided by grammatical rule-systems; and it overcomes the philosophy of the subject when it traces the achievements of the knowing and acting subject, who is bound up in his linguistic practices, back to the foundational structures and generative rules of a grammar. Subjectivity thereby loses the power of spontaneously generating a world. Levi-Strauss, who extends this approach into anthropology, maintains that the mirror of savage thought exposes the philosophy of the subject as the groundplan for the illusory self-understanding of modern societies. Of course, this destruction is not yet extended to the observing scientist himself; the ethnologist's gaze does not err when it penetrates familiar phenomena and grasps them as the anonymous work of unconsciously operating mind.

When the *poststructuralist* thinkers surrender this scientistic self-understanding, they also surrender the only moment that was still retained from the concept of reason developed in the modern period. They follow the lead of the later Heidegger and begin with a model of language that treats it as an occurrence of truth; the philosophy of the subject is overcome when the modern interpretation of the world is comprehended as one event in an epochal discourse that both prejudices and makes possible all innerworldly occurring—whether one conceives of it as an event within a directed history of metaphysics, as Derrida still does, or instead as an event in the contingent up-and-down of power-knowledge formations, as Foucault does. The later Heidegger conceives of language as the house of self-adaptive (*sich schickenden*) 'being'; hence, the various stages in the understanding of 'being' still retained for him a transcendent relation to a 'being' that always remains *itself*. Foucault eliminates even this last weak connotation of a philosophy of history related to truth. *All* validity claims become immanent to particular discourses. They are simultaneously absorbed into the totality of some one of the blindly occurring discourses and left at the mercy of the "hazardous play" among these discourses as each overpowers another. This conception demands that "the subject of knowledge be sacrificed." Science is shoved aside by genealogy, which "gives rise to questions concerning our native land, native language, or the laws that govern us[;] its intention is to reveal the heterogeneous systems which, masked by the self, inhibit the formation of any form of identity."[3]

In the wake of the disintegration of transcendental subjectivity, the analysis is directed to an anonymous occurring of language, an occurring that releases worlds from within itself and swallows worlds back up, which is superordinate to every ontic history and to every innerworldly practice, which reaches through everything, through the now porous borders of the ego, of the author, and of his work. This kind of analysis "permits the dissociation of the self, its recognition and displacement as an empty synthesis, in liberating a profusion of lost events."[4] For Foucault, for Derrida, for the poststructuralists, the issue is treated as if it were settled: "The breakdown of philosophical subjectivity and its dispersion in a language that dispossesses it while multiplying it within the space created by its absence is probably one of the fundamental structures of contemporary thought."[5] In passing through structuralism, this movement of thought has made transcendental subjectivity disappear *without a trace,* and indeed in such a way that one also loses sight of the system of world relations, speaker perspectives, and validity claims that is inherent in linguistic communication itself. Without this reference system, however, the distinction between levels of reality, between fiction and reality, between everyday practice and extra-ordinary experience, and between the corresponding kinds of texts and genres becomes impossible and even pointless. The house of 'being' is itself sucked into the maelstrom of an undirected linguistic current.

This radical contextualism reckons on a language made fluid, one that continues to exist only in the mode of its flowing, so that all innerworldly movements first emerge out of this flow. This concept finds only weak support in the philosophical discussion. It is primarily based upon aesthetic experiences or, to be more precise, on evidence from the domains of literature and literary theory.

III

Italo Calvino, who is both an imaginative storyteller and a knowledgeable analytical thinker who participates above all in the French discussion, addresses the topic of the "Levels of Reality in Literature" from the point of view of an author considering the sentence: "I write that Homer tells that Ulysses says: I have listened to the Sirens' song." Calvino analyzes the various levels of reality that the writer generates when he (1) reflexively refers to his act of writing by (2) fabricating another storyteller who (3) has one of the characters appearing in his story report an experience with contents (4). The levels (2) through (4) are reality levels within the work, or fabricated levels of reality. For this region the text does not lay claim to the credibility of a historical report, a documentation, or the statement of a witness but to "the kind of credibility peculiar to the literary text, in parentheses, as it were, matched on the reader's part by an attitude Coleridge defined as 'suspension of disbelief'."[6] A literary text is marked by the fact that it does not come forth with the claim that it documents an occurrence in the world; nonetheless, it does want to draw the reader into the spell of an imagined occurrence step by step, until he follows the narrated events *as if* they *were* real. Even the fabricated reality must be capable of being experienced by the reader as a reality that is real—otherwise a novel does not accomplish what it is supposed to.

Now, since the literary text bridges the gap between fiction and reality in this manner, Calvino is interested in the question of whether a text could be reflexive in such a way that it could even bridge the reality gap separating the text itself, as a body of signs, from the empirical circumstances of its *own* surroundings—could, as it were, absorb everything that is real into itself. It would thereby expand itself into a totality behind which one could not go. In any event, the idea of a linguistic reality that posits itself in the work as something absolute and that encompasses everything is what makes Calvino's reflections relevant in our context.

If the text is to totalize the fabricated world in this way, it has first to capture reflexively three world-relations in which it is itself embedded: the relation to the world in which the author lives and has put the text together; then the relationship between fiction and reality in general; finally, the relation to the reality that is intended in the narrative, which must at least be capable of appearing to be the real reality. The text intersects with a reality that is outside of it in these three places: wherever it distinguishes itself from the thoughts of the author; wherever it causes a difference to emerge between the fictional world and reality in general; finally, wherever the believability of the text depends upon the reader relating what is depicted in the narrative to a world that is *supposed* by him *as real* and independent from the text.

(1) The interval between text and author can be bridged by the text when it takes the author up into itself as a first-

person narrator. Following the schema of the aforementioned representative sentence, Calvino thematizes the element "I write that . . ." in terms of a famous example:

> Gustave Flaubert the author of the complete works of Gustave Flaubert projects outside of himself the Gustave Flaubert who is the author of *Madame Bovary,* who in turn projects from himself the character of a middle-class married woman in Rouen, Emma Bovary, who projects from herself that Emma Bovary whom she dreams of being.[7]

In the end the semantic circle between text and author must close itself, according to Flaubert's classic remark: *"Madame Bovary, c'est moi."* The author must be seen as a dependent variable within the series of his own products, and as that alone:

> How much of the "I" who shapes the characters is in fact an "I" who has been shaped by the characters? The further we go toward distinguishing the various levels that go to make up the "I" of the author, the more we realize that many of these levels do not belong to the author as an individual but to collective culture, to the historical period or the deep sedimentary layers of the species.[8]

The conclusion that Calvino draws from this sounds like a sentence out of Foucault or Derrida: "The starting point of the chain, the real primary subject of the verb 'to write,' seems ever more distant from us, more rarefied and indistinct. Perhaps it is a phantom 'I,' an empty space, an absence."[9]

(2) The text is capable of engulfing not only the author but, by making the operation of generating a new world within itself transparent, it can engulf the categorial distinction between fiction and reality as well. Calvino clarifies this with reference to the second element of his representative sentence: "I write that Homer tells. . . ." The storyteller can introduce a figure who experiences and assimilates the collision of incompatible worlds: "The character of Don Quixote clears the way for the clash and encounter of two antithetical languages, or, rather, of two literary worlds without any ground in common: the chivalric-supernatural and the picaresque-comic."[10] Cervantes does not simply open up a new dimension in this way; rather, he allows a new, quixotic reading of the world as a whole to emerge from within the experiential horizon of a

character who stands at the intersection of two worlds that are preformed in literature. In this character, the text self-referentially mirrors the selfsame operation of world-disclosing that makes the text itself into a literary text.

(4)   With reference to the last element of the representative sentence, ". . . I have listened to the Sirens' song," Calvino discusses the possibility of building a final bridge. Once again, the text pushes against a reality that is external to it wherever it fabricates the object-relation of the narrated experiences and actions; for the text to be believable, the world its characters are related to must be capable of being presumed as objective. The reader must be able to regard what is depicted as real. Now at this point Calvino slips into speculation, because a gap opens up that the text cannot easily close. In order always to fit in with its readers' expectations about reality, the text would have to control and steer their horizon of ontological expectations. An author is a contemporary of his own text, and he experiences the repercussions of his product in a different way than a reader experiences an alien text that he approaches from a context completely different from its own, without being bound to it in advance though internal strands of effective history. Calvino reasons that in relation to this exposed flank the text could perhaps secure itself by closing itself upon itself reflexively—that is, by reflecting itself as a whole in one of its parts: "What do the Sirens sing? One possible hypothesis is that their song is nothing more or less than the *Odyssey*."[11]

But this becoming reflexive of the semantic content is a defensive reaction, one that alerts the reader to the plan. How the text might also capture the reality suppositions of the narrated occurrences themselves is a problem that can only be solved through the relation of the text to the reader. Whether the text is able to effect that peculiar 'suspension of disbelief' depends upon the reader's suppositions about reality.

(3)   I have not yet mentioned the reader-relation of the text as a fourth world-relation. Calvino treats it (not very plausibly) in terms of the third element of his representative sentence, "Ulysses says. . . ." He refers to the principle of the enframing narrative that imports fictitious readers or hearers into the story's occurrences. But the ladies and gentlemen whom Boc-

caccio has fleeing before the plague from Florence to a bucolic country seat in the year 1348 cannot *represent* a German reader from the year 1888 or a Japanese reader from the year 1988, especially not with respect to the authenticating ontological preunderstanding with which these readers approach the text. Calvino, then, also concludes his brilliant investigation more cautiously. As a literary theorist he does not give in to the temptation to infer from the reflexive encapsulation of fictional worlds a model that would elevate language to the rank of a temporalizing original power: "literature does not recognize Reality as such, but only *levels*"—that is, the fictional levels of reality within the universe of the written words, in which that "credibility peculiar to literary texts" resides.[12]

But it is otherwise with Calvino the writer. In one of his novels he introduces a writer who develops the poststructuralist idea of language in his diary. This writer feels the desire to hand himself over to the pull of an anonymous and all-encompassing linguistic occurrence that directs everything from behind the scenes: "For the writer who wants to annul himself in order to give voice to what is outside him, two paths open: either write a book that could be the unique book, that exhausts the whole in its pages; or write all books, to pursue the whole through its partial images." With Silas Flannery, his image of the ideal writer, Calvino opts against the first, the metaphysical concept, and for a radicalized historicism of language: "The unique book, which contains the whole, could only be the sacred text, the total word revealed. But I do not believe totality can be contained in language; my problem is what remains outside, the unwritten, the unwritable. The only way left me is that of writing all books, writing the books of all possible authors." With the novel from which this passage is taken, Calvino undertakes the literary experiment of capturing in literature itself the appropriation of literature by the reader.[13] He wants, in literary practice itself, to make the border between fiction and reality perceptible as mere appearance, as a difference that is generated by the text itself—and to make this text (like every other) recognizable as a fragment of a *universal* text, a primordial text, which knows no limits because the dimensions of possible delimitations, space and time, first emerge from within it.

IV

If on a winter's night a traveler is a novel composed of the beginnings of ten novels. These are set in an enframing narrative that depicts a male reader and a female reader hunting for the continuations of the fragments, searching for the lost original. Artfully interwoven with this metanarrative is in turn a meta-reflection of the author of the seventh incipient novel, whose voice Calvino uses to reveal to us, in the conversation of the ideal author with the ideal (female) reader, the intentions that guide Calvino himself in the construction of the multiply self-referential text. Surface motives pop up first here. Doesn't the jaded reader put down every new novel out of boredom after the first thirty pages anyway? Worse yet: doesn't the author himself have the feeling after a few pages that he has already said everything? Couldn't a novel that puts the reader on the trail of ten further novels reduce the unhappy complexity of the growing torrent of books? But another motive should already be taken more seriously: the desire to submit the reader to an exercise that is otherwise required only by serialized novels. Calvino has his reader cross the border between his everyday life and an alien fictional world ten times, and ten times he tears him away, at the high point of the suspense, from an illusion that then turns out not to have been one; ten times he drops him roughly on the ground of trivial everyday practice with unsatisfied curiosity about the continuation of the story that has been withheld:

I feel [notes Flannery] the thrill of a beginning that can be followed by multiple developments, inexhaustibly. . . . The romantic fascination produced in the pure state by the first sentences of the first chapter of many novels is soon lost in the continuation of the story. . . . I would like to be able to write a book that is only an *incipit*, that maintains for its whole duration the potentiality of the beginning. . . . Would it be the beginning of one tale inside another, as in the *Arabian Nights?* (177)

However, the heart of the matter is first reached only by a further consideration: "I, too, would like to erase myself and find for each book another I, another voice, another name, to be reborn; but my aim is to capture in the book the illegible world, without center, without ego, without I." (180) The identifiable person of the author, the unity of a work that is localizable in space and time and has a beginning and an end, the rootedness of the written work in the context of its genesis—this illusion of individuation gets in the way of the truth of literature, the truth of a book that wants to be "the written counterpart of the unwritten world" (172):

> How well I would write if *I* were not here! If between the white page and the writing of words and stories that take shape and disappear without anyone's ever writing them there were not interposed that uncomfortable partition which is my person! . . . If I were only a hand, a severed hand that grasps a pen and writes. . . . Who would move this hand? The anonymous throng? The spirit of the times? The collective unconscious? I do not know. It is not in order to be the spokesman for something definable that I would like to erase myself.[14] Only to transmit the writable that waits to be written, the tellable that nobody tells. (171)

In this longing to strip away all that is subjective, to become an impersonal scrivener, two things are expressed: the genuine experience of the process of world-disclosing, or the linguistic innovation that allows us to see with other eyes what happens in the world; but also the desire to *overdraw* this aesthetic experience, to totalize the contact with the extra-ordinary, to absorb the everyday. Everything that piles up as problems in the world, that is resolved or is left undone, is supposed to be reduced to a mere function of the opening of ever newer horizons of experience and of different ways of seeing things. Such a need is only satisfied by the concept of the book that writes itself: "'I read, therefore *it* writes.'" (176)

Calvino takes experiences of the world-disclosing productivity of linguistic artworks and totalizes them in a concept of language that, not accidentally, coincides with Derrida's theory. This theory is, as it were, acted out in the search for the continuations that have disappeared in so mysterious a way, the continuations that would complete the received fragments and return to them their original form and integrity—which they have never possessed and will never be able to achieve. Ludmilla, the reader who is read, dives with relish into every new novel and lets herself be consumed by every new world with the expectation that this world will form a whole with beginning and end; this Ludmilla has indeed understood that the person of the author has little to do with the role of the author, that books emerge almost naturally, are namely "produced" in the same way "as a pumpkin vine produces pumpkins." (189) Yet her hunt for the continuations also lets us recognize what the ideal reader has not yet understood: that there has never been an original. Only her alter ego, the scheming translator Marana, who counterfeits all manuscripts, knows that. Marana dreams of a "plot of apocryphers" (193), and this dream reveals the truth *about* literature.

With his machinations Marana fights against the idea "that behind each book there is someone who guarantees a truth in that world of ghosts and inventions by the mere fact . . . of having identified himself with that construction of words." He dreams of "a literature made entirely of apocrypha, of false attributions, of imitations and counterfeits and pastiches." (159) Marana/Derrida systematically produces uncertainties about the identity of works, authors, and generative contexts. He makes sure that two copies of a novel that look completely alike contain two completely different novels and that counterfeits circulating under the successful author Flannery's name resemble the original down to the last detail. He replaces one manuscript with another and mixes up works and authors, languages, and places of origin. He knows the secret that Calvino would like his reader to discover: that pages continually migrate from one book to another. Calvino turns the search for the books that have apparently disappeared into an exercise that is supposed to bring to light the truth *about* literature: there are no originals, only their traces, no texts, only readings, no fictional worlds *in contrast to* a reality.

If the text dissolves into the event that is the search for apocryphal texts, however, then it can never exist except in the fleeting act of being received. The book lives only in the moment of its being read. It is the recipient who steers the production. The writer, who knows the truth about literature and extinguishes himself as author, tries to plug into the circuitry of his readers: "perhaps the woman I observe with the spyglass knows what I should write . . . what she knows for certain is what she expects, what void my words would have to fill."[15] He feels the need "to write anything at all, but thinking that it must pass through *her* reading." (172)

These are the ideas from the aesthetics of reception that Calvino incorporates into his novel as commentary at the metareflexive level. This theory, which feeds on an aesthetic experience and yet shoots far beyond the realm of the aesthetic, still has to prove itself (and here Calvino is more consistent than Derrida) in aesthetic practice itself. Calvino must first *carry through* the experiment of a novel that is consistently written in the second person before he can *show* that the relation of the novel to the reader need not remain external to the text. The theory requires proof, worked through in practice, that the literary text is able to dissolve its identity, which is determined through the difference to everyday life, by somehow incorporating within itself its reception by the reader—and that it is thus able to redeem literature's claim to encompass everything. If the experiment were to succeed, then it would also no longer be correct to speak of a theory in the strict sense. What I at first called theory would then prove to be a piece of literature, such as that which also appears in the novel. Literature and literary theory would be assimilated.

V

The novel in the second person turns the reader into a member of the cast of characters who hovers between a fictional world and his real world, who is both inside and outside: inside as one among several fabricated persons, but at the same time outside, because the character of the reader who is read refers to the actual reader and to this extent establishes a reference beyond the book. By reflecting its relation to the reader, the novel hubristically bursts the limits of fiction, even as it uses the ways and means of fiction.

The borders of the novel are marked by the beginning and the end of its encounter with 'the' reader. Calvino captures this circumstance in his novel. Calvino's *If on a winter's night a traveler* begins with the reader in a bookstore buying a copy of Calvino's *If on a winter's night a traveler* hot from the press and immediately submerging himself in a reading that literarily ends with the last sentence on the last page of the book. Now Calvino takes up a dual relationship to his reader. He narrates how 'the' (male) reader meets a (female) reader, how he becomes entangled with her in an adventurous story (the search for the lost books), how during this time he falls in love with her, sleeps with her, and marries her. To this extent the two occupy the normal roles of characters in a novel, whose lives the author controls without any limitation. This sovereignty is grammatically hemmed in, at least, when the real reader is addressed in the second person; for now the latter is in a position to reply. The autonomy of the reader grows with a threefold refraction of this relation to the author.

The author, who is identical with the first-person narrator of the enframed incipient novels, first takes the reader by the hand and cunningly leads him into these fictional worlds. Surrealistically, the world of the reader who is read is interpenetrated by the world that starts to disclose itself to him through his reading, and it forms a web that holds present the process of working into and submerging into the second-order fictional occurrences. The first novel within the novel begins with the words: "The novel begins in a railway station, a locomotive huffs, steam from a piston covers the opening of the chapter, a cloud of smoke hides part of the first paragraph. There is someone looking through the befogged glass, he opens the glass door of the bar. . . ." (10) At the same time, the reader who is read and the real reader each has the voice of the author in his head: "Your attention, as reader, is now completely concentrated on the woman, already for several pages you have been circling around her, I have—no, the author has—been circling around the feminine presence. . . ." (20)

On the next level of reflection, the author lets the reader in on just this artful construction of bringing the reader into the novel. The author directs himself for example to Ludmilla, who 'the' reader has in the meantime met as a sympathetic soul:

What are you like, Other Reader? It is time for this book in the second person to address itself no longer to a general male you, perhaps brother and double of a hypocrite I, but directly to you who appeared already in the second chapter as the Third Person necessary . . . for something to happen between that male Second Person and the female Third . . . (141)

The level of the recipients must take on its own life if the lone reader appearing in the novel is not to remain the bare mirror image of the author.

To be sure, it is only on a third level of reflection that the male reader and the female reader obtain the autonomy of taking a position with "yes" or "no" toward the reflections of their opposite number and of putting their *own* ideas into play. Curiously enough, they become autonomous when they confront the author Calvino not in the role of the second person but as third persons within the diary entries of the writer Flannery (Calvino's theorizing alter ego). It is noteworthy that the male reader and the female reader do not owe this independence to the grammatical role that is ascribed to them here, that of a triply enframed character in a novel; rather, they derive it from their social role as partners in conversation with a writer who draws them into *argumentation,* into an almost literary-theoretical discussion. Calvino achieves the goal of incorporating the reader-relation into the literary text, therefore, not with literary means but only insofar as he succeeds in motivating his real readers to forget the world of the novel for a moment and to take the arguments that are stated in it by fictional characters seriously *as arguments.* He has to put the laws of the novel into abeyance in order to capture in the novel that which belongs to its environment, namely, the possible reactions of *a* reader. For it is only in the role of a participant in argumentation that *the* reader—the one Calvino provides himself in thought—is transformed into that of *any* reader whatsoever.

The eminently clever Calvino naturally sees exactly the problem that would have to be solved. In order to hold his place open for every real reader, the depicted reader must, on the one hand, be an abstract placeholder. 'The' reader therefore remains nameless. One has to wonder whether as a man he is not already defined too specifically or too narrowly, or whether he is not too precisely identified by the acquisition of a copy of Calvino's latest novel "hot off the press," or by the urban milieu, the white-collar career, etc. On the other hand, 'the' reader has to take on his own specific characteristics and, despite all precautionary measures, step out of his anonymity, because as a character in a novel he cannot prevent himself from becoming entangled in a story. Calvino hopes that he can resolve this problem of effecting a grammatical division of labor by treating it in terms of content, namely, by dividing the reader's role between one partner who is masculine and anonymous and another who is feminine and vividly depicted. He finally tells 'the' other reader, 'the' female reader:

This book so far has been careful to leave open to the Reader who is reading the possibility of identifying himself with the Reader who is read: this is why he was not given a name, which would automatically have made him the equivalent of a Third Person, of a character (whereas to you, as Third Person, a name had to be given, Ludmilla), and so he has been kept a pronoun, in the abstract condition of pronouns, suitable for any attribute and any action. Let us see, Other Reader, if the book can succeed in drawing a true portrait of you, beginning with the frame and enclosing you from every side, establishing the outlines of your form. (141–142)

The vigorous yarn-spinner Calvino, who erects one arch of tension after another (and leaves them hanging in the air uncompleted), succeeds wonderfully at this, but only at the price of having gradually to take the anonymity of the fabricated reader away from him once he has fallen under Ludmilla's influence. On the level of the recipients, the story will become progressively more polarized. The one pole is formed by the dynamics of the action, which increasingly individualizes even the abstract you of 'the' reader, fills in the empty place of the singular term 'you' more and more with flesh and blood, and moves the second-person pronoun further and further into the vicinity of a proper name; the other pole is formed by a desperately defensive effort to preserve the grammatical fiction

of 'the' reader from the concretion of life, to keep his love for
Ludmilla, his first night with her, and his decision to marry
her as bland as possible, to place all this in brackets or, at best,
to illuminate it with the reflected light of parallel actions that
are being played out on other levels. The novel does not get
beyond the limits of the novel.

The fiction that transcends itself falls prey to the laws of
fiction. What Calvino wanted to demonstrate *with* the novel has
instead to be portrayed *within it:* the transition of the novel into
life and the presentation of life as reading. In Ludmilla, Calvino *depicts* the person whose life disappears into reading. He
depicts the power the written word has over life by accompanying Ludmilla with the foil provided by her sister, who
defends herself in vain against the pull of an irresistible textual
happening. Lotaria, the woman of '68, is placed under the
postmodern light of an ironic distancing. She regards literature
as a waste of time, continues to track the tendencies of the age,
and still wants to "solve problems." But she too is captured in
the end by the frequencies of her own word lists, by the frenzy
of signifiers. And even Irnerio, the nonreader on principal,
does not escape the world of books; the papier-mâché sculp-
tures that he makes out of Ludmilla's books end up in the
hands of art critics and on the pages of art catalogues. 'The'
reader is prompted: "You concentrate on your reading, trying
to shift your concern for her to the book, as if hoping to see
her come toward you from the pages." (140)

In short, Calvino *tells* a story whose scenes are literally played
out in the world of the book—in bookstores and publishing
houses, in literary-theory departments, in the studies of writers,
before shelves of books, in double beds that are dominated by
nighttime readings. But in the end he still remains the only
director of this world and gazes down from above upon his
male reader and his female reader, who remain third persons
even when they are second persons. No one hinders the sovereignty of the author: "Now you are man and wife, Reader
and Reader. A great double bed receives your parallel readings." (260) Ludmilla closes her book and asks her reader:
"'Turn off your light, too. Aren't you tired of reading?'" In

my copy this final page has no number. A last, vain attempt to *blur* the transition from the one world into the other?

VI

It is also an indication that even Ludmilla is let go into everyday life. The contact with the extra-ordinary remains limited to an interim; it can neither be made constant nor be blown up into a totality. Everyday life continues to place limits around literary texts, and neither they nor the aesthetic experiment that is made with them furnishes any corroboration for conceiving language as a universal textual occurrence that levels the difference between fiction and reality and overwhelms everything that is in the world. But what does literature refer to without being able to capture it? In what sense does everyday life *place limits* around literature?

In everyday communicative practice speech acts retain a force that they lose in literary texts. In the former setting they function in contexts of action in which participants cope with situations and—let's say it—have to solve problems. In the latter setting they are tailored to a reception that removes the burden of acting from the reader; the situations that he encounters, the problems that he faces, are not immediately his own. Literature does not invite the reader to take a position of the same kind that everyday communication invites from those who are acting. Both are caught up in stories (or histories), but in different ways. One angle from which this difference can be made clear is the connection between meaning and validity.

Throughout the prose of everyday life, the claims that are made for the truth of statements, the rightness of norms, the truthfulness of expressions, and the preference for certain values, all concern both the speaker and the addressee. The validity claims that appear within a literary text, on the other hand, possess this same binding force only for the persons appearing *in* it, not for the author and the reader. The transfer of validity is interrupted at the boundaries of the text; it does not extend through the communicative relation all the way to the reader. Literary speech acts are in this sense illocutionarily *disempowered*. The internal relation between the meaning and the validity of what is said survives intact only for the characters in the novel, for those in the third person or for those in the second person transformed into third persons (the depicted readers), but not for the real readers.

This decoupling keeps the reader from directing certain questions to the text: e.g., whether the Japanese versions of Flannery's novels, which Calvino has a person in the novel (the translator Marana) produce and at the same time denounce as counterfeits, are *in fact* counterfeits. The reader knows that what the author calls "counterfeit Flannerys" are counterfeit Flannerys. For the reader it is just not possible to "seize the function of the author." He alone determines what is valid and what is not; only he can credibly assure us that "there is no truth outside falsification."[16] (193) As soon as the author concedes to the reader the possibility of judging for himself whether what Flannery says to Ludmilla and how Ludmilla replies to Flannery is in fact accurate, he leaves behind the sovereign position of a literary author—but at the price of producing a *different* kind of text. When a reader takes a position toward the validity claims inside of the text just as he does "outside" in everyday life, he reaches right through the text to some subject matter (*Sache*)—and destroys the fiction.

It is in this way that the reader relates to philosophical and scientific texts. These texts elicit from him a kind of criticism that is directed to the validity claims raised within the text. His criticism does not refer *to* the text and the operation of world-disclosing that it carries out, as aesthetic criticism does; rather, it refers to what is said *in* the text about something in the world. The burden of action is also removed in a way from theoretical texts, but unlike literary texts, they distance themselves from everyday practice *without stopping the transfer of validity at their margins* and so without releasing the reader from the role of being addressed by the validity claims that are raised in the text itself.

The philosophical and the scientific author leave behind the sovereign position of the literary author, who pays for this position with another kind of dependence. The literary author's dependence on the eye-opening power of a language that is not at his disposition, to which he must also surrender himself in the contact with the extra-ordinary, is Calvino's theme. The scientific author, too, cannot free himself from this dependence completely—the philosophical author even less so. Adorno regarded the striking aphorism as the most appropriate form of presentation. *As a form* the aphorism is capable of expressing in language his secret ideal of knowledge, a Platonistic thought that cannot be expressed, at least not without contradiction, in the medium of speech that gives reasons: knowledge must actually burst the prison of discursive thought and terminate in pure intuition.[17] Blumenberg's inclination to the anecdotal betrays a different literary model, perhaps Georg Simmel, in any case not Nietzsche. Here, too, there is a correspondence between literary form and philosophical conviction: one who understands the rootedness of theory in the lifeworld in contextualist terms will want to discover the truth in the metaphors of the narrative.

But even Blumenberg's "philosophical narratives" and reflections do not cause the distinction between genres to disappear. They do not give up the orientation toward questions of truth. Unlike literary texts, one of which can parody another, repeat it while displacing it, or comment upon it, philosophical texts can *criticize* one another. Thus, for example, Blumenberg criticizes (without naming him) Adorno:

> To the extent that the opposition of science to error disappears because, namely, the results of science no longer meet with prejudices commensurate with them, then the acute urgency to be freed from something fades away. It was an extremely clear symptom when the outbreak of discontent with science was accompanied by a 'final attempt' on the part of those who live from science to maintain, by merely adding the epithet 'critical' to every possible discipline and to science as a whole, precisely the impression that they are still dealing with an opponent that is becoming ever more secretive and underhanded.[18]

One can refer to *Minima Moralia* to find out how Adorno would have replied to this metacritique.

Postscript

Even our reviewer, who discusses—in the same forum a half year later—Karl Kraus, has in the meantime come to see this and warns against the consequences of falsely turning science and philosophy into literature: "The prattle which Kraus heard from the press has now found its way into the sciences, the loci of rationality. Philosophers and historians, *Geisteswissenschaftler* in general, believe that they can dispense with arguments and are beginning to speak in fictions."[19]

Notes

1. F. Schirrmacher, "Das Lachen vor letzten Worten. Hans Blumenbergs 'Die Sorge geht über den Fluß'," *Frankfurter Allgemeine Zeitung* (November 17, 1987).

2. H. Schlaffner, "Ein Grund mehr zur Sorge," *Merkur* (April 1988), 328ff.

3. Michel Foucault, "Nietzsche, Genealogy, History," in *The Foucault Reader,* ed. Paul Rabinow (New York: Pantheon, 1984), 95.

4. Ibid., 81.

5. Michel Foucault, "Preface to Transgression," in *Language, Counter-Memory, Practice,* trans. and ed. Donald Bouchard and Sherry Simon (Oxford: Blackwell, 1977), 42.

6. Italo Calvino, "Levels of Reality in Literature," in *The Uses of Literature,* trans. Patrick Creagh (New York: Harcourt Brace Jovanovich, 1986), 105.

7. Ibid., 112.

8. Ibid., 113.

9. Ibid.

10. Ibid., 114.

11. Ibid., 118.

12. Ibid., 120.

13. Italo Calvino, *If on a winter's night a traveler,* trans. William Weaver (New York: Harcourt Brace Jovanovich, 1981), 181. [In what follows, numbers in parentheses in the text refer to page numbers in this book.]

14. [Translator's note: Habermas and the German translation have "something indefinable" (*etwas Undefinierbares*) where the English translation has "something definable."]

15. [Translator's note: The English has: "what she knows for certain is her waiting, the void that my words should fill." (171)]

16. [Translator's note: The English version has "certitude" in place of "truth" (*Wahrheit*).]

17. Herbert Schnädelbach, "Dialektik als Vernunftkritik," in Ludwig von Friedenburg and Jürgen Habermas, eds., *Adorno-Konferenz 1983* (Frankfurt: Suhrkamp, 1983), 66–93.

18. Hans Blumenberg, *Die Sorge geht über den Fluß* (Frankfurt: Suhrkamp, 1987), 75.

19. F. Schirrmacher, "Wie Worte Taten gebären," in the literary supplement of the *Frankfurter Allgemeine Zeitung* (March 29, 1988).

Index

Abduction, 100, 106–107, 174
Absolute, 32, 129
Absolute negativity, 121
Absolute spirit, 39, 130, 157
Absolute subject, 129
Abstraction, 30–31
Accountability, 143
Action. *See also* Communicative action
  accountable, 181
  categories of, 45
  contexts of, 34
  oriented toward understanding, 48, 58
  plan of, 79, 100
  purposive, 104
  situation of, 79
  social norms of, 69
  strategic, 65, 74, 79, 80, 82, 84, 192
  subjects capable of, 14, 47
  teleological, 59, 78
  theory, 59, 78
  and thought, 97
Adorno, Theodor W., 5, 120, 123, 142
  and the critique of ideology, 28
  Minima Moralia, 206, 225
  negative dialectics of, 37, 130
  as a writer, 205–206, 225
Aesthetic experience, 40, 210, 216, 218
Aesthetics of reception, 218
Analytic philosophy, 4–5, 7, 37, 208
Anaximander, 206
Anthropology, 37, 133, 208
Apel, Karl-Otto, 49, 107, 136
Aquinas, St. Thomas, 29, 128, 151
Arabian Nights, 215
Architectonic, 35, 41, 94–95, 162
Architecture, postmodern, 3

Argumentation, 103, 132
  and agreement, 109
  and autonomy, 220
  game of, 68
  and ideal communication, 104
  procedure of, 38
  and proof, 101
  rational form of, 102
  and truth, 98
Aristotelianism, 4
Aristotle, 13, 206
Art, 17–18, 39, 216
Artaud, Antonin, 206
Assertions, 67, 70
Assertoric force, 66, 72
Assertoric sentences, 66–70, 76
  and constative utterances, 69, 77
  content of, 74
  logical genesis of, 99
  truth-claim of, 20, 50, 66, 89, 95
  as unit of semantic analysis, 61
  and verification rules, 68
Augustine, St., 29, 128, 166
Austin, J. L., 46, 62, 66, 74
  and illocutionary acts, 64, 69–71
Author, 213, 217–219, 224–225
Autonomy, 192
Avowals, 76, 165

Bachelard, Gaston, 5
Beck, Ullrich, 195, 197–199
Beethoven, Ludwig van, 10
Behaviorism, 8, 21, 58
Being
  of beings, 13, 121
  determinate, 122–123, 153

Being (cont.)
Hegel's degrees of, 151
and the later Heidegger, 42, 207, 209
opposition to nonbeing, 120
and Parmenides, 30
Bennett, Jonathan, 58
bios theoretikos, 32, 119
Bloch, Ernst, 5, 123
Bloomfield, Leonard, 58
Blumenberg, Hans, 206, 225
Body, 19, 45, 154
Borges, Jorge Luis, 206
Buddhism, 32, 119–120
Burckhardt, Jacob, 205
Büchner, 37
Bühler, Karl
functional scheme for language, 57–60,
64, 73, 75–76
organon-model of language, 58
on sign functions, 59

Calvino, Italo, 211–225
and absolute linguistic reality, 211
and aesthetic practice, 218
and Derrida, 216–218
on fictional levels of reality, 210, 214
If on a winter's night a traveler, 215, 219
"Levels of Reality in Literature," 210
and the reader-relation, 213, 220
Capitalism, 199
Cerberus, 89
Cervantes, Miguel de, 212
Christianity, 25, 32, 165
Coleridge, Samuel T., 211
Common sense, 18, 38, 104
Communication. *See also* Language,
Speech acts
context of, 34
evolution of, 177
forms of, 50
gestural, 175, 178
ideal, 104, 184
linguistic, 88, 91, 107, 110, 145, 162,
175, 178, 210
mode of, 24, 178, 189
networks of, 141
nexus of, 108
participants in, 36, 43, 46, 62, 76
and Peirce, 88–111
and prayer, 167
process of, 60, 74
public, 102
purposive-rational explanation of, 65
and role of the subject, 96
and self-understanding, 183
structures of, 200

theory of, 182, 188, 193
unifying power of, 93
Communication community, 184, 186,
188, 192
Communicative action. *See also* Action,
Speech acts
and actor as a social object, 172, 190
and assertoric sentences, 90
and autonomy, 190
concept of, 74
idealizing presuppositions of, 144
and indirect communication, 83
and the lifeworld, 9, 43, 142
and linguistic turn, 44
other's perspective in, 24
primacy of, 64
sincerity conditions of, 82, 84
and strategic action, 79–80
and subjectivity, 26
theory of, 34
and universal pragmatics, 139, 191
and unlimited communication
community, 192
Communicative practice, 39, 47–48, 50,
142, 223
Communicative reason, 116, 139, 142,
144–146
Community. *See also* Communication
community
of citizens, 35
and ego, 187
ideal, 136
and individualism, 186
of inquirers, 35
interpretive, 95, 96
of investigators 92, 96, 103–104
without limits, 104
linguistic, 23–24, 43, 103, 135–138,
162
and the person in Peirce, 108
voice of the, 185
will of the, 181
Compensation theory, 132–133
Competence, 58
Comprehensibility conditions, 71
Concept
of the concept, 119
detranscendentalization of, 34
of individuality, 158, 162, 167
of law, 160
of rationality, 136
of reason, 116–117, 125, 133, 141–142,
208–209
and totalizing thought, 36
Concrete universal, 130
Concretism, 30, 119

Confession, 166–169
Conscience, 151
Consciousness. *See also* Philosophy of
  consciousness, Self-consciousness
  critique of modern positions on, 25
  empirical, 41
  Henrich on, 11
  historical, 34, 131
  and introspection, 23, 96
  and logic, 93
  monadic, 42, 97
  and naturalism, 45, 106
  semiotic interpretation of, 94
  theory of, 13, 22–23
Consensus, 110, 138, 140
  formation of, 74
  ideal ("final opinion"), 98, 103–105
  linguistically-attained, 48
  Peircean concept of, 184
Constative speech acts. *See* Speech acts
Contemplation, 32
Context, interactive, 24
Contextualism, 49, 117, 139, 225
  and logocentrism, 50
  moderate, 132
  of postanalytic philosophy, 5
  radical, 115–116, 134–135, 141, 210
  and truth, 116
Counterfactual conditionals, 67
Critical theory, 7
Critique of ideology, 28, 123
Critique of metaphysics, 115, 117, 123,
  128, 144
Critique of reason, 121
Critique of the understanding, 122
Cusanus (Nicholas of Cusa), 29, 128

Darwin, Charles, 20, 45
Dasein, 41–42
Davidson, Donald, 5
Deconstruction, 17, 37, 206
Derrida, Jacques, 5, 37, 140, 206, 209–
  210, 212
  and Calvino, 216–218
  metaphysical thought of, 121
Descartes, René, 29, 31, 158, 178, 208
Determinate being. *See* Being,
  determinate
Dewey, John, 171, 173–174, 188
de Man, Paul, 206
Dialectic, 39
Dialectical materialism, 18
Dialogue roles, 46
Difference, 30, 32, 117, 121
Dilthey, Wilhelm, 19, 37, 40, 49
Don Quixote, 212

Doubt, Cartesian, 97
Dualism, 18, 132
Dummett, Michael, 58, 67–68, 77
Duns Scotus, John, 122, 155
Durkheim, Emile, 110, 149, 150, 182

Eco, Umberto, *Name of the Rose*, 107
Effective history, 4, 7, 36, 139
Ego, 120, 197, 199
  empirical, 127, 158
  and identity, 188
Egohood, 161
Eighteenth century, 33, 166
Elkana, Yehuda, 133
Emancipation, 15, 197
Embodiment, 7
Empiricism, 4, 29, 31, 98
Enzensberger, Hans Magnus, 140
Epistemology, 133
Ethical life, 15
Ethical self-understanding, 183
Ethics, 14, 185, 191
Ethnocentrism, 136, 138
Everydayness
  and contexts, 34
  and life, 223
  and practice, 17, 143, 210
Evolution, 93, 106, 109
Existential illumination, 37
Existential relation, 99
Experience, 98, 100–103, 107, 210
Expert cultures, 18, 39, 49
Explanation, 30, 78, 119
Extraordinary, the, 48, 51

Facticity, 39, 41, 164
Facts, 61–62
Fallibility, 104
Family, 197–198
Felicity conditions, 71
Female labor power, 197
Feuerbach, Ludwig, 19, 39, 110
Feyerabend, Paul, 133
Fichte, Immanuel Hermann, 29, 170
  on concept of individuality, 159–162,
    165, 168
  and problem of intersubjectivity, 161–
    162
  and problem of self-objectification, 24–
    25, 44, 160–162, 171, 207
  on self-consciousness, 10, 44, 178
  on self-positing consciousness, 158–162
  Sittenlehre, 160, 170
  Wissenschaftslehre, 25, 160, 162, 170
Fiction, 206, 210–213, 216–219, 223–
  226

Fiction (cont.)
  grammatical, 221
  levels of reality in, 214
Finiteness, 32, 34, 120
Finitude, 39, 123
First philosophy. See *Prima philosophia*
Flaubert, Gustav, 212
"For us" / "for me", 17, 131
"For us"/ "for them", 131, 137–138
Forms of life. *See also* Lifeworld, World,
    Worldview
  exemplary, 32
  and individuals, 128
  intersubjectively recognized, 181
  and justification, 136
  and language, 63, 69, 163
  and lifeworld, 16, 115
  particular, 103, 106
  and philosophical theory, 127
  pluralization of, 115, 140
  reification and functionalization of, 34
  and relation-to-self, 180
  and transcendental subjects, 40
  universalistic, 186
  and utopia, 145–146
Foucault, Michel, 5, 149, 210, 212
  empirico-transcendental thought of, 40
  on power-knowledge formations, 209
Foundationalism, 96
Frankfurter Allgemeine Zeitung, 206
Frankfurt Institute for Social Research,
    5
Freedom, 15, 123, 126–127, 129, 149,
    152, 159–161, 183, 192, 208
Free will, 160, 181, 187–188, 190
Frege, Gottlob, 19, 21, 44, 46, 58, 61–
    62, 66–67, 71, 93
Freud, Sigmund, 5, 45, 120, 180, 205–
    206

Gadamer, Hans-Georg, 7, 19, 49, 138
Game theory, 21
Gehlen, Arnold, 12, 19, 149
Genealogy, 15, 17, 199, 207, 209
Genus and specific difference, 122
Geometry, 30, 119
German Idealism, 31
Germany, 15
Gerth, Hans, 152
Gestures, 173
Grammar, 208
Grammatical facts, 23
Grammatical rule-systems, 43, 47
Grammatical structures, 7
Gramsci, Antonio, 5
Grice, H. P., 58–59, 65

Hegel, Georg Wilhelm Friedrich, 4, 12,
    28–29, 33, 40, 123, 140, 142, 205,
    208
  on absolute subject, 129
  Aesthetics, 151
  and dialectical logic, 156
  Differenzschrift, 121
  logic of, 32
  and Hegelian Marxism, 7
  and history, 117, 130
  and individuality, 150–151, 157
  influence on Peirce, 94
  and metaphysical thinking, 128, 130
  on the nonidentical, 130
  Phenomenology of Spirit, 10
  and philosophy of history, 157
  and philosophy of right, 157
  and post-Hegelian thought, 44
  and pragmatism, 18
  on reflection, 129
Heidegger, Martin
  Being and Time, 4, 41, 207
  on Being-in-the-world, 41, 207
  on *Dasein*, 41–42
  and the destruction of the history of
    metaphysics, 28
  on language as the house of Being,
    209–210
  later philosophy, 37, 42, 206–207, 209–
    210
  "Letter on Humanism," 4
  metaphysical thinking of, 121
  on Nietzsche, 13
  and politics, 12
Henrich, Dieter, 10, 12–14, 18–19, 22–
    23, 25–26
Herder, Johann Gottfried von, 128, 176
"Hermeneutical manslaughter," 133
Hermeneutics, philosophical, 49
Hesse, Mary, 205
Historicism, 37, 40, 117, 131, 214
History, 32, 34, 36, 39, 42, 124, 127–
    131, 164, 209
History of ideas, 134
Homer, 210, 212
Horkheimer, Max, 6, 15, 16, 120, 123
Hölderlin, Friedrich, 10, 206
Human sciences, 37, 131–133, 205
Humanism, 116, 146
Humanities, 34–36
Humboldt, Wilhelm, 19, 45, 128
  and communications-theoretic
    approach, 208
  on individuation and socialization, 144,
    152–153

and intersubjective understanding, 48,
 159, 208
on language, 162–165
linguistic philosophy, 21
on "reciprocal conversation," 163
Hume, David, 19, 31
Husserl, Edmund, 6, 33, 40–42, 44–45,
 60, 93, 206
analysis of the lifeworld, 7, 49
Experience and Judgment, 98
Fifth Cartesian Meditation, 42, 161
Logical Investigations, 4
Hypotheses, 36

Icon, 99, 107
Id, 180
Idea, 94, 96, 102, 125
Ideal essences, 36
Idealism, 15, 29–31, 39, 44, 115, 117–
 122, 129, 154
metaphysical, 116
semiotic, 107–108
Idealization, 46, 136, 143, 186
Ideas of reason, 126–127, 130, 134–135,
 143, 156
Identity, 30, 32, 117, 121, 124, 126, 197,
 209
Identity thinking, 29, 31, 33, 44
Ideology, 12, 16
Illocutionary acts, 64, 69–71, 75, 77, 81–
 82, 84, 143, 144, 169, 189. *See also*
 Locutionary acts, Speech acts
Illocutionary force, 72–74, 77, 95, 102
Imagination, 124
Imperatives, 67, 76, 81, 83–84
Individual, 31, 122, 149, 150, 154
Individualism, 140, 150, 186
Individuality, 15, 41, 44, 111, 151, 154,
 158, 168, 169
Individualization, 152, 184, 194
Individuation, 26, 152, 154, 182
Infinite, 30, 32, 120, 126, 129
Infinitesimal calculus, 155
Information, 100, 101, 103, 105
Instinct, 176
Instrumental reason, 123, 208
Intellectual intuition, 31, 45
Intentional objects, 45
Intentionalism, 58
Interpretive process, 90
Intersubjective agreement, 92
Intersubjective recognition, 170
Intersubjectivity, 47, 109, 141
of an agreement, 137
fractured, 140
and individuality, 162

linguistic, 25
and objectivity, 101–103, 136
problem of, 42, 161
of understanding, 48, 145
and the world, 42–43, 46, 74, 101, 105,
 109
Introspection, 172
Intuition, 15, 47, 124
Intuitionism, 96

Jaspers, Karl, 37, 120
Jesus, 120
Joyce, James, 206
Judgment, 13, 68, 71, 77, 96, 98, 100,
 124, 127, 166–167, 184, 186
aesthetic, 14, 17
Justice, 50, 143
Justification, 17, 33, 36, 49, 134, 136–
 138, 166, 169,

Kant, Immanuel, 17, 40, 101, 115–117,
 125–128, 130–131, 144, 155, 158,
 168, 184–185, 205, 208
Critique of Pure Reason, 17, 125
and the critique of reason, 13
and Darwin, 20, 45
and idealism, 29, 117
and the Ideas of Reason, 127, 134, 156
and metaphysics, 10, 13–14, 18, 28–29,
 115, 125, 128
and the moral world, 126, 142, 185
semantic transformation of his
 thought, 93–94
and transcendental synthesis, 124–125
and the "thing-in-itself," 97
and the transcendental dialectic, 28
and transcendental illusion, 126
and the transcendental subject, 41, 158
and unity, 125, 162
Kenny, Anthony, 66
Kierkegaard, Søren, 39, 131, 164–167,
 169–170
on the ethical stage of life, 165
and individuality, 143, 152
and the life history of the individual,
 117, 162, 164
on the Other, 164
and self-choice, 159
"Sickness unto Death," 24–25
Kingdom of ends (Kantian), 126, 185
Knowledge, 31, 37, 42, 48–49, 61, 65,
 67, 78, 83, 96, 97, 225
background, 63
concept of, 124
of essences, 36
everyday, 38

Knowledge (cont.)
  expert, 17, 50
  fallible, 18
  indirect, 68
  intersubjective, 66, 208
  intuitive, 36
  of nature, 35
  nomological, 36
  objective, 135
  performative, 169
  philosophical, 36
  pretheoretical, 20
  scientific, 35
  semiotic model of, 103–104
  subject of, 22
  of success conditions, 72, 83
  systematic, 125
  theoretical, 32
  of truth conditions, 68
  as universal, 13
Kolakowski, Leszek, 37
Kraus, Karl, 225
Kuhn, Thomas, 5, 49, 133

Lacan, Jacques, 5, 47
Language, 12, 19, 21, 36, 42, 45–46,
  50–51, 57, 60–61, 65, 70–72, 96, 103,
  105–108, 115, 128, 132, 136, 145,
  153, 180, 183, 188, 193, 205, 207–
  210, 212, 214, 216–217, 224–225.
  See also Communication, Language
  games, Linguistic turn, Speech acts
  boundaries of, 70, 72
  Bühler's functional scheme for, 57–60,
    64, 73, 75–76
  and fiction, 214, 223
  Heidegger on, 209–210
  Humboldt on, 162–165
  ideal, 138–139
  and justification, 136
  as a medium of understanding, 42–43,
    58, 62, 80–82, 84, 97, 110, 116–117,
    134, 140, 144, 153, 161–162, 178,
    192, 208
  natural, 43, 64, 77, 134
  ordinary (everyday), 4, 64, 205
  philosophy of, 5, 7, 34, 44, 116, 134,
    159, 178, 207
  pragmatics of, 19, 46, 63, 69, 78, 153
  religious, 25, 51
  representational function of, 49, 60,
    62, 69, 106
  and the self, 191
  semantic analysis of, 60, 66
  and signs, 89–91
  strategic use of, 82–83

and socialization, 63
structuralist analysis of, 47
and subjectivity, 178, 210
theory of, 21, 23–24
therapeutic treatment of, 37
as a tool, 45, 58–59, 63
and transcendental consciousness, 19
use-theoretical approach to, 62–63
and validity, 78
world-relation of, 8, 45, 61–62, 69–72,
  74–75, 78, 90, 95, 105, 134–135, 138,
  142, 153, 209
Language games, 7, 63–64, 72, 115, 139
  Cartesian, 19
  grammatical rules of, 69
  local, 49
  natural history of, 69
Last Judgment, 166
Law, 17, 39
  natural, 33, 35
  universal, 127
Learning processes, 104–109, 138, 153
Lebensphilosophie, 40
Legal theory, 33
Leibniz, Gottfried Wilhelm, 13, 29, 128,
  155–157, 168, 186
Levi-Strauss, Claude, 5, 7, 208
Life, 14, 39–40, 50–51
Life-history 153, 164–165, 167, 186
Lifeworld, the, 18, 21–22, 132, 141–142,
  145, 199, 225. See also Forms of life,
  World, Worldview
  background of, 34, 63, 143
  certainties of, 97, 100
  concept of, 16
  concrete, 50
  of the contextualist, 136
  deformations of, 50
  detraditionalized, 193, 195
  familial, 198
  horizon of, 17, 168
  Husserl's analysis of, 7, 49
  intersubjective, 83, 190, 192
  linguistically structured, 43
  and philosophy, 38–39
  practices of, 51
  rationalized, 197, 199
  symbolically structured, 9, 20, 107
  text of, 133
  totality of, 48, 143
  traditional, 194, 196
  unity of, 115
Linguistic analysis, 4, 12, 21, 46, 49, 60,
  188
Linguistic community. See Community,
  linguistic

Linguistic expressions, 47, 59–60, 62
Linguistic interaction, 25
Linguistic signs, 59
Linguistic symbols, 23
  archeology of, 99
Linguistics, 133
Linguistic turn, 6, 8, 21, 43–47, 134,
  139, 162, 207
Literary text, 211, 224
Literary theory, 210
Literature, 205–207, 210, 213–214,
  216–218, 223, 226
Lived experience, 45, 76
Locutionary acts, 69–71. *See also*
  Illocutionary acts, Speech acts
Logic, 22, 37, 44, 46, 93, 153, 207
Logical empiricism, 6, 21
Logical grammar, 134
Logocentrism, 6, 8, 20, 48, 50
Luhmann, Niklas, 22, 194
Lukács, Georg, 5
Lyotard, Jean-François, 115

McCarthy, Thomas A., 137
Madame Bovary, 212
Malesherbes, M. de, 166
Manifold, 125
Many, the. *See* One, the, and the many
Marcuse, Herbert, 8
Marriage, 197–198
Marx, Karl, 20, 39, 51, 108, 117, 131,
  193, 208
Marxism, 4–5, 8, 16
Materialism, 21, 29, 33, 37, 44, 123
Material production, 39
Mathematics, 37, 46
Matter, 31, 123, 126, 154
Maturana, 22
Mead, George Herbert, 7, 19, 91, 136,
  144, 163, 170
  on autonomization, 152–153, 185–186
  "Definition of the Psychical," 171
  on differentiation, 152, 185
  on individuation through socialization,
    26, 110, 144, 149–153, 171–194, 197,
    199–200
  "Social Consciousness and the
    Consciousness of Meaning," 171
  "Social Self," 171
Meaning, 23, 62, 70
  content of an utterance, 60
  contexts of, 42
  formal-pragmatic explanation of, 78
  intended, 64
  linguistic, 58
  literal, 64

theory of, 57, 60
  truth-semantic conception of, 62
  use-theory of, 62
  utterance, 64
  and world-disclosure, 43
Meaning-conferring acts, 60
Mediation, concept of, 32
Mentalism, 13, 31
Mental representation, 95–96
Merleau-Ponty, Maurice, 4, 19, 49
Metaphysical thinking, 13, 29–31, 33,
  34, 37, 115–117, 120–121, 123, 128,
  130, 141, 157. *See also* Metaphysics
Metaphysics, 9, 12, 17–18, 25, 32, 34–
  39, 44, 49–51, 119–122, 124, 126–
  127, 130–131, 140–141, 152–153,
  157. *See also* Metaphysical thinking
  critique of, 15, 28, 115, 117, 123, 128,
    144
  demarcation of, 6
  history of, 28, 31, 208–209
  Kant's ambiguous relation to, 10, 13–
    14, 18, 28–29, 115, 125, 128
  and modernity, 11
  of morals, 14
  and naturalism, 19
  negative, 28, 116, 144–145
  normative content of, 142
  and obscurantism, 15
  overcoming of, 11
  post-Kantian, 10, 14, 18
  problematization of, 29
  renewal of, 28
  return to, 11, 37, 115
  and science, 49
  as science of the universal, 13
  starting point of, 31
  and the subject, 11
Mills, C. Wright, 152
Mind-body problem, 19–20
Mirandola, Pico de, 29
Model, logical and mathematical, 13
Modernity, 3, 6, 9, 14, 17, 50, 101, 129,
  149–150, 187
  connection with metaphysics, 11
  normative content of, 12, 20
Mohammed, 120
Moleschott, Jakob, 37
Monad, 97, 156–157
Moore, Edward C., 88
Moore, George E., *Principia Ethica*, 4
Moral consciousness, 182, 184
Morality, 15, 17–18, 35, 39
Moral law, 126, 158
Moral theory, 33, 185
Morris, Charles W., 21, 58

Mysticism, 108
Myth, 29, 37
Myth of the given, 98
Mythological powers, 120
Mythological thinking, 117
Mythology, 118–119, 151

Narration, 30
Narrative, 70, 213, 225
Natural attitude, 21, 32
Natural history, 39
Naturalism, 10, 11, 19–22, 45
Natural language. See Language, natural
Natural law. See Law, natural
Natural numbers, 14
Natural science. See Science, natural
Nature, 20, 32, 34, 36, 39, 106, 108, 127, 130, 141
Necessity, 31, 39–40
Negation, 120, 123
Negative dialectics. See Adorno
Negative metaphysics. See Metaphysics, negative
Negativism, 28
Neo-Platonism, 29
Neurophysiology, 21
Newton, Isaac, 131
Nicholas of Cusa. See Cusanus
Nietzsche, Friedrich, 5, 6, 28, 44, 119, 121, 208, 225
  and the critique of reason, 40
  as metaphysical thinker, 13
Nineteenth century, 34, 37, 131
Nominalism, 29, 31, 106, 122
Non-assertoric sentences, 66
Non-being, 31, 36, 120, 123, 129
Non-identical, the, 48, 115, 123, 130, 158
Normative content, 47
Normative expectations, 190
Normative rightness, 50, 71, 75, 223
Nous, 121, 129

Objectification, 48
Objectivating attitude, 81
Objective spirit, 134
Objective world. See World, objective
Objectivism, 135–136, 208
Objectivistic fallacy, 139
Objectivity, 39, 99–101, 103
Obscurantism, 15
Occam, William of, 154
Odyssey (Homer), 213
One, the
  idealism and, 121

as origin and ground, 115, 119, 123, 143
and the many, 30, 32, 115–118, 120–121, 126, 129
Plotinus on, 119, 121, 129, 156
and the whole, 30, 33, 118, 145
Ontological difference, 41, 121
Ontological thinking, 13
Ontology, 12, 19, 22, 31, 153
  Cartesian, 18
  empiricist, 21
Order, 15, 30
Ordered multiplicity, 30
Origin, 17, 30, 33, 117–121
Ought-validity 71

Paradigm, 23, 25, 31, 46, 84, 171
  concept of, 12
  of consciousness, 22
  linguistic, 22, 118, 208
  of mutual understanding, 22, 43
  philosophical, 22
  of the philosophy of consciousness, 96
  of representative thinking, 94–95
Paradigm shift, 7, 34
Parmenides, 13, 30, 118, 120
Parsons, Talcott, 149, 194
Participant perspective, 36, 91, 131, 136, 138
Peirce, Charles Sanders, 7, 19, 46, 88–111, 136, 173
  concept of the person in, 108
  critique of the philosophy of consciousness, 93–94, 98
  critique of psychologism, 93
  "Fixation of Belief," 101
  Harvard Lectures of 1865, 92–93
  on ideal consensus, 98, 101–103, 105, 110, 184
  Lowell Lecture of 1866, 90, 95
  "On Time and Thought," 94
  and pragmatism, 49, 92, 94–95, 97
  semiotics of, 21, 88–111
  semiotic idealism of, 107–108
  "Speculative Grammar," 89
  on synthetic inferences, 98, 100
  theory of presymbolic representation, 98–99
Perception, 94, 104, 152
Perceptual judgment, 98, 100
Performative attitude, 24, 48, 66, 80–81, 144, 163, 165, 167, 172, 174, 177, 179–180, 189
Performative self-contradiction, 135
Performative sentences, 62, 70, 81, 189

Perlocutionary effects, 82–84
Person, 15, 150
Perspectivistic thesis, 135
Phenomenalism, 97
Phenomenological anthropology, 19
Phenomenology, 3–5, 7, 8, 37
Philosophy, 3, 8, 14–18, 28, 34, 140,
    153, 205, 207. See also Philosophy of
    consciousness
  ancient, 29
  concepts of, 128
  of history, 115, 131–132, 142
  and individuality, 111
  as "interpreter," 14
  of language, 5, 7, 23, 34, 44, 116, 134,
    159, 178, 207
  and literature, 9, 205–210, 224–226
  movements of, 4
  of nature, 33, 108, 142
  of origins, 28, 29, 120
  political implications of, 12
  postanalytic, 3
  reconstructive tasks of, 14, 146
  of reflection, 170, 208
  and relationship to science, 14, 36–39,
    48–51, 134
  of science, 5
  as specialized knowledge, 48
  of the subject, 45–46, 115, 133, 141,
    152–153, 160, 188, 208–209
  texts of, 224–225
  theoretical role of, 14
  transcendental, 19, 40, 43
  twentieth-century, 3, 6
Philosophy of consciousness, 12–13, 24,
    31, 122, 153, 158, 170–171. See also
    Prima philosophia
  and mental representations, 96
  object-directedness of, 61, 160
  Peirce's critique of, 93–94, 98
  premises of, 59–60, 124
  and traditional metaphysics, 33, 160–
    161
  transition to the philosophy of
    language, 7, 21, 23, 34, 44–45, 98,
    134, 207–208
Physics, 21, 133, 205
Piaget, Jean, 5, 7, 45
Pico, Della Mirandola, 128
Plato, 13, 29–30, 115, 136
Platonic anamnesis, 38
Platonic concept of the person, 93
Platonic doctrine of Ideas, 29, 31, 33,
    121
Platonic Idea, 30–31, 120, 122–123
Platonic idealism, 128

Platonism, 4, 6, 11, 15, 25, 109, 225
Play impulse, 157
Plessner, Helmut, 19
Plotinus, 29, 115, 118–119, 121, 128–
    129, 156
Politics, 12
Popper, Karl, 76
Positivism, 6, 28, 37, 117
Post-Marxists, 3
"Posties," 4
Postmetaphysical thinking, 6, 8, 28, 29,
    34, 39, 44, 51, 116, 124
Poststructuralism, 3, 5, 209–210, 214
Power claim, 82–84
Power-knowledge formations, 209
Practical reason. See Reason, practical
Practice, 34, 97–98, 100, 209
Pragmatics, 138, 153
  formal, 46, 78
  linguistic, 20, 26
Pragmatic turn, 47, 92, 94, 96
Pragmatism, 7, 18, 24, 33, 49, 60, 74,
    110, 178
Prayer, 166–167
Predicative determinations, 154
Predicative sentences, 95, 98–99
Prelinguistic level of gestural
    communication, 175
Prelinguistic sphere, 47
Prepredicative experience, 98, 100
Prescientific practice, 49
Presymbolic representation, 98–99
Preunderstanding, ontological, 42
Prima philosophia, 31, 36, 129. See also
    Philosophy of consciousness
Primitive society, 182
Private-language argument, 102
Probability theory, 101
Problematization, 16, 29, 173
Procedural rationality. See Rationality,
    procedural
Productive imagination, 124
Promises (intention sentences), 70, 76,
    156, 170
Propositional attitude, 66
Proust, Marcel, 206
Psychological perspective, 95
Psychologism, 21, 93
Psychology, 20, 37, 57, 173, 174
Putnam, Hilary, 135, 137

Quine, W. V. O., 5, 19, 21, 49

Rationalism, 4
Rationality, 17, 18, 35, 66, 74, 80, 121,
    134–139

Rationality (cont.)
  communicative, 50
  home of, 75
  problem-solving, 35
  procedural, 6, 33–39, 100–101
  theory of, 38
Rationalization, 120
Rational reconstruction, 38
Reader, 221
Realism, metaphysical, 109
Reality, 109, 131, 193
  and fiction, 210–214, 217, 223
  and knowledge, 97,
  and language, 61, 66, 99, 106
  linguistic, 211, 135
  and signs, 98–99, 105
  as transcendent, 103
  and truth, 92, 103–104
Reason, 32, 34–35, 49–50, 119, 124–
  125, 132, 134, 139–140, 142, 161
  attempts to detranscendentalize, 43
  chimerical, 39
  communications-theoretic approach to,
    208
  concept of, 39, 44
  critique of, 5, 8, 16
  dialectical, 32
  foundationalist, 32
  historical, 40
  incarnated bodily, 39
  instrumental, 8, 12, 44
  modern, 12
  practical, 126, 127
  productive, 32
  pure, 127
  situated, 6, 8, 19, 39–40, 49, 139
  theoretical, 34, 126
  unity of, 9
Recollection, 17
Referential expressions, 58
Referential model of language, 61
Regulative idea, 92, 139
Relation-to-self, 24, 178, 180
Relativism, 132, 135
Religion, 17, 25, 51, 93, 145
  world, 15, 32, 119
Religious experience, 93
Religious language, 51
Religious speech, 25, 153
Representation, 95
  of facts, 69
  symbolic, 95
Representing subject, 59
Revelations, 76
Rhetoric, 207
Rightness, normative, 50, 71, 75, 223

Rilke, Rainer Maria, 206
Ritter, Joachim, 132
Romanticism, 128
Rorty, Richard, 5, 115, 133, 135–138
  contextualism of, 135
  and the deconstruction of the "mirror
    of nature," 133
Rousseau, Jean-Jacques, 127, 166–167,
  169, 183–184, 206
Rousseauism, 26
Rule-following, 68
Rule-guided conduct, 68
Rules, underlying system of, 47
Russell, Bertrand
  Principia Mathematica, 4

Salvation, 15, 32, 191
Sanction conditions, 84
Sartre, Jean-Paul, 4, 8, 42, 161
Saussure, Ferdinand de, 5, 45, 47, 89,
  206, 208
Savigny, Friedrich Karl von, 205
Scheler, Max, 7, 49
Schelling, Friedrich W., 13, 24, 29, 123–
  124, 129
Schelsky, Helmut, 133
Schiffer, Stephen, 58, 65
Schiller, Friedrich, 157
Schleiermacher, Friedrich, 128
Schmitt, Carl, 12
Schnädelbach, Herbert, 12
Science, 6, 8, 14, 16–18, 20, 33–39, 48,
  131, 134, 209, 225
  empirical, 6, 28, 35–38
  fallibilism of, 36
  hermeneutical, 36
  and the humanities, 35
  and literature, 205–207, 226
  natural, 21, 35–37, 132–133
  postempiricist theory of, 49, 133
  realism of, 104
  social, 21, 133, 141
  self-reflection of, 49–50
  system of, 29, 38, 50
  theory of, 21, 46, 117, 131
Scientific culture, 50
Scientific texts, 224
Scientific theories, 36
Scientism, 8, 131, 209
Searle, John, 71–73
Self, 11, 25, 50, 97, 164, 171, 177, 180,
  185, 187, 189, 209
Self-consciousness, 12, 23, 25, 31, 32,
  44, 95–96, 119, 124, 129, 158–159,
  168, 170–173, 175, 177–178, 207–208
Self-constitution, 159

Self-critique, 137
Self-deception, 168
Self-determination, 162
Self-interpretation, 11
Self-knowledge, 127, 207
Self-objectification, 141
Self-preservation, 11
Self-reference, 129
Self-referential expression, 188
Self-referential thought, 36
Self-reflection, 49, 179, 188
Self-relation, 25, 172
Self-transcendence, 119
Self-understanding, 14–15, 17–18, 21,
    38, 141, 169, 193
  intersubjectively mediated, 15, 153
  objectivistic, 34
Semantic analysis, 46
Semantic form, 72
Semanticism, 46
Semantic orientation, 24
Semantic perspective, 95
Semantics, 44, 64
  formal, 46, 58, 60
  Fregean, 6
  intentionalistic, 58, 63
  referential, 61
  truth, 66–67
Semiosis, 91, 106–107
Semiotics, 47, 89, 92–93
  circle of, 105–106
  idealism and, 107–108
  and mediation, 96
  and thought, 88
  universal, 89
Sentence form, 24
Seventeenth century, 33
Sexism, 198
Sherlock Holmes, 107
Sign(s), 60, 66
  and communicability, 90
  natural, 108
  operations, 91, 93
  Peirce on, 21, 88–92, 94, 96–98, 101,
    103–107, 109, 111
  representative function of, 90
  world-disclosing function of, 103, 106
Simmel, Georg, 225
Sincerity, 84, 143
Sincerity condition, 71, 73, 82
Situating reason, 6, 8, 19, 39–40, 49,
    139
Situation interpretations, 79
Skepticism, 13, 15, 16, 29, 49, 97, 116
Skinner, B. F., 58
Social acceptability, 69

Social individualization, 196, 199
Social interaction, 139
Social relations, 39
Social sciences, 21, 133, 141
Social theory, 16, 26
Socialization, 18, 26, 63, 135, 152–153
Societal modernization, 116
Society, 39, 140, 141
Sociobiology, 21
Sociology, 37, 151, 193
Socrates, 120, 155
Space-time coordinates, 154
Speaker(s), 23–24, 47–48, 58, 69
  illocutionary aims of, 80
  intentions of, 46, 72
  perspective of, 48
Speech act(s), 63, 74, 83, 89, 143. See
    also Communication, Illocutionary
    acts, Locutionary acts
  binding effects of, 72–73, 80
  comprehension of, 74
  commissive, 73
  constative, 69, 71–72, 169
  elementary, 74
  expressive, 73, 76, 189
  formal-pragmatic analysis of, 73
  and intentions of the speaker, 46, 58
  literary, 223
  perlocutionary effects of, 82, 84
  regulative, 76–77, 142
  sincerity condition of, 71, 73, 82
  theory of, 64, 69–71, 75–76
  validity of, 71, 77–78, 80, 190
Speech situation, 46, 117, 138
Spinoza, Baruch, 13, 29, 128
Spirit, 32, 35, 39, 129–130, 142, 151–
    152
State of affairs, 7, 61, 66, 69, 90, 95, 99,
    199
Stenius, Erik, 66
Strauss, Leo, 12
Strawson, P. F., 65
Structuralism, 4–5, 7, 47, 89, 207–208,
    210
Subject, 13, 18, 19, 20, 23–24, 35, 41,
    124
  acting, 59, 181
  causal intervention of the, 59
  empirical, 142
  perceiving, 31
Subjectivism, 29
Subjectivity, 12, 19, 39, 47, 59, 102, 171,
    207–208
  and contingency, 139
  and idealism, 31–32
  and intersubjectivity, 42, 96

Subjectivity (cont.)
  and language, 178, 210
  prelinguistic, 25
  principle of, 13
  retreat into, 11
  of self, 25
  theory of, 12
  transcendental, 7, 40–41, 43, 157, 209–
    210
  world-constituting, 35, 45, 59, 97, 153,
    155–158, 208
  world-projecting, 41–42
Success conditions, 72–73, 83
Supratemporality, 31, 39, 40
Suspension of disbelief, 213
Symbol, 94–95, 99
Symbolic forms, 107
Synthetic inferences, doctrine of, 98
Synthetic judgments, 13
Systems theory, 21, 22

Taste, 50
Technology, 34, 39
Temporal reference, 94
Theodicy, 123
Theology, 127
Theoros, 33
Theory, 6, 29, 32–33, 34, 48, 206
Thing-in-itself, 97
Thinking. *See also* Metaphysical
    thinking, Postmetaphysical thinking
  identity, 29–30
  precritical, 39
  representational, 97
  totalizing, 33
  transcendental, 139
  unitary, 30, 139
Thought games, 21
Time, 94, 118, 188
Totality, 18, 33–36, 38–39, 118, 130,
    144, 156
  of beings, 35, 49
Totalization, 16
Trakl, Georg, 206
Transcendental apperception, 163
Transcendental consciousness, 7, 19, 41,
    141
Transcendental ego, 41, 127, 161
Transcendental idea, 143
Transcendental illusion, 126, 143–144
Transcendentalism, 108
Transcendentalist, 93
Transcendental philosophy, 19, 40, 43
Transcendental subjectivity, 7, 40–41,
    43, 157, 209–210
Transcendental synthesis, 40

Transcendental unity of apperception,
    125
Truth, 49, 67, 69, 89, 92, 98, 100, 108,
    143, 206, 217–218
  as acceptability, 136
  and contextualism, 116, 135–138, 209
  correspondence theory of, 135
  and ideal consensus, 103–105
  philosophy and access to, 32, 38, 48
  subjective, 50, 75
  and validity, 71, 96
Truth-claim, 20, 95
Truth-conditions, 61, 67–68, 75, 77
Truth-semantics, 69, 71–72, 75
Tugendhat, Ernst, 12, 170

Ulysses, 210
Understanding, 8, 23, 43, 78, 79, 124–
    125
Unity, 31, 117, 134, 140
Universalism, 140, 186
Universality, 31, 39–40
Universals, 109
Utopia, 145, 188

Validity, 51, 78, 81, 223–224. *See also*
    Validity claims
  criteria of, 18, 49
  and forms of life, 139
  inheres in language, 78
  intersubjective, 45
  meaning and, 69
  Putnam on, 137
  of sentences, 62, 69, 96
  spectrum of, 50
  syndrome of, 17
  and truth, 71
Validity claims, 71, 75, 78, 143, 210. *See
    also* Validity
  and consensus, 43
  context-dependent and transcendent,
    139
  Foucault and, 209
  and idealizations, 47
  intersubjective acknowledgment of, 74,
    80
  in literary texts, 223–224
  local standards of, 47
  normative, 73, 84
  of results, 35
  of a rule, 68
  spectrum of, 9
  speech acts and, 71, 77–78, 80, 190
  in texts, 224
  transcendent, 142
  universal, 71

Verification rules, 67–68
Vienna Circle, 6, 37
Vygotsky, Lev S., 7

Weber, Max, 120, 208
Welby, Lady, 89
Weltanschauungen, 6, 37
Whitehead, Alfred North, 4, 185–186
Will, 39, 191
Wittgenstein, Ludwig, 4, 19, 37, 46, 69,
   71, 136, 172–173
   and builders, 62–63
   and language games, 7, 63, 72
   Philosophical Investigations, 4, 62
   private language argument, 102
   on rule-following, 68
   Tractatus Logico-Philosophicus, 4
   and use-theory of meaning, 58, 62–64
Work of art, 156
World, 30, 41, 45, 90, 108, 207, 210. *See
   also* Forms of life, Lifeworld,
   Worldview
   of appearances, 125
   concept of, 76, 128
   constitution of, 40–42, 126, 157
   decentered understandings of, 29
   disclosure of, 42, 213, 216
   fictional, 211–213, 216–219, 223–224
   and history, 120, 131, 151
   horizon of, 50, 173
   and intersubjectivity, 42–43, 46, 74,
      101, 105, 109
   and language, 8, 45, 61–62, 69–72,
      74–75, 78, 90, 95, 105, 134–135, 138,
      142, 153, 209
   and meaning, 43
   moral, 126, 142, 185
   natural attitude toward, 21
   objective, 75–76, 95
   postmetaphysical thinking's concept of,
      39–43
   and process, 22, 120
   rationally structured, 34–35
   and religion, 15, 32, 119, 145
   and signs, 103, 106
   social, 75, 76
   and spirit, 157
   subjective, 95–96
   and subjectivity, 35, 41–42, 45, 59, 97,
      153, 155–158, 208
   of symbolic forms, 94, 107
   as totality, 18
   transcendent creator-god, 30
   unity of, 30, 117–119

Worldview, 119, 163. *See also* Forms of
   life, Lifeworld, World
   closed, 28, 29
   linguistic, 42, 135
   of metaphysics, 39, 143
   natural-scientific, 37
   religious, 51, 193

Young Hegelians, 39, 110, 124

Studies in Contemporary German Social Thought
Thomas McCarthy, General Editor

Theodor W. Adorno, *Against Epistemology: A Metacritique*
Theodor W. Adorno, *Prisms*
Karl-Otto Apel, *Understanding and Explanation: A Transcendental-Pragmatic Perspective*
Seyla Benhabib and Fred Dallmayr, editors, *The Communicative Ethics Controversy*
Richard J. Bernstein, editor, *Habermas and Modernity*
Ernst Bloch, *Natural Law and Human Dignity*
Ernst Bloch, *The Principle of Hope*
Ernst Bloch, *The Utopian Function of Art and Literature: Selected Essays*
Hans Blumenberg, *The Genesis of the Copernican World*
Hans Blumenberg, *The Legitimacy of the Modern Age*
Hans Blumenberg, *Work on Myth*
Susan Buck-Morss, *The Dialectics of Seeing: Walter Benjamin and the* Arcades Project
Craig Calhoun, editor, *Habermas and the Public Sphere*
Jean Cohen and Andrew Arato, Civil Society and Political Theory
Helmut Dubiel, *Theory and Politics: Studies in the Development of Critical Theory*
John Forester, editor, *Critical Theory and Public Life*
David Frisby, *Fragments of Modernity: Theories of Modernity in the Work of Simmel, Kracauer and Benjamin*
Hans-Georg Gadamer, *Philosophical Apprenticeships*
Hans-Georg Gadamer, *Reason in the Age of Science*
Jürgen Habermas, *On the Logic of the Social Sciences*
Jürgen Habermas, *Moral Consciousness and Communicative Action*
Jürgen Habermas, *The New Conservatism: Cultural Criticism and the Historians' Debate*
Jürgen Habermas, *The Philosophical Discourse of Modernity: Twelve Lectures*
Jürgen Habermas, *Philosophical-Political Profiles*
Jürgen Habermas, *Postmetaphysical Thinking: Philosophical Essays*
Jürgen Habermas, *The Structural Transformation of the Public Sphere: An Inquiry into a Category of Bourgeois Society*
Jürgen Habermas, editor, *Observations on "The Spiritual Situation of the Age"*
Axel Honneth, *The Critique of Power: Reflective Stages in a Critical Social Theory*
Axel Honneth and Hans Joas, editors, *Communicative Action: Essays on Jürgen Habermas's* The Theory of Communicative Action
Axel Honneth, Thomas McCarthy, Claus Offe, and Albrecht Wellmer, editors, *Philosophical Interventions in the Unfinished Project of Enlightenment*
Hans Joas, *G. H. Mead: A Contemporary Re-examination of His Thought*

Reinhart Koselleck, *Critique and Crisis: Enlightenment and the Pathogenesis of Modern Society*

Reinhart Koselleck, *Futures Past: On the Semantics of Historical Time*

Harry Liebersohn, *Fate and Utopia in German Sociology, 1887–1923*

Herbert Marcuse, *Hegel's Ontology and the Theory of Historicity*

Guy Oakes, *Weber and Rickert: Concept Formation in the Cultural Sciences*

Claus Offe, *Contradictions of the Welfare State*

Claus Offe, *Disorganized Capitalism: Contemporary Transformations of Work and Politics*

Helmut Peukert, *Science, Action, and Fundamental Theology: Toward a Theology of Communicative Action*

Joachim Ritter, *Hegel and the French Revolution: Essays on the* Philosophy of Right

Alfred Schmidt, *History and Structure: An Essay on Hegelian-Marxist and Structuralist Theories of History*

Dennis Schmidt, *The Ubiquity of the Finite: Hegel, Heidegger, and the Entitlements of Philosophy*

Carl Schmitt, *The Crisis of Parliamentary Democracy*

Carl Schmitt, *Political Romanticism*

Carl Schmitt, *Political Theology: Four Chapters on the Concept of Sovereignty*

Gary Smith, editor, *On Walter Benjamin: Critical Essays and Recollections*

Michael Theunissen, *The Other: Studies in the Social Ontology of Husserl, Heidegger, Sartre, and Buber*

Ernst Tugendhat, *Self-Consciousness and Self-Determination*

Mark Warren, *Nietzsche and Political Thought*

Albrecht Wellmer, *The Persistence of Modernity: Essays on Aesthetics, Ethics and Postmodernism*

Thomas E. Wren, editor, *The Moral Domain: Essays in the Ongoing Discussion between Philosophy and the Social Sciences*

Lambert Zuidervaart, *Adorno's Aesthetic Theory: The Redemption of Illusion*